T0065110

'Difficult to ignore for any armchair mountaineer, let alone anyone objectively looking at the events on and after the K2 attempts.'

Suburban Mountaineer

'Conefrey gives a compelling account of the first attempt to conquer "Savage Mountain"... exploring both the practical side... and the people brave enough to attempt the climb.'

History Revealed

'A worthy successor to *Everest 1953*... scholarly yet accessible.'

Footsteps on the Mountain

'Exhilarating... offers a new twist to its controversial first ascent.'

Library Journal

'Most of us will never experience K2. Conefrey leaves readers with both tremendous admiration for and an appreciation of the consequences for those who succeed in an adventure so physically, mentally, and emotionally taxing.'

Kirkus

ABOUT THE AUTHOR

Mick Conefrey is the author of *Everest 1953, How to Climb Mont Blanc in a Skirt* and *The Adventurer's Handbook*. An internationally recognized filmmaker, he has produced several BBC documentaries on mountaineering and exploration, including the prize-winning 'The Ghosts of K2'. He lives in Oxford, England.

GHOSTS
of K2

*The Race for the Summit of the
World's Most Deadly Mountain*

MICK CONEFREY

A Oneworld Book

First published in North America, Great Britain and the
Commonwealth by Oneworld Publications, 2015

This paperback edition published 2016

Reprinted, 2018, 2023

Copyright © Mick Conefrey 2015

The moral right of Mick Conefrey to be identified as the
Author of this work has been asserted by him in accordance
with the Copyright, Designs, and Patents Act 1988

A CIP record for this title is available from the British Library

ISBN 978-1-78074-873-3
ISBN 978-1-78074-596-1 (eBook)

Typeset by Tetragon, London
Maps Drawn by Adam T. Burton
Printed and bound in Great Britain by Clays Ltd, Elcograf S.p.A.

Oneworld Publications
10 Bloomsbury Street
London WC1B 3SR
England

Stay up to date with the latest books,
special offers, and exclusive content from
Oneworld with our newsletter

Sign up on our website
oneworld-publications.com

To Michael F.

CONTENTS

Character List   ix

List of Illustrations   xi

Prologue: The Mountain with No Name   xiii

1   The Beast and the Prince   1

2   The Harvard Boys   31

3   A Climbing Party   67

4   High Ambition   93

5   The Fall Out   107

6   Unfinished Business   133

7   Teamwork   149

8   Man Down   165

9   The Old Road   183

10   The Flowers of Italy   205

11   The Spoils of Victory   233

12   The Base Lie?   247

Epilogue: Living up to Your Name?   273

Acknowledgements   291

Notes   293

Bibliography   303

Index   307

Character List

The Pioneers

T.G. Montgomerie British surveyor who identified and named K2 in 1856

Henry Godwin-Austen British surveyor who measured and mapped K2; on some maps it is known as 'Mt Godwin-Austen'

Sir Martin Conway British art historian who led the first mountaineering expedition to K2 in 1892

The 1902 Expedition

Aleister Crowley co-leader, poet

Oscar Eckenstein co-leader, engineer

The climbing team *Jules Jacot-Guillarmod*, doctor; *Guy Knowles*, student: *Heinrich Pfannl*, judge; *Victor Wessely*, barrister

The 1909 Expedition

The Duke of Abruzzi, Luigi Amadeo Savoia expedition leader

Vittorio Sella expedition photographer

The 1938 Reconnaissance

Charlie Houston expedition leader

Bob Bates deputy leader

The climbing team *Paul Petzoldt*, mountain guide; *Bill House*, forester; *Dick Burdsall*, engineer; *Norman Streatfeild*, British liaison officer

The 1939 US Expedition

Fritz Wiessner	expedition leader
Oliver 'Tony' Cromwell	deputy leader
Pasang Kikuli	head Sherpa, 'sirdar'
The climbing team	*Jack Durrance*, student; *Chapel Cramner*, student; *George Sheldon*, student; *Dudley Woolfe*, yachtsman; *George Trench*, British transport officer
The Sherpa team	*Pasang Lama*, Fritz Wiessner's summit partner; *Tse Tendrup*, deputy sirdar; *Phinsoo, Tsering Norbu, Sonam, Pasang Kitar, Pemba Kitar, Dawa Thondup*

The 1953 US Expedition

Charlie Houston	expedition leader
Bob Bates	deputy leader
The climbing team	*George Bell*, physicist; *Bob Craig*, ski instructor, *Dee Molenaar*, mountain guide and artist; *Pete Schoening*, chemist; *Tony Streather*, British transport officer; *Arthur Gilkey*, geologist
Pakistani liaison officer	*Dr Mohammed Ata-Ullah*
High altitude porters	*Ghulam, Hidayat, Haji Bey, Mohammad Ali, Hussain, Vilyati*

The 1954 Italian Expedition

Ardito Desio	expedition leader
Achille Compagnoni	climbing leader and summiter
Lino Lacedelli	Compagnoni's summit partner
Guido Pagani	expedition doctor
Mario Fantin	expedition photographer
Pakistani liaison officer	*Dr Mohammed Ata-Ullah*
The climbing team	*Erich Abram*, engineer; *Ugo Angelino*, salesman; *Walter Bonatti*, guide; *Cirillo Floreanini*, draughtsman; *Pino Gallotti*, engineer; *Mario Puchoz*, guide; *Ubaldo Rey*, guide; *Gino Soldà*, guide; *Sergio Vitto*, guide

LIST OF
ILLUSTRATIONS

Map 1 K2, 1902   7

Map 2 The overland route to K2   40

Map 3 The ridges around K2   48

Map 4 Fritz Wiessner's camps, K2   81

Map 5 K2, 1953   137

Map 6 The Gilkey Rescue, 10 August 1953   170

Map 7 The final Italian camps on K2   215

THE MOUNTAIN WITH NO NAME

On a small hill, next to a huge mountain on the border of Pakistan and China, there's a unique monument: a stone cairn some 10 ft high. It was built in 1953 to commemorate the death of a young American climber, Art Gilkey. In the decades since, it has been turned into a memorial for all the men and women killed trying to climb K2.

It is covered with small plaques. A few are elegantly embossed metal, cast thousands of miles away and then brought over by friends and relatives; others look as if they were hammered out on the spot from old tin plates. Some commemorate climbers who died on the way up, others remember those who perished on the way down. Several are famous names in the mountaineering world – Alison Hargreaves, Nick Estcourt, Tadeusz Piotrowski – others are less well known but equally missed. When the wind blows, and it often does, the plaques rattle against the rocks like sails in a marina.

Several hundred feet away, the brightly coloured tents of base camp stand out on the Godwin-Austen glacier, tiny specks in a timeless landscape of grey-brown rocks and endless fields of snow and ice. In the late spring there can be dozens of expeditions, but as the summer wears on they gradually leave, until there is nothing left but the wind and the snow.

Up above rises the huge mass of K2, over two vertical miles of rock and ice. Occasionally the summit is revealed but for much of the time it is hidden behind dense layers of cloud. Though in theory K2 does not suffer the huge monsoon snowfalls that make climbing on Everest so difficult, the weather is very unpredictable and when storms come they can be severe. In January the temperature can drop to below −50° C. Combine that with hurricane-force winds of up to 70 miles per hour and it's not surprising that no one has ever climbed K2 in winter.

At 28,251 ft, it is second in height to Everest and only just taller than its nearest rival, Kanchenjunga, but over the last century K2 has exerted a particular fascination upon the world's climbers. It is the 'mountaineer's mountain', the ultimate challenge: relentlessly steep slopes, extreme altitude, a remote location and unpredictable weather. On Everest there is a well-worn 'yak route' to the top but on K2 there is no easy way up or down.

It is easy to see how K2 acquired its reputation as the toughest mountain in the world – in the fifty years after the first ascent, 247 men and women reached the summit and 54 died trying.[1] In more recent years, advances in equipment and technology have made K2 marginally safer to climb, but it still hits the headlines every few years with stories of the latest 'K2 tragedy'.

K2 was first located by Lieutenant Thomas George Montgomerie, a British officer working for the Great Trigonometrical Survey of India, one of the finest legacies of the British Raj. On 10 September 1856 he climbed Haramukh, a 16,000 ft peak in Kashmir, to set up a survey station. Some 130 miles away, he spotted two prominent peaks in the middle of the Karakoram, a long chain of mountains to the north west of the Himalayas.

After taking bearings, Montgomerie drew a small sketch in his notebook and named them K1 and K2, the 'K' standing for Karakoram. As the survey progressed, several more 'K' numbers were added to his list. In most cases, local names were subsequently found but K2 was just so remote, so hard to get to, that there was no agreed local name. In the end, despite several attempts to rechristen it, K2 has retained its original designation, an austere name for an austere mountain.

In the decades that followed Montgomerie's first sighting, several travellers got closer to the mountain but no one attempted to climb it; their purpose was military rather than sporting. Britain and Russia were rivals in the so-called Great Game – the Imperial struggle for the heart of Asia. The Russians, or so the British feared, wanted to spread south and eventually get a foothold in India; the British, or so the Russians feared, wanted to extend their empire north to the rich trading grounds of Central Asia. In order to gain the upper hand should either of these scenarios come to pass, both nations sent out soldiers and officials on secret missions to explore the unmapped regions.

The first of those explorers to see K2 was the British soldier Henry Haversham Godwin-Austen. In 1861 he set off on a mission to probe the glaciers of the Karakoram and determine whether K2 lay entirely within, or marked the northernmost border of, Kashmir. He got no closer than 16 miles to 'the great Peak K2', but came back claiming to be the first European to get a proper look at the mountain. In his honour, the glacier that runs along the eastern flank of K2 today bears his name, and on some maps the peak itself is called Mount Godwin-Austen.

A full twenty-six years later, Godwin-Austen was followed by another dashing young Sandhurst graduate, the splendidly named Francis Younghusband. As the remarkable climax to an epic journey across mainland China, Younghusband was asked by his superiors in British Intelligence to take a closer look at the Karakoram mountains from the Chinese side. For the twenty-four-year-old Younghusband, it was a perfect piece of derring-do for the glory of the British Empire:

> *I had no experience of mountaineering, and no Alpine equipment – not even a pair of nailed boots, still less an ice-axe. And I had no money. I had already travelled nearly 3,000 miles across the Desert of Gobi and the plains of Turkestan. And now I was asked to cross the Himalaya by an unknown pass. It was just the kind of call I liked.*[2]

On 8 September 1887 Younghusband left Yarkand in China with eight men and thirteen ponies. Two weeks later they got within sight of K2. Though he never had any intention of climbing it, Younghusband wrote the first great literary homage to the mountain:

I chanced to look up rather suddenly, and a sight met my eyes
which fairly staggered me. We had just turned a corner, which
brought into view, on the left hand, a peak of appalling height,
which could be none other than K2, at 28,278 in height second
only to Mount Everest. Viewed from this direction, it appeared
to rise in an almost perfect cone, but to an inconceivable height.
We were quite close under it – perhaps not a dozen miles from
its summit – and here on the northern side, where it is liter-
ally clothed in glacier, there must have been from fourteen to
sixteen thousand feet of solid ice. It was one of those sights
which impress a man forever, and produce a permanent effect
upon the mind – a lasting sense of the greatness and grandeur
of Nature's works – which he can never lose or forget.[3]

Younghusband went on to explore the high passes and glaciers of the
Karakoram range before finally returning to his regiment in India,
eighteen months after he had left it. His journey won him a gold medal
from the Royal Geographical Society and further boosted interest
in K2.

Britain and Russia weren't the only nations active in the region. The
Schlagintweit brothers from Bavaria published several large volumes
covering their travels through the Karakoram and the Himalayas in the
same period, and there was a long tradition of Italian interest, beginning with the Jesuit priests who were active in the 1700s and moving
on to the Marchese di Cortanze, an Italian aristocrat and tea-planter
who explored Baltistan and Ladakh in the late nineteenth century.
There is some anecdotal evidence that the first person actually to set
foot on K2 might have been Roberto Lerco, a wealthy alpinist from
northern Italy. Around 1890, at the end of a long solo expedition to
the Himalayas and the Karakoram, he reached K2 and, according to
members of his family, actually attempted to climb its south east ridge.
Lerco did not, however, publish anything and his diary was lost in a
house fire, so it is impossible to be sure of this.

The last of Britain's great nineteenth-century expeditions to K2, by
contrast, produced a very famous book, *Climbing and Exploration in*

the Karakoram-Himalayas. Its author was William Martin Conway, an art historian who in his spare time was a keen mountaineer. Conway's 'civilian' team included the redoubtable Lieutenant Charles Granville Bruce, who would win fame on the first two British Everest expeditions.

Having read the accounts of Younghusband and Godwin-Austen, Conway left England in February 1892 aiming to map the glaciers adjacent to K2 and obtain a collection of geological and anthropological specimens. The official artist was the well-known painter A.D. McCormick; the expedition's mountaineering contingent was headed by Oscar Eckenstein, an outstanding rock climber.

High on Conway's wish list was to bring back a painting of the by now famous K2, but his ambition was continually thwarted by clouds and intervening ridges. When he finally came face to face with the mountain he had read so much about, Conway was shocked to discover that rather than being the 'majestic peak' of his imagining, it was what he called an 'ugly mass of rock, without nobility of form'.[4] A.D. McCormick did produce one rather striking image of K2 from the Throne glacier but, having by then fallen out with and dismissed Oscar Eckenstein, Conway did not dare to set foot on the mountain itself.

By the end of the nineteenth century, K2 had been located, measured, mapped and painted. All that remained was for someone to climb it. This book is the story of that first ascent and the expeditions that led up to it. It is based on diaries, letters and contemporary documents, and interviews with mountaineers and their relatives.

This is one of the great sagas in mountaineering history and includes some of its most intense characters: the Duke of Abruzzi, the greatest explorer of the early twentieth century; Charlie Houston, the brilliant but tortured Harvard expedition leader; Fritz Wiessner, the German émigré who revolutionised climbing in the USA; Achille Compagnoni, the Italian ski champion and soldier; and his nemesis, Walter Bonatti, acclaimed as one of the greatest climbers ever. For each of them K2 became an obsession that lasted all their lives but left no one happy.

It is a fascinating and unusual tale, not just because it involves so much human drama but because unlike the other two Himalayan giants, Everest and Nanga Parbat, respectively the national obsessions of Britain and Germany, the first ascent of K2 is very much an international story. Over the course of six decades mountaineers from Austria, Switzerland, Italy, the United States, Germany and Britain came together to try to climb the world's second-highest mountain, each building on the previous attempts and each bringing their own national characteristics to the ascent.

The early history of K2 has spawned some notable books: Charlie Houston's and Bob Bates' accounts of their two expeditions in 1938 and 1954, *Five Miles High* and *The Savage Mountain*, are regarded as mountaineering classics, as is Filippo de Filippi's account of the 1909 Abruzzi expedition. There have also been a number of very good general histories, including books by Jim Curran, Ed Viesturs, Leonardo Bizzaro and Roberto Mantovani. So why write another one?

The answer is because new archival material has now emerged which shines a light on some of the most interesting, and most controversial, episodes in K2's history. Fritz Wiessner's 1939 expedition, for example, has long been the subject of fierce and highly polarised debate, a lot of it founded upon inaccurate and incomplete factual information. Over the last few decades, a mass of documents, diaries and letters have become available which now make it possible to write a much more detailed version of the story, and solve at least some of the mysteries.

If the arguments that followed Wiessner's expedition were intense, then nothing in the history of mountaineering can match the 1954 Italian expedition for bitterness and rancour. For fifty years its members and organisers argued with each other over almost every aspect of what occurred, from finances to film making to the specific timetable of events on the mountain. The longest-running and most personal battle was between Walter Bonatti, who went on to be acclaimed as one of the greatest climbers of the twentieth century, and Achille Compagnoni and Lino Lacedelli, the two Italians who first set foot on K2's summit.

Over the last ten years, a consensus has emerged in Italy which endorses Bonatti's position, and condemns Compagnoni and Lacedelli as liars. The new evidence that I have uncovered, however, both photographic and written, suggests the story is not quite so black and white, and that Compagnoni and Lacedelli may very well have told the truth. To reveal that the two protagonists of a story were *not* liars does not sound like a typical bit of revisionist history, but, as will become clear, in the topsy-turvy world of K2 expeditions, the atypical is the norm.

This story begins, however, in 1902, long before the first ascent was debated in the bars and piazzas of Milan and Turin, with the first expedition to set foot on K2. Fittingly, for a mountain that would later be called 'cursed', it was co-led by the most famous occultist of the twentieth century: Aleister Crowley, 'the Great Beast, 666'.

Chapter 1

THE BEAST AND THE PRINCE

Aleister Crowley was a flamboyant, bisexual drug fiend with a fascination for the occult. He was not a typical twentieth-century mountaineer, but for a few years at least he was a very keen one.

He was born Edward Alexander Crowley in Leamington Spa in 1875, the son of fundamentalist Christian parents. After his father's death in 1887, the eleven-year-old Crowley quickly rebelled and spent his teenage years being enrolled in and then withdrawn from a series of schools before ending up at Cambridge University in the mid-1890s. Inheriting a huge private fortune, he was soon indulging his passion for prostitutes, chess, poetry and 'magick', and occasionally making forays into the mountains.

Crowley began climbing in Scotland in his teens before graduating to the dangerous chalk cliffs of Beachy Head on the south coast of England. Like most British climbers, before long he found himself in the Alps, which by then had become, in the words of the famous Victorian writer Sir Leslie Stephen, the 'Playground of Europe'. Unlike the majority of his fellow travellers, Crowley was never keen on hiring professional Alpine guides, preferring to climb solo or with like-minded friends. Though he was talented and enthusiastic, he never joined the Alpine Club, then the mainstay of British mountaineering.

In 1898, at the age of twenty-three, Crowley met Oscar Eckenstein, the climber who would eventually become his co-leader on the first recorded attempt on K2. Eckenstein was another classic outsider and eccentric, though of a different kind. The son of a well-known Jewish Socialist who had fled from Germany to London after the revolutions of 1848, Eckenstein was a chemist turned railway engineer. Though seventeen years older than Crowley, the two men soon became firm friends, in spite of their very different backgrounds and temperaments.

In appearance they were equally ill matched. Eckenstein was short and muscular and, according to the British writer Geoffrey Winthrop Young, 'had the beard and build of our first ancestry'.[1] He dressed scruffily, wore sandals in town and when not practising the bagpipes invariably had a tobacco pipe hung from his mouth, surrounding him in a dense fug of Rutter's Mitcham Shag, one of the strongest and coarsest tobaccos available. Crowley, by contrast, dressed like a dandy and had the lean emaciated look of a Victorian aesthete, a huge flop of hair crowning his haunted face.

Though the two men were fascinated by the nineteenth-century explorer and mystic Sir Richard Burton, Eckenstein had no interest whatsoever in Crowley's 'magick'. Whereas Crowley was gregarious and intellectually curious, Eckenstein was dour and rational. When it came to climbing, they respected each other's talents, but approached the sport very differently. Eckenstein was an innovator who designed new types of ice-axes and crampons and treated climbing as if it were an engineering problem, always looking for the most efficient way to scale a peak or a boulder. Crowley by contrast was instinctive and impetuous, the very opposite of Eckenstein as he acknowledged:

> His climbing was invariably clean, orderly and intelligible; mine can hardly be described as human.[2]

The one thing that linked them together was their common distaste for the Alpine Club and the mountaineering establishment. After being proposed and rejected by the club in 1895, Crowley developed a lifelong antipathy toward what he called its 'impostors'. Both he and Eckenstein were particularly scathing about guided climbing, which they regarded as fundamentally dishonest.

Though a singularly odd couple, the two men formed a solid climbing partnership that took them from the crags of the Lake District to the Alps of Switzerland. In 1901 they ventured further afield, spending the spring in Mexico. They made ascents of the Pico de Orizaba, its highest point, and Popocatépetl, its most famous volcano; they even made an attempt on a recently erupted volcano, Colima. Only when their boots started to burn did Crowley and Eckenstein accept that it was time to turn round. Buoyed by their success and happy with each other's company, they began to plan a much bigger expedition in the following year – to K2.

For Aleister Crowley it would be his first visit to the Karakoram but for Oscar Eckenstein it was a chance to settle an old score. In spring 1892 he had been part of Martin Conway's expedition to the Himalayas and Karakoram, but it had not been a happy experience for the expedition leader or its star climber. Eckenstein thought he had signed up for a sporting trip to the world's most challenging mountains, but all that Conway seemed to want to do was cover as much ground as possible, stopping only occasionally to raid a local cemetery to add to his collection of skulls or let the expedition artist knock off another watercolour.

By June, Eckenstein was getting bored. In spite of being surrounded by amazing mountains, as he wrote in a letter home, they had climbed 'practically nothing whatsoever'.[3] When the expedition reached Askole, the final village before K2, the tension between the two men came to a head. According to Conway's subsequent account:

> Eckenstein had never been well… It was evidently useless for him to come further with us, so I decided that he'd better return to England.

Eckenstein, however, told it differently:

> We had a sort of general meeting, at which it was arranged that I should leave the expedition. There had been a good deal of friction from time to time, and, as we had now been some two and a half months in the mountains without making a

single ascent of importance, having only crossed two previ-
ously known passes, I was not anxious to go on, and accord-
ingly we agreed to separate.[4]

While Conway carried on toward K2, aiming to paint not scale its summit, Eckenstein turned back. Lacking companions, equipment and supplies, he was unable to do any mountaineering, so he made a leisurely return, stopping occasionally to stage climbing competitions in local villages. He reached Srinagar, the capital of Kashmir, at the end of August and spent two months on a houseboat on Dal Lake, getting to know the local merchants and haggling over antiques.

Back in Britain Conway's account made no mention of tensions on the expedition, but in Eckenstein's book *The Karakorams and Kashmir* there were frequent swipes at his former leader, noting, for example, how Conway needed to rope up between two guides just to cross a bridge and complaining repeatedly about all the mountains that he had not been allowed to climb. Conway made no public reply, but nor did he forget the insults.

Unsurprisingly, when he heard the story, Aleister Crowley was sympathetic to Eckenstein and hostile to a pillar of the climbing establishment like Martin Conway. Though he had never been to the Karakoram or tackled anything higher than 19,000 ft, he became convinced that they would scale K2, show up Martin Conway, and come back with a new world altitude record.

Once they had agreed upon their goal, Crowley left Eckenstein to recruit the rest of the party. His team selection was unusually cosmopolitan. From Austria came Heinrich Pfannl and Victor Wessely, judge and barrister respectively and, by reputation, two of their country's finest rock climbers. From Switzerland came Dr Jules Jacot-Guillarmod, enlisted as both climber and expedition doctor. The final participant was Guy Knowles, a twenty-two-year-old Cambridge student who had climbed with Eckenstein in the Alps. Though he had less mountaineering experience than the others, Knowles was said to be very fit, and known to be very rich – an important attribute for any K2 expedition in those days.

In the contract drawn up by Crowley and Eckenstein, all participants were required to obey their leader's orders 'cheerfully and to the best of their ability', except when it meant putting their own lives at stake. Any disputes were to be resolved by a show of hands, though the leader (either Eckenstein or Crowley) had the casting vote. Remembering an incident on his last visit to Kashmir, when he tried to purchase a jewelled dress and ended up buying the woman inside it, Eckenstein added an extra clause compelling members to keep well away from local females and not to buy anything without his specific approval.

When the press heard about the expedition they approved wholeheartedly, though it is clear from a report in the *Daily Chronicle* of May 1902 that K2 had not yet acquired its reputation as the most dangerous mountain in the world:

> *The main object of the expedition is a sporting ambition to break all former records in mountaineering, but scientific observations will also be made and the flowers and fauna of the Himalayas, of which scientists have so little knowledge, will not be neglected. The first summits to be attempted will be the Godwin-Austen (K2), 28,250, and then Dapsang,[5] 28,265. If success crowns the initial attempts Mount Everest, at 29,002 the highest mountain in the world and the goal of ambitious alpinists, will be tried, but this last part of the programme has not been settled yet.[6]*

It is obvious that the climbers were equally ignorant of what they were getting into. Guy Knowles explained at the beginning of his unpublished journal that Eckenstein and Crowley chose K2 not because it was such a huge challenge but because it presented 'no technical difficulties of a climbing kind to contend with'. As far as Knowles was concerned, the main qualification for anyone attempting K2 was that they had plenty of time and enough money for a year-long holiday in the East.

Today all this sounds very naïve but in the early twentieth century very little was known about the high mountains of the Himalayas or the Karakoram and the dangers of climbing at altitude. Scientists and mountaineers had a general sense that the air grew thinner the higher you went but no one had any concept of the 'death zone'[7] or any real understanding of mountain sickness. Eckenstein and Crowley had climbed in the Alps and in Mexico and were ambitious for something new; Everest was out of bounds because Nepal and Tibet, the two countries either side of it, were closed to foreigners, but Kashmir was open, so K2 was the next best choice.

While Eckenstein looked after the logistics and detailed planning, the carefree Crowley headed off to Ceylon and India where he studied yoga, saw the sights and wrote poetry. In order to prepare the expedition and the long hike in through 'Mahommedan' lands, he grew a beard and taught himself never to touch his face with his left hand. Other than that, his preparations were minimal. On Sunday 23 March 1902 he hopped on board a mail train for Rawalpindi in northern India where they had all arranged to meet, and by happy coincidence found himself on the same service as the others. The Eckenstein Crowley K2 expedition was under way.

Rawalpindi was one of the busiest towns in the region, a major military base for the British Indian Army, and the end of the line as far as the train network was concerned. Eckenstein's men spent five days breaking down their 3 tons of supplies and equipment into more easily transported units and then set off for Srinagar, the famously beautiful capital of Kashmir. They travelled in small, primitive carts called *ekkas*, which were really little more than boxes on wheels. According to student Guy Knowles, the *ekka* was 'as near the elementary vehicle as I can imagine must be seen today'. The Austrian barrister Victor Wessely was so uncomfortable that he developed severe back pain, and had to hire a much better appointed, and more expensive, carriage called a *tonga*. Then the real problems began.

After stopping one night at a village en route, Crowley woke up to find a British police inspector sitting at his bedside. Though the slightly embarrassed official could not explain quite why, he told Crowley that he was under orders to detain everyone. A few hours later the deputy commissioner of Rawalpindi arrived with slightly more detailed orders to hold Eckenstein but let the others continue. Their co-leader was not formally under arrest, the district commissioner assured them, but nor would he be allowed to continue on to K2.

Rather than halt the expedition in its tracks, Eckenstein agreed to return to Rawalpindi to find out was going on. He hoped that everything could be sorted out quickly and that he would soon be able to rejoin his comrades, but if not, he told Crowley to assume total leadership. It was not an auspicious start to the expedition.

Thankfully, for Crowley and the others, the next stage was less eventful. In those days Kashmir was what was known as a 'princely state': one of the hundreds of small kingdoms within and on the edges of British India that enjoyed a limited form of independence. Local rulers wielded domestic power but were not allowed to maintain an army or conduct a foreign policy. Kashmir, with its dramatic mountains and lakes, was a popular retreat for British colonials. Crowley was surprised at how similar its landscape was to that of Mexico and Switzerland. Jacot-Guillarmod, the Swiss doctor, marvelled at the extensive forests and everyone was enchanted by Srinagar's houseboats, elegant bridges and floating gardens.

Map 1   K2, 1902

For two weeks they had a leisurely time, alternating between sight-seeing and trips to the bazaar, and more long hours reorganising their supplies and equipment. During the next stage of the journey, every-thing would have to be carried by pony, or more frequently by human porter, so no single load could weigh more than 53 lbs. To supplement the vast quantities of dried food procured by Eckenstein in England, which Crowley dismissed as 'fit only for soldiers', they bought fresh fruit and vegetables.

Then on 22 April, three weeks after his arrest, Oscar Eckenstein reappeared, happy to be free but none the wiser about the reason for his detention. Some said that because of his name, he had been mis-taken for a Prussian spy. Others maintained that he'd been stopped because of stories in the press that he was heading for Everest, not K2. Eckenstein's own suspicion, shared by both Crowley and Knowles, was that his old enemy Martin Conway, now the president of the Alpine Club and a well-connected public figure, had played a role in it. Eckenstein couldn't prove anything, but when he had threatened to make a stink in the press, it didn't take long for British officials to offer their excuses and let him proceed.

Hoping that their luck was now due to change, on 28 April the full party left Srinagar with a small staff of personal servants, around 150 Kashmiri porters and a troop of Pathan mercenaries from the Punjab, hired to impress and intimidate. Ahead of them lay an estimated 330 miles to the base of K2.

The first stage was almost Alpine in its landscape but once they crossed into Baltistan, then a province of Kashmir, the landscape sud-denly changed. Gone were the lush pine-clad hills and endless forests, replaced by a much harsher landscape of bare rocky hills, criss-crossed by narrow paths. Apart from the occasional village with its own irriga-tion system, there was hardly any vegetation at all.

Their marches were short but frequently exhausting. Though each stage might not represent a great distance on the map, there was usually so much ascent and descent, and so many diversions from the main direction of travel, that it could take several hours to get just a few miles. Along the way, they were greeted and entertained by local rajahs;

Aleister Crowley noted that in Baltistan the term 'king' could refer to anyone from the headman of the local tribe to an absolute monarch who ruled over hundreds of thousands of people.

Eckenstein remembered several occasions in 1892 when he had encountered British and American hunters in the remotest parts, but this time they encountered no other Westerners apart from a British missionary at the village of Shigar. Predictably, Aleister Crowley was not impressed with what he called a 'Christian serpent in a Mahommedan Eden'.

After two and a half weeks on the trail, they reached Skardu, the biggest town in Baltistan, and stopped for several days to reorganise their equipment for the third and final time, before the final stages to Askole, the last village before K2. After that, there would be no chance of resupply, so in the words of Crowley they 'bought every pound of everything eatable in the valley and employed every man available'. As they had come to realise, the problem with this kind of expeditionary mountaineering was that you not only had to find porters to carry your food and equipment, but you also needed another set of porters to carry food for your luggage bearers. Dr Jacot-Guillarmod estimated that after Askole, a third of their porters were employed to carry chapatti flour, the staple diet of Baltistan, for other porters.

With manpower expensive and in short supply, Eckenstein asked each member of the team to limit their personal gear to no more than 40 lbs, prompting an unexpectedly bitter argument with Aleister Crowley. The problem was his large collection of books. Other mountaineers, he said, might be willing to forego such intellectual pleasures and behave like savages 'when travelling through a savage country', but Crowley insisted that he could not live without his Milton and the rest of his books. He would rather endure physical than intellectual starvation, he exclaimed with a flourish. The argument got so heated that Crowley threatened to resign rather than give up his portable library.

In the end Eckenstein conceded and 'Literature' won the day, but by the time they left Askole there were already signs that the expedition was becoming a little ragged. Guy Knowles, the youngest member of the party, was not coping well with the travelling and Crowley was getting increasingly irritable. With tempers fraying, the two Austrians, Pfannl and Wessely, asked Eckenstein for permission to leave with three days' worth of provisions for a quick trip up the Baltoro, the huge, 39-mile glacier that runs through the heart of the Karakoram mountains, followed by a rapid dash up and down K2. Eckenstein, unsurprisingly, refused their unrealistic request.

When the group finally left Askole after another ten days of organising and re-organising, their caravan had grown to almost 230 people, and now included four cooks, twelve personal servants, a small herd of goats and sheep and a local dignitary, the Wazir of Alchori. The final stretch of their journey would be the hardest. The arid wasteland and endless up and down of Baltistan were nothing compared to the hardships of the Karakoram mountains.

Europe's ranges looked Lilliputian in comparison. Eckenstein's men crossed vast glaciers, covered in huge rocks, riven by streams up to 100 ft wide. In Switzerland a typical glacier might culminate with a rocky terminal moraine a few hundred feet high, but here, according to Crowley, some of them soared up to 1500 ft. The goats and sheep seemed to enjoy the challenge, but for everyone else the terrain was sheer torture.

Progress became so slow that Eckenstein resolved to split the party. Crowley, he decided, would lead the charge, heading directly for K2 with a small group of porters, followed at intervals by the others. Eckenstein selflessly agreed to hold up the rear and arrange the transport of food and provisions until he was ready to join them. In order not to antagonise Wessely and Pfannl, Eckenstein told Crowley not to begin the attack on K2 until everyone was assembled.

For his part, Aleister Crowley was only too pleased to leave them behind for a few days at least. Never one to suffer fools gladly, he had developed an intense dislike of one of the Austrians, Wessely. In particular he was appalled by his eating habits. Wessely was, according to Crowley, a 'perfect pig' who was so short-sighted that in order to eat 'he would bend his head over his plate and, using his knife and fork like the blades of a paddle wheel, would churn the food into his mouth with a rapid rotatory motion'.[8] Precisely what Wessely made of his young British colleague is hard to know, but the fact that he later left Crowley out of his account of the expedition speaks as loudly as any insult.

Though he liked being the spearhead of the expedition, the further Crowley travelled up the Baltoro glacier, the less he enjoyed the experience. At night the temperature could drop to as low as −30° C but during the day it was scorching hot. Like many climbers and trekkers to come, Crowley had to abandon his Western notions of hygiene. For eighty-five days in a row, he did not wash and allowed his hands and face to become coated with grease. He found it disgusting at first but he soon realised that this was the best way to keep his skin moisturised. Lice, he noted, were an occupational hazard, their stocks continually replenished whenever he came in contact with one of his porters.

Crowley was, however, much more willing to forgive the idiosyncrasies of local people than those of his European comrades. He was fascinated in particular by Balti cooking. The mainstay of the local diet was the chapati, a kind of flatbread made by smearing watery flour paste around large stones heated in the campfires. The porters would make the dough in the morning and then wrap the stones in their shawls so that when they stopped at the end of the day the chapattis were ready to eat. For footwear, they wore crude shoes called *pabu*, made from wedges of straw, or rags, held in place by leather thongs. *Pabu* worked well on rocks and soft snow but were not at all safe on ice. Instead of protective goggles, they grew their hair Tibetan style, with long plaits that could be held in front of their eyes when conditions demanded.

After a two-week march, in mid-June Crowley's party finally reached Concordia, the dramatic natural amphitheatre where five glaciers come together and huge mountains ring the skyline. Crowley was amazed at how different the surrounding peaks looked – Marble Peak, with its sharply pointed summit, Mitre Peak, with its twin spires, Crystal Peak, with its thick mantle of snow. K2, or Chogori as Crowley preferred to call it,[9] was not yet visible, but after another few hours marching up the Godwin-Austen glacier, the long river of rock and ice that leads from Concordia to the south east flank of the world's second-highest mountain, it finally came into view.

Looking up at its enormous south face, at first Crowley could not see a direct route to the top or even a stopping place for a high camp, but after a day observing K2 through his binoculars, he came to the opposite conclusion. As he later told Eckenstein, there would be no great difficulty in climbing the south east ridge as far as a high snowy shoulder and from there to ascend the final rocky pyramid to the summit. Full of optimism he sent a note back to the others, and then continued up the glacier to find a suitable base camp.

Over the next four days the other members of the party gradually made their way up the Godwin-Austen glacier to join him. They weren't all quite so optimistic. When Jacot-Guillarmod saw K2 for the first time it stopped him in his tracks:

> It was as if we were paralysed, subjugated. We stayed silent, and couldn't find words to express how we felt… the more we looked at it, through the naked eye or binoculars, at both the parts in shadow and in the sun, the more we realized how unlikely it would be to fall to our first attack.[10]

By 20 June everyone had assembled at base camp, apart from Eckenstein who was still several days away organising relays of food. For the next week they stayed put, making forays onto the glacier while waiting for their leader to arrive. The weather was capricious, alternating between fine, dull and stormy days with no apparent logic.

With base camp at over 16,000 ft,[11] Jacot-Guillarmod noted how everyone found it hard to breathe, particularly with any kind of exertion. Headaches were commonplace though not too severe. Just a few minutes outside the tent without tinted goggles were enough to cause snow-blindness. On a lighter note, Jacot-Guillarmod observed that reduced atmospheric pressure also meant that champagne bottles – a surprisingly common feature of early expeditions – no longer popped and that water boiled at just 82° C, hence it took much less time to cook rice and vegetables.

When Oscar Eckenstein finally reached base camp a few days later, he came laden with fresh meat and bread, but it was obvious to all that their leader wasn't well. A heavy smoker throughout his life, he suffered from lung problems. Jacot-Guillarmod diagnosed influenza, and added Eckenstein's name to a growing sick list that now included Crowley, who had recently endured an attack of malaria on the Baltoro glacier, and the young Guy Knowles who appeared to be developing some kind of altitude sickness.

Nevertheless, they were all keen to get going, so, on the following day, Eckenstein convened a meeting and decided that on 29 June they would make their first attempt on the summit. Crowley, Pfannl and Jacot-Guillarmod would form the first summit party, supported by Knowles, Wessely and a small number of porters. The ill Oscar Eckenstein would stay in camp – for the moment at least.

Their plan was simple and highly optimistic. They would rig up an improvised sledge out of skis and load it with a tent and three days' worth of provisions. Then they would start on the route that Crowley had identified, aiming to reach a prominent band of yellow rock midway up the south east ridge. There they would set up a small camp and send their Balti porters down to get more supplies. On the following day, the Europeans would climb to the summit. Just like that.

Anticipating a hungry day to come, Jacot-Guillarmod cooked up a quarter of a freshly slaughtered sheep, while the others sorted out their gear. Then the weather changed. In the early afternoon, the north easterly wind grew to hurricane strength, battering their camp and temporarily filling the cook tent with snow. It calmed down in the early evening but that night it was so gusty there was no hope of sleep. Instead, they stayed up into the early hours, playing chess. It was not the best preparation for an attack on the world's second-highest mountain.

The following morning was a predictable anti-climax. They were due to set off at 5.00 a.m. but it was so cold and windy that even the normally eager Crowley suggested delaying departure for a few hours. No one disagreed but, rather than go back to sleep, Pfannl and Wessely strapped on their skis and headed further up the glacier to investigate another of K2's ridges several hundred feet higher up the

Godwin-Austen glacier. The two Austrians came back reporting that in their opinion the north east ridge looked marginally easier than the south east. Crowley protested that it would take longer to climb and, from what he could see, was more dangerous, but he was overruled. He was the only one who liked their current base camp and, after being stuck there for almost ten days of very mixed weather, no one else wanted to remain at 'Misery Camp'.

On 1 July Pfannl and Wessely left to establish a new base. The others planned to join them the next day, but the bad weather returned. Jacot-Guillarmod's description of camp life during a four-day storm on K2 would be repeated in one form or another many times over the following decades:

> *The days pass more or less monotonously. The sky is usually covered in cloud, with storms and squalls coming frequently, adding their harsh tones to the sound of avalanches. In the occasional clear periods, we get out of our tents and expose our damp clothes and sleeping bags to the sun or take a walk around the camp, just to warm the blood and loosen up our joints.*[12]

By the time the weather improved, and they were ready to move up, Crowley was again showing signs of malaria. He was still eager to make an attempt, however, so on 8 July he set off with Jacot-Guillarmod for Pfannl and Wessely's new base camp. Five hours later, they arrived after a difficult journey. Crowley rallied and even felt well enough to make a solo dash toward the north east ridge on the following day, but it was the last climbing he would do on the expedition. His malaria, contracted a year earlier in Mexico, returned with a vengeance and for the next month he was more or less confined to his tent, tormented by chills, fevers, breathlessness and nausea.[13]

With Crowley out of action and Eckenstein and Knowles still down at the lower camp nursing his influenza, it was left to Jacot-Guillarmod and the two Austrians to make the expedition's first proper attempt on the north east ridge. On the morning, Pfannl announced that he too felt ill and elected to stay in camp rather than join Wessely and Jacot-Guillarmod. In spite of this they started the day optimistically, cheered by good weather and the confidence that the summit was within reach.

It was not long before reality, or at least a semblance of it, set in. Unlike Crowley's preferred route up the south east ridge, which had a relatively easy start, their new approach required them first to climb a very tall, steep snow slope up to a knife-edge ridge, which they hoped would eventually take them all the way to the shoulder of K2 and then up to the summit. However, just reaching that ridge was a trial in itself, which left Wessely panting for breath every few steps. When after several hours they finally reached the top of the slope, they realised that the way ahead was both very exposed and covered in uncomfortably deep snow. To add to the risk, it was periodically interrupted by overhanging cornices, huge wind-blown accumulations of snow and ice, attached to the top of the ridge, which looked as if they might break off at any minute.

When they reached a point estimated at 22,000 ft, just 800 ft below the world altitude record set on Aconcagua in 1897, Wessely decided that it was time to turn back.[14] Jacot-Guillarmod later complained that it was a decision brought on by laziness, but they had already been climbing for several hours and, as Wessely argued, they could come back the following morning and use the steps that they had chopped to reach the crest more quickly. Their return was much more rapid than their ascent, climaxing with an 1800 ft glissade, or slide, which took them virtually back to their tents.

It had been an exhilarating day. In spite of Wessely's problems, Jacot-Guillarmod was surprised at how good they felt when they reached the top of the ridge. Any discomfort he put down to the intensely cold air, not the altitude. The awkward thing about the north east ridge was not whether they could get back up, which they both felt was possible, but whether their porters would be able to follow in their wake, burdened down with tents and supplies.

So instead of retracing their steps, with the newly arrived Oscar Eckenstein's agreement, Wessely and a seemingly recovered Pfannl took five porters and went in search of an easier way up. They left on the morning of 12 July full of energy and determination, but three days later a messenger rushed back into camp with news that Pfannl had taken a severe turn for the worse. Jacot-Guillarmod skied over and found him lying in his tent, coughing up a nasty-looking river of pink froth. He diagnosed pulmonary oedema, a very dangerous condition in which the lungs fill up with fluid. The only cure was to take him down the mountain to a lower altitude, but Pfannl was so weak that he could barely stand up.

When they finally got him back to the others, Pfannl's condition worsened. In his delirium, he called Aleister Crowley into his tent and told him that he felt as if he was being split into three parts: the first two seemed relatively friendly, but the third was a huge threatening-looking mountain with a dagger in its hand. He was clearly very ill but, curiously, Guy Knowles put Pfannl's illness down to the pitfalls of overtraining:

> *Ever since he got on the boat at Suez he has never ceased taking exercise on every opportunity. The result was that he arrived on the glacier trained fine but did not have the resources to withstand the very bad weather we experienced.* [15]

Jacot-Guillarmod looked after him as best as he could, but their new base camp was still far too high for Pfannl to stand any chance of recovery. So two days later, Jacot-Guillarmod left with the two Austrians, aiming to escort them back down to the Baltoro glacier.

The British members of the team elected to stay but in reality they too were in no fit state for mountaineering. Crowley still hadn't shaken off his malaria, Eckenstein's influenza was no better and Guy Knowles had developed an acute ear infection and angina. Quite why they didn't just pack up and leave, it is difficult to know. Perhaps the altitude had dulled their judgment as well as their appetites. They were certainly behaving very strangely, with a feverish Aleister Crowley at one point brandishing his revolver, before he was swiftly disarmed by Knowles. [16]

When Jacot-Guillarmod returned after escorting the Austrians down to a lower altitude, he was shocked to see how emaciated everyone looked. The already thin Guy Knowles had lost almost 33 lbs and Jacot-Guillarmod himself had lost 26 lbs. When he took samples of their blood and analysed them with a portable haemoscope, he discovered that their haemoglobin levels had reached a distinctly alarming 80–85 per cent. An increase in the proportion of red blood cells was expected at high altitude, but these were extraordinarily high levels. Not wanting to alarm them, the good doctor Jacot-Guillarmod kept his test results to himself.

They were clinging on and it was clear that they would soon have to give up. On 1 August 1902 Eckenstein wrote a gloomy letter to his friend Douglas Freshfield, who had visited the Himalayas a few years earlier:

> Our present storm has gone on for over 96 hours, and shows as yet no sign of abatement. At our camp there are over five feet of fresh snow. Our prospects of ascending a high mountain, or any mountain, are consequently practically nil on this occasion.[17]

The final straw came later that day when a troop of porters arrived, sent up by Pfannl and Wessely. They brought fresh stocks of bread and meat and, far less welcome, news that an epidemic of cholera was raging in Baltistan. Twenty people had already died in Askole and there were rumours that the whole region was about to be quarantined, making any return to Srinagar impossible. With his pen as stiff as his upper lip, Guy Knowles recorded in his diary:

> It is rather bad luck that this cholera epidemic should come on us on the top of our other troubles.[18]

There was no alternative but to send for fresh porters from another village just outside the cholera zone and use the men who had just arrived to take down as much of their equipment as possible. Three days later they broke camp and began the long haul back down to the Baltoro glacier.

When a Balti post-runner met them on the way down, he had no more news of the cholera outbreak but he did have something equally unexpected: a fresh batch of mail from Europe. For Jacot-Guillarmod it meant three weeks' worth of his local newspaper, the *Gazette de Lausanne*, and series of letters from friends back home, congratulating him in advance on what they assumed to be his successful ascent of K2.

For a brief moment Jacot-Guillarmod was gripped by an intense desire to head back up the Godwin-Austen glacier to make a final dash for the summit. Even if he couldn't go all the way, he assured Eckenstein that he would break the world altitude record. If none of the other Europeans were up to it, maybe some of the porters would accompany him for extra pay. Eckenstein refused to allow him. Over the last couple of days, his good doctor had also been suffering from flu, and obviously it had gone to his head. The expedition was over.

It was a miserable, despondent team that trudged back down to Concordia and then the Baltoro glacier to Pfannl and Wessely's camp. Jacot-Guillarmod felt personally insulted by Eckenstein's rejection of his plan and sensed that everyone was embarrassed by the expedition's failure. Crowley was still very sick, suffering from repeated bouts of vomiting and diarrhoea.

When they reached Pfannl and Wessely, initially the two halves of the team were very pleased to see each other until Eckenstein realised that the two Austrians had eaten most of their reserve food supplies. Upon investigation, it turned out that Wessely, the Austrian barrister, was the main culprit. Though it was a perfect act of futility for a team on the way down from the mountain, Wessely was called to give an account of himself and then expelled from the expedition.

The 1902 Crowley–Eckenstein expedition was breaking up, and no one was going home happy. Wessely had been rudely ejected from the team and Pfannl had chosen to leave with him, Jacot-Guillarmod had fallen out with Eckenstein, and Knowles was only too glad to reach the end of what would be his first and only high-altitude expedition. The only good news was that the cholera epidemic seemed to have abated, but Eckenstein and Knowles were still so worried about catching the disease that they refused to enter Askole and took a longer route back to Srinagar.

It had been a remarkable act of perseverance. They had spent sixty-eight days on the glacier and only enjoyed eight days of good weather and never more than two good days in a row. The only thing that had kept them going was the deluded idea that K2 would be an easy mountain to climb. Even at the end when Jacot-Guillarmod went to Eckenstein, he still thought that all he needed was a few good days of sunshine, a few willing porters and the summit would be his.

Ultimately, although in print Crowley was scathing about the climbing abilities of what he called the 'international' contingent, the only men who actually got anywhere on the mountain were Wessely and Jacot Guillarmod. Eckenstein was sick for virtually the whole period at base camp and Crowley suffered repeated bouts of malaria. The world's first documented attempt on K2 had not gone well.

Back in Europe, the failed expedition received little coverage. Wessely wrote articles for Austrian climbing journals and several pages from Crowley's diary were reprinted in *Vanity Fair*. Eckenstein does not appear to have published anything at all about K2. He continued to climb but over the next two decades his health declined. When he died of suspected TB in 1921 there were no eulogies in the national press. Eckenstein's young friend Guy Knowles did not go on any further expeditions but did eventually, in his late sixties, join the Alpine Club and was honoured with an obituary in the *Alpine Journal* in 1959. At one point he seems to have considered publishing his K2 diary, but though it exists in typewritten form it was never released.

As for Aleister Crowley, though he did not have a very happy time in 1902, his energy and enthusiasm for mountaineering remained undiminished. Three years later he came back to India to make the first attempt on Kanchenjunga, the world's third highest mountain. It was an even more chaotic and rancorous expedition than K2, climaxing with the death of three porters and the Swiss climber Alexis Pache. Though he came back claiming a new world altitude record, Crowley was not widely believed. After Kanchenjunga, he did very little climbing but he dedicated almost two chapters of his 'autohagi-ography', *The Confessions of Aleister Crowley*, to his adventures in the mountains.

Unsurprisingly, Victor Wessely and Heinrich Pfannl had nothing to do with him after K2 but, for a few years at least, Crowley remained good friends with Jacot-Guillarmod. The Swiss doctor made a memorable visit to Crowley's eccentric mansion next to Loch Ness and even went to Kanchenjunga with him in 1905. When that expedition imploded, Crowley denounced Jacot-Guillarmod as a mutineer and never forgave him.

As for the Swiss doctor himself, he published a long detailed account of the K2 expedition in 1904, illustrated with numerous photographs. Though never translated into English, it made quite an impact in Europe and eventually came to the attention of the next key character in the history of K2: the Italian prince Luigi Amadeo Savoia, more commonly known as the Duke of Abruzzi.

The cousin of the reigning King of Italy, the Duke was, in the words of the great Victorian climber Edward Whymper, 'A Right Royal Mountaineer'. Tall and thin with a handsome face and 'far away' eyes, Abruzzi was a slightly troubled soul, who preferred expeditions to the formality of aristocratic life. Between 1897 and 1906 he attempted to reach the North Pole, made the first ascent of Mount St Elias in Canada and led a long and successful expedition to the Ruwenzori, the fabled 'Mountains of the Moon' that straddle Congo and Uganda, in which he made several first ascents. Then once he had become the most famous explorer in the world, he fell in love – with a woman he couldn't have.

Katherine Elkins was the beautiful daughter of a US senator and reputed to be the heiress to a vast fortune. For two years American newspapers were full of stories of her impending wedding to the dashing Italian prince, but Elkins was neither royal, Catholic, nor Italian – and for the Duke's aunt, Queen Margherita, that made her an impossible match. Things came to a head at the end of 1908 when pressure from without, and possibly within, led to the break-up of their relationship.

A few months later, US newspapers announced that the lovelorn prince was off on his travels again, hoping to mend his broken heart by making the first ascent of K2. He'd been encouraged by the positive tone of Jacot-Guillarmod's book. Though candid about the failings of the 1902 expedition, the Swiss doctor maintained that K2 could indeed be climbed, and with Nepal and Tibet still closed to foreigners, it remained the biggest challenge available for a dedicated mountaineer in need of a distraction.

In contrast to the ad hoc internationalism of the Eckenstein expedition, Abruzzi's team was all-Italian and most of its members were trusted lieutenants from his previous adventures. He took four experienced Alpine guides: the brothers Alexis and Henri Brocherel and the father and son team, Joseph and Laurent Petigax, along with three porters, from his home region of Val d'Aosta. The expedition doctor and official chronicler was Filippo de Filippi, who had accompanied the Duke to Mount St Elias, and the 'new boy' on the team was Federico Negrotto, a trained topographer. The final member of the Duke's party was his regular collaborator, the fifty-year-old Vittorio Sella, then regarded as the greatest mountain photographer in the world.

Vittorio Sella was the nephew of Quintino Sella, the founder of the Italian Alpine Club. He was a very gifted climber and a truly exceptional photographer. During a mountaineering career spanning over thirty years, he and his cameras travelled the world from the Caucasus of Eastern Europe, to the St Elias range of Alaska and the Ruwenzori mountains. He accompanied Abruzzi on most of his major expeditions but increasingly became more and more focused on photography. By 1909, he had begun to tire of the Duke, who always seemed to be in a rush, but a trip to K2 was too good an opportunity to turn down. Sella agreed to go but insisted that he should be given a set of porters of his own, so that he could work independently of Abruzzi's main party whenever necessary.

On Easter Sunday 1909, after a two-week trip from Europe, the Duke and his men arrived at Rawalpindi, the military cantonment in northern India that was rapidly becoming the starting-off point for any trip to the Karakoram. Their baggage consisted of no fewer than

132 separate loads, each weighing 80 lbs. The combined total came to 10.5 tons, over three times as much food and equipment as Eckenstein had taken.

Two days later, having sent the baggage off in advance, they climbed into a pair of landau carriages and set off for Srinagar in high style. This time there were no morning visits from local policemen or travel bans. Instead Abruzzi was warmly welcomed by Kashmir's official British Resident: the K2 pioneer, now peer, Sir Francis Younghusband. For the next week, Abruzzi was wined and dined at the British Residency.

At Younghusband's suggestion, the Duke had hired a local man, A.C. Baines, to act as his transport manager. It was a wise move. An experienced traveller, Baines handled all the hiring and firing of porters along the route, as well as organising social encounters with local rajahs and maharajahs.

The Duke followed the same route as Eckenstein from Kashmir through Baltistan to the Karakoram. His only variation came at the beginning when, with due pomp and ceremony, he and his men left Srinagar in two splendidly appointed official boats, with fifteen brightly uniformed rowers apiece and the maharajah's admiral of the fleet. Abruzzi and his team spent their night afloat being royally entertained before disembarking the following day and continuing their journey by pony and boot.

The trek in went smoothly and uneventfully. It took fifteen days to get to Skardu and a further seven to reach Askole, about a week less than Eckenstein and Crowley. Everything worked with well-oiled efficiency: Baines rode ahead of the team, setting up their camps and making sure that when Abruzzi and the others arrived there was plenty of tea and tiffin.

When they reassembled their equipment at Askole, they were delighted to see that after a twenty-two-day march over 295 miles, they had not lost a single item in spite of several changes of porters. Then two days later they were off for the final leg of the approach march, with a vast caravan of over 250 people flanked by a small herd of goats and sheep, taken along to provide fresh milk.

Even though the Duke's party was very well travelled, and had seen some of the most spectacular mountains in the world, they were amazed at the scale of the glaciers and the huge variety of mountains that surrounded them. De Filippi was reminded of the Arctic, though he found the Karakoram even more impressive:

> *Instead of the monotonous horizons of the far north, all the landscape around K2 has the richest variety of design, the greatest majesty of form and an infinite diversity of plane and perspective... The scale is far too vast for one to receive an impression of the whole at once. The eye can only take in single portions.*[19]

When they reached Urdukas, the oasis of flowers and grass banks halfway up the Baltoro glacier where Pfannl and Wessely had spent their final weeks recuperating, they sent back half their porters, retaining just over 100 men to go all the way to K2 base camp. Thirty-five of the youngest and fittest-looking were hired for the duration of the expedition, ten to remain with the Duke, and twenty-five to stay with Baines at Urdukas and hump regular supplies of fresh food and fuel to base camp.

Abruzzi was keen to carry straight on but a heavy fall of overnight snow made any travel on the following day impossible. Not wanting to waste an unexpected day off, Vittorio Sella took a party of men down to the Baltoro glacier to build up a pyramid of stones while Negrotto, the topographer, fixed its position. Two months later, when they returned to Urdukas, they repeated the sightings and were amazed to discover that the glacial flow had carried their marker 361 ft downstream in sixty-two days.

The next morning, the weather still looked uncertain, but they took a risk and headed back up the glacier. A day and a half later they found themselves staring up at their goal: K2. Like Jacot-Guillarmod, de Filippi was both entranced and intimidated, and, like Francis Younghusband, his first sight inspired another of the great literary descriptions of a mountain:

Down at the end, alone, detached from all the other moun-
tains soared up K2, the indisputable sovereign of the region,
gigantic and solitary, hidden from human sight by innumer-
able ranges, jealously defended by a vast throng of vassal
peaks, protected from invasion by miles and miles of glaciers.
Even to get within sight of it demands so much contrivance,
so much marching, such a sum of labour.

It fills the end of the valley with nothing to draw the atten-
tion from it. All the lines of the landscape seem to meet and
converge on it. . .

We gazed, we minutely inspected, we examined with our
glasses the incredible rock wall. All the time our minds were
assailed with increasing doubt, culminating almost in cer-
tainty, that this side of the mountain was not accessible, and
did not offer even a reasonable point of attack.[20]

The Duke was not quite so pessimistic. Without more ado, he and his
guides set off to make a rapid reconnaissance. It was impossible to
reach the north face on the Chinese side, but they managed to get a
good look at K2 from every other angle. Everyone agreed that the faces
were too steep and avalanche-prone to offer a safe route, but three of
the ridges looked as if they might 'go'. In the first instance, like Aleister
Crowley, the Duke was principally interested in attempting K2 via the
south east ridge.

He quickly devised a plan of attack. First they would build a small
supply depot at the foot of the ridge. Then he and his Italian guides
would make their way to the band of red and yellow rock at around
22,500 ft. Once the route had been prepared, their Balti porters would
come up with equipment and supplies and help build an intermediate
camp from which the Duke would strike out for the top. If absolutely
necessary they would take the means to set up one further camp, but
Abruzzi hoped to climb K2 in just three stages.

As with Eckenstein and Crowley, the Duke's plan was optimistic.
Though he claimed that one purpose of the expedition was to investigate the effect of high altitude on the human body, he didn't seem to

think that it would slow down his or his team's climbing. On the other hand, he was realistic enough to acknowledge that they might not reach the actual summit and thought that getting to the Shoulder, the prominent flat area 3000 ft below, would be an achievement in itself. Certainly it would be enough to win him his coveted world altitude record.

On the morning of 30 May they were ready to start. For the first attempt, the Duke decided to take only his Alpine guides, the Brocherels and the Petigaxes, and to leave Vittorio Sella and the other members of the scientific team at base camp. Having had a second look at the ridge, he didn't think there would be enough space to move everyone up to the higher camp. Besides which, if he failed on the first attempt, the others could follow and take advantage of the tents already in position.

Everyone accepted this arrangement, though de Filippi admitted that when the Duke left he was very worried:

> *The simple fact is that these are not mountains like other mountains, and one cannot look at them without disquiet and foreboding.*[21]

At first it went reasonably well. The Brocherels and the Petigaxes forged ahead and found a sheltered spot about 18,200 ft up the ridge, big enough to set up two tents. The Duke soon joined them but then elected to stay back to look after the slightly nervous Balti porters, while his guides climbed on as far as a small rock saddle 1000 ft higher up. They were still 4000 ft below the band of yellow rock and more than 8000 ft below the summit but it was a positive start. They cached their bags and then descended to the tents for a good night's sleep.

Next morning, the Balti porters were persuaded to go further and follow the Italians up the ridge to the saddle. Then once again the guides left them behind and continued on, putting up 350 ft of safety rope over the most difficult sections. At 3.00 p.m. they turned round and headed back to the warmth of their tents.

It had been another good day, but it was becoming clear that the south east ridge was going to take a lot longer than anyone had anticipated. So Abruzzi sent six of the porters back to base camp for more food and equipment. On the next day, he stayed in camp again while his guides rapidly climbed up to the rock saddle and then re-ascended the icy gully. When they reached the top, however, it only got harder. Above was a very narrow and very exposed crest. Make a slip on one side, and they would fall straight back down the icy gully. Make a slip on the other, and they'd find themselves some 3000 ft down on the glacier below.

The Brocherels and the Petigaxes were proud Alpine guides and didn't want to turn back, but as they made their way slowly and gingerly upwards, they began to realise that it was impossible to judge distances correctly. The band of yellow rocks always seemed to be close, but never was. Slopes that looked easy from a distance turned out to be sheer cliffs, demanding total concentration. After three hours, Joseph Petigax finally decided that enough was enough and that K2 would not be climbed via this particular route. On the way down, he collected the rope that they had fixed in the gully, confident that the Duke would not object. Abruzzi didn't take much convincing: even if they could get further, he agreed with Petigax that their Balti porters would never be able to climb a ridge that seasoned Alpine guides found so difficult.

On 2 June, four days after they had left, Abruzzi and the others returned to base camp to the relief of the men they had left behind. Their first foray onto K2 had not been a great success, but at least they had returned unscathed and there was still plenty of time to investigate other options. None, however, turned out to be as accessible as their first choice. When they moved operations to the other side of the mountain, Abruzzi succeeded in climbing a steep snow slope to the north west ridge, but in the words of de Filippi, the view from the top was enough to 'utterly annihilate the hopes with which we had begun the ascent'. Returning to the other side, they headed up the Godwin-Austen glacier toward the north east ridge, under which Eckenstein and Crowley had camped for all those weeks in 1902.

Before they reached it, they came across a pile of boxes and climbing equipment: the detritus of Eckenstein's last camp. When the Duke compared its current position to the map in Jacot-Guillarmod's book, he realised that in the intervening seven years the glacier had carried Eckenstein's leftovers almost a mile downstream.

For almost two weeks, they explored the labyrinth of ridges, glaciers and passes to the north east of K2 looking for a chink in its armour. Vittorio Sella obtained some very striking panoramic views, the cartographer Negrotto gathered data for a detailed map, and the Duke managed to reach 21,650 ft on nearby Skyang Kangri, 'Staircase Peak', from which he took a classic photograph of K2's east face. He did not, however, find a better route to the summit. By the end of June, the Duke had had his fill of K2. He and his men had accumulated a mass of topographical and meteorological data, had investigated the mountain from three sides and made one, albeit limited, attempt to reach the summit. All that remained was the small question of that world altitude record.

Fortunately, the Duke had a plan B. On the way up to K2 he had seen several peaks over 26,000 ft but all had looked equally difficult. So like Martin Conway, Abruzzi decided to focus his attention on the southern end of the Baltoro glacier. He didn't want to repeat Conway's attempt on the Golden Throne, which was too low to break any record, but close by there was another higher mountain called Chogolisa, or Bride Peak.

Like K2, it proved a lot harder than anticipated, with both bad weather and growing fatigue playing a significant role, but on 18 July, just over two weeks after leaving K2, he and his guides managed to reach 24,600 ft, over 1200 ft above the then-current altitude record. They were 500 ft below Chogolisa's summit but the slopes above them were shrouded in mist and on one side there was an unstable-looking cornice. For two hours the Duke waited, hoping that the weather might improve but it didn't. So reluctantly he turned back.

Abruzzi and his companions had set a record that would last until 1922 but he would have far preferred to do so by reaching Chogolisa's summit, rather than by stopping just short of it. When they broke camp on 20 July to begin the long journey home, their Balti porters could not have been happier, but the Italians left the Karakoram, as de Filippi recorded, 'silent and depressed, under the evil fate that had snatched from the Duke the prize of so much labour and perseverance, after it had lain almost within his grasp'.[22]

On the way back to Europe the sombre mood continued. According to an Italian journalist quoted in the *New York Times*, the Duke spent most of his time on the voyage home

> *writing in the music room of the steamer, or else stretched out on his deck chair. Even when he took a walk on deck with the Marquis or another of his friends, he scarcely spoke at all. His eyes, said the Italian, seemed fixed on something far away, as if planning new expeditions to remote parts of the world.*[23]

Whether he was thinking about K2, his next big trip, or his old American flame, Katherine Elkins, no one could tell.

Ultimately, Abruzzi had got no higher on K2 than Pfannl and Jacot-Guillarmod in 1902 but the impact of his expedition on the subsequent history of the mountain was far greater. In 1912, after three years of painstaking labour, Filippo de Filippi's 469-page official history was published in Florence, New York and London. Accompanying the main volume was an extraordinary set of maps and photographs, many of them panoramic views. It was a monumental work that would become a key reference point for the expeditions that followed, and further elevate Vittorio Sella's reputation as the greatest mountain photographer of his era.

Like Eckenstein and Crowley, Abruzzi had vastly underestimated the scale and difficulties of K2. Immediately afterwards he was widely quoted as saying it was simply impossible to climb. However, as de Filippi made clear in the conclusion of his book, on reflection he did not think that there was any absolute limit to the altitude that a climber might ascend. Nor did he think that K2 was simply too steep or too complicated. The real problem came from its isolation: according to de Filippi, K2 was simply so remote, and its climate so hostile, that no one could properly lay siege to it.

In the future, though, if a quicker way could be devised to get to K2 and if it became possible to stay longer, who could tell? Perhaps following on from the 'Golden Age of Alpine Climbing' of the mid-nineteenth century, when most of the high mountains of the European Alps were climbed, there would be a Golden Age of Himalayan climbing. As the Duke's friend, the Norwegian Arctic explorer Fridtjof Nansen, liked to say:

> *The difficult is what takes a little time. The impossible is what takes a little longer.*

The epic saga of K2 had begun. Montgomerie had come up with the name, Eckenstein and Abruzzi had written the introductory chapter. Far away across the Atlantic, the next set of suitors were still in shorts, but they would build on the work of their predecessors and their stories would turn out to be even more extraordinary.

Chapter 2

THE HARVARD BOYS

So, they turned the wastepaper basket over and propped Vittorio Sella's photographs around the edge. Then they walked around it, two Harvard boys and a Yaley, looking for a way up the world's second-highest mountain.

The north side? No. The south? No. East? West? No and no again; there was no obvious route. Give up now? Hell no – in a few months they'd be on their way to India, hoping to prove Abruzzi wrong, and Nansen right. It was March 1938 and the American Alpine Club were on their way to the world's second-highest mountain and nothing was going to stop them now.

In the twenty-nine years since Abruzzi came back empty-handed, there had been no further expeditions to K2 but there had been plenty of activity in the Himalayas. Between 1921 and 1937 there had been six Everest expeditions, three attempts on Kanchenjunga,[1] and three on Nanga Parbat, the world's third- and ninth-highest mountains respectively. None of them were successful, but two British teams had got within 1000 ft of the summit of Everest, smashing Abruzzi's altitude record by over 3000 ft.

In Europe mountaineering was big news, but in spite of all the country's natural riches, the sport had been slow to take off in the United States. In the 1930s, however, that began to change, albeit slowly. Climbing clubs appeared at several of the Ivy League colleges on the East Coast including Yale and Dartmouth. The biggest and most influential club was founded at Harvard in 1924, and that's where our two Harvard boys, Charlie Houston and Bob Bates, come into the story.

Charles Houston, or Charlie as he was universally known, was born in 1913 in New York. His father was a successful lawyer who specialised in maritime law, his mother the daughter of an ancient Scottish family that had settled in the American South several generations earlier. Charlie grew up on Long Island and went on to the prestigious Hotchkiss School. He got his first taste of climbing at the age of twelve when his father took the Houstons for a family holiday in the Alps. After enrolling at Harvard in 1931, he joined the mountaineering club and was soon spending his weekends scaling the walls of local rock quarries.

Bob Bates came from the academic side of America's middle classes. His father, a professor of Greek at Pennsylvania University, was a keen outdoorsman, and his mother, a teacher turned housewife, shared that passion. The Bates spent their summers in the White Mountains of New Hampshire and let their children roam free in the woods. Bob met Charlie at Harvard in the early 1930s. After their first major expedition to Mount Crillon in Alaska in 1933, they formed an enduring friendship that would last a lifetime. For both of them, Alaska was their training ground and a showcase for their ambition and skill. Charlie Houston led the first ascent of Mount Foraker and Bob Bates partnered fellow Harvard alumnus Brad Washburn on the gruelling ascent of Mount Lucania in the Canadian Yukon.

Bob had never climbed outside of America, but by 1938 Charlie was already a Himalayan veteran. In 1936 he and two other Harvard chums, Farnie Loomis and H. Adams Carter, had the temerity first to apply to the British authorities to make an attempt on Kanchenjunga, the third-highest mountain in the world, and then, when their request was turned down, to seek a permit for Nanda Devi. Ringed by an almost impenetrable barrier of mountains at 25,643 ft, it was one of India's highest and holiest mountains and considered one of the great prizes in the world of mountaineering. Just to get to the foot of Nanda Devi was an epic in itself, and here they were setting off to climb it and enlisting two of the most famous figures in mountaineering to help them: Britain's Bill Tilman and Noel Odell. These Harvard boys might have lacked experience, but they had no shortage of confidence.

Though it was Odell and Tilman who ultimately reached the summit of Nanda Devi, Charlie Houston returned to the US at the tender age of twenty-three hailed as one of the United States' leading mountaineers. In 1937 he was the star turn at the American Alpine Club's annual dinner in Boston, along with German émigré Fritz Wiessner. Charlie gave a speech about his adventures in the Himalayas while Fritz recounted his dramatic first ascent of Mount Waddington in Canada. Neither man knew it at the time, but over the next decades their destinies would be closely entwined and revolve around K2.

In character and style they were utterly different. Charlie was short and stocky, with tight curly hair, an intense gaze and a serious air. Fritz was thirteen years older, with a prominent bald head and a broad chest. Charlie was an Anglophile, his mountaineering heroes British through and through. Fritz was unmistakeably German in his accent and his manner. Charlie was old money, Fritz was an immigrant hoping to make his millions in the New World.

Both were very talented, but there was no question that Fritz was the more gifted technical climber. Already well known in Germany, in the early 1930s he had taken the American climbing world by storm, bringing in new techniques and introducing American climbers to some great but ignored mountains in their own backyard. Fritz was an organiser and an enthusiast. Throughout his life he loved to inspire and encourage young climbers and put climbing parties together. In 1932, three years after arriving in the US, he helped organise the first German expedition to Nanga Parbat, the 26,660 ft peak that would become known as Germany's 'mountain of destiny'. Fritz brought two Americans along too: Elizabeth Knowlton, a journalist and one of America's foremost female climbers, and Rand Herron, a scion of a very wealthy family who had recently become interested in mountaineering. The expedition did not go particularly well, but it introduced Fritz to the vagaries of Himalayan weather and gave him his first experience of high-altitude climbing.

Four years later, in 1936, he tried to organise an American Alpine Club expedition to Nanga Parbat, but was refused permission by the British authorities who controlled access to the region. Another

Austro-German expedition had been approved and they didn't want a second team on the mountain. So Fritz set his sights higher and put in an application, again via the American Alpine Club, to make an attempt on K2. This time the British authorities eventually gave their approval, but they took so long to make up their minds that when the permit came through, Fritz was no longer available.

For almost a decade he had been trying to get a business off the ground and 1938 looked like it was going to be very busy. A chemist by training, he had run a small chain of pharmacies in Germany and was now trying to set up a factory in America to manufacture ski wax. Having lobbied for the K2 permit long and hard, the American Alpine Club didn't want to give it up, so they came up with a compromise plan. In 1938 they would send out a reconnaissance party, tasked with finding a route up the mountain, and in the following year Fritz would return with the main team. The best man to lead that reconnaissance, as everyone agreed, was Charlie Houston.

Charlie leapt at the chance. He had been thrilled by his visit to Nanda Devi and was ambitious for more. He knew from his British friends that no American party would ever get access to Everest while the Empire still reigned in the East, so for everyone else, K2 was still mountaineering's biggest challenge. Now all he needed was a team.

His first call was to Bob Bates. Even though Bob had just started a new teaching job and was hard at work on a PhD, he said yes straight away. For a while they talked about bringing some British climbers on board – perhaps Bill Tilman again or Freddy Spencer Chapman, the well-known Greenland explorer. Neither was available, so Charlie and Bob turned to two Americans whom Fritz had already approached: Dick Burdsall, who had been part of the American team that climbed Minya Konka in China in 1932, and Tony Cromwell, a stalwart of the American Alpine Club. Family reasons prevented Cromwell from going but Dick Burdsall signed up.

Charlie tried to get Farnie Loomis, another Harvard boy and a member of his 1936 Nanda Devi team. Initially he said yes but a few weeks later Loomis discovered that he couldn't make it, so he suggested Paul Petzoldt, a respected mountain guide who ran a guiding company in the Grand Teton National Park. A self-proclaimed 'Wyoming cowboy', his background was very different from everyone else's, but Loomis was so confident in Petzoldt's climbing abilities that he offered to cover his costs.

Securing the final member of the team was the trickiest part. With the 1938 and the 1939 expeditions both recruiting, Charlie and Fritz Wiessner were competing for the best climbers – in particular they were both after Bill House, a very strong twenty-five-year-old and the former president of the Yale mountaineering club. Bill had been Fritz's partner on the first ascent of Mount Waddington but Charlie wanted him for his reconnaissance expedition. Though it would have made sense for the reconnaissance and the main expedition to share members, because of the high cost in time and money, it was very unlikely that House, or any other climber, would be available for two years in a row, so who would get him?

In spite of their mutual respect as mountaineers, Charlie and Fritz had never really been that comfortable with each other and the tussle over Bill House only made things worse. Back in 1936 when Charlie got his permit for Nanda Devi, officials at the American Alpine Club had encouraged him to invite Fritz onto the team. But Charlie had refused, on the grounds that a German would not fit into an Anglo-American party.[2] Fritz for his part blew hot and cold about Charlie – he had climbed and skied with him and considered him a friend but they were never very close.

In the end, Bill House signed up for Charlie's 1938 reconnaissance, but even though he had won that particular battle, Charlie and his deputy, Bob Bates, increasingly started to feel that Fritz was using them. They would go out in 1938, do all the hard work and then he would return in the following year, follow their route to the summit and come back with all the glory. The only way to stop that happening, they decided, was to get to the top themselves.

Once Charlie had his team, the next hurdle was finance. Though the 1938 reconnaissance was an 'official' American Alpine Club expedition, the participants had to cover the costs themselves. In Britain, there was so much interest in mountaineering that Everest expeditions were largely funded by selling newspaper rights to *The Times* of London. In the United States, there simply wasn't the same level of interest, so prospective climbers had to be well off or well connected if they wanted to test themselves against the high mountains of the Himalayas or the Karakoram.

Charlie came from a privileged background but he was still a student and depended on his parents for support. Fortunately for Charlie, his father Oscar was very interested in mountaineering; fortunately for Oscar, Charlie's natural instincts were toward frugality. He set the budget at $9000, and asked each man to contribute what he could. The majority would have to be made up at the end through newspaper articles, lecture fees and private donations. Unlike the Duke of Abruzzi, who employed a host of transport managers and minions, Charlie and Bob had to do most of the preparatory work themselves.

Ever the Anglophile, Charlie ordered most of their clothing and equipment from Britain: boots from Robert Lawrie and Co. of Marble Arch in London, Shetland wool underwear and windproof outer clothing made from specially treated Grenfell cloth from a factory in Burnley in the north of England.

Bob Bates looked after expedition food. His tastes were more eclectic: heat-resistant chocolate called Javatex, dried vegetables made from a secret recipe by a Massachusetts firm and 50 lbs of pemmican from Denmark. A mixture of fat, dried beef and raisins, pemmican had for many years been the staple food of Arctic expeditions. It was ideal for K2, but Bob was worried that there might be problems crossing Hindu India with large quantities of tinned beef, so he removed the labels and passed the tins off as spinach and pumpkin.

Bob's method of choosing expedition biscuits would have made Salem's witch-hunters proud: he dropped them from a second-floor window to judge their crackability and then left them out overnight in the rain to see how quickly they became soggy. In the end he ordered 100 lbs of the same brand, which was water-resistant yet easy to break. For special moments, Bob's treats box was small but luxurious: four plum puddings, two tins of caviar, a batch of kippered herrings and two bottles of rum.

After five very busy months of preparations, the whole team finally came together in New York for a farewell meal with their friends and family on 14 April 1938.[3] Fritz Wiessner was invited but he couldn't make it. Then at midnight they embarked on the SS *Europa* for France where they would connect with a second ship to India. Though dinner was paid for by his father Oscar, Charlie did not accompany the others. With his medical exams coming up, he was planning to fly out a few weeks later to meet them at Rawalpindi in northern India.

The voyage to Europe was a good opportunity for team bonding. Bob Bates quickly became firm friends with Bill House and Dick Burdsall, but though everyone tried hard to make Paul Petzoldt feel welcome, the self-styled 'Wyoming cowboy' was very conscious of being an outsider. Tall and square-jawed, Petzoldt both looked the part and lived it. He had grown up in rural Idaho, the son of a poor farmer who died when he was just a toddler leaving his mother to bring up nine children alone. While Charlie and Bob, 'Eastern Nabobs' according to Petzoldt, were being educated in the best schools and colleges in the US, he had worked variously as a mortuary attendant, gambler, ranch hand and hotel dishwasher.[4] In between odd jobs, he climbed his first mountain, the Grand Teton, in 1922 and instantly found his niche and his passion.

When Petzoldt got the invitation from Charlie Houston to join his K2 team, he said yes straight away but it rankled that he was so much poorer than the other guys. This feeling wasn't helped when, just before leaving, he found an unsigned memo at the American Alpine Club in amongst the expedition papers which questioned whether a 'Wyoming packer and guide' would have the social skills for planned meetings with members of the British and French Alpine Clubs.

In fact, when a week later in Paris they met Pierre Allain, the president of the French Alpine Club, Petzoldt easily held his own. Behind his rough exterior, he was a much more intelligent character than most people realised and was not easily intimidated – not by Harvard boys, big mountains or club presidents.

The French Alpine Club had been responsible for the last big expedition to the Karakoram, a well-funded attempt on Hidden

Peak, one of K2's smaller neighbours, in 1936 by a team of highly experienced climbers. It had failed utterly after a huge storm trapped the climbers in their tents for two weeks. When club members had heard about the forthcoming K2 expedition by what they considered a bunch of American greenhorns, they were very sceptical and joked that they were bringing far too much food because they would not last long.

The young Americans didn't take the bait but after a little good-humoured mockery, they did visit a French climbing shop to purchase a bag of climbing pitons, then considered essential by most Continental climbers. After that, Bates and the others took a train to Marseille where they embarked on the SS *Comorin* for the voyage to India.

In Bombay they made time for a little more last-minute shopping – for climbing rope. There was plenty on offer in the bazaar, but nothing was graded for strength. The only way to test a rope was to tie one end of a sample to something solid, throw the other end over a beam and then for everyone to hang off it. The first couple of batches didn't survive the combined bulk of three well-fed Americans, but eventually Bob Bates found one type of rope that did and bought several hundred feet.

After a brief unexpected meeting with two members of the latest German team on their way to Nanga Parbat, they took the *Frontier Mail* to Rawalpindi. On 9 May they were reunited with Charlie Houston, not quite so fresh from his medical-school exams and the journey out to India. During the course of a hectic two weeks, he had crossed the Atlantic on the *Queen Mary*, made a multi-stop flight from London to Karachi and embarked on a twelve-hour train journey through the burning heat of the Sindh Desert. No one could doubt his dedication to K2.

At Rawalpindi, they also met the final members of the team: Norman Streatfeild, the British transport officer assigned to their expedition by the colonial authorities, and six Sherpas. Streatfeild was a tall, cheerful Scot. He had played the same role on the 1936 French expedition to Hidden Peak, and made it clear from the start that he wanted to be a full member of the climbing team. In return, Streatfeild's contribution to expedition stores included a large Stilton cheese and a portable rubber bath.

The Sherpas hailed from Darjeeling, many miles away in the north east of British India. This was the first time that they had been employed on K2 but by the mid-1930s they had become a vital part of any Himalayan expedition. Originally from Tibet, the Sherpas, or 'People from the East', had migrated across the Himalayas into Nepal during the previous 300 years. Many had then made a second migration to Darjeeling in search of work. Very strong and tough, over the last two decades Sherpas had established themselves first as general porters and then as a kind of elite high-altitude porter, whose role was to carry equipment when the main body of local 'coolies' had been dismissed. Two of the six who turned up at Rawalpindi had been on Charlie's Nanda Devi expedition in 1936 and one, Pasang Kikuli, had been his 'personal' Sherpa.

Houston planned to follow the same route as Abruzzi and Eckenstein, going from Rawalpindi to Srinagar, the capital of Kashmir, then across Baltistan to Askole, before heading up the Baltoro glacier to K2. This time round, rather than cramming into *ekkas* or carriages, they hired two large cars and a lorry for the 180-mile journey to Srinagar. Many bumpy hours later, they arrived at Nedou's Hotel, a few miles from the famously beautiful Dal Lake. It was surrounded by pine trees and flower meadows but there was no time to enjoy the view or go sightseeing. Task number one was to unload their supplies and equipment. Unlike Abruzzi, who had sent his stores from Europe in pre-packaged bundles, they had to break down 4 tons of supplies into 55 lb porter loads and assemble a set of flatpack wooden boxes.

To their relief, almost everything was intact, apart from a few casualties. A 5 lb tin of jam had burst and decorated everything in its path and Charlie Houston's fur-trimmed wind-suit was soaked in sticky honey from another damaged container. He was not pleased.

Three days later, they left Srinagar in two large lorries and set off along the last 18 miles of usable road. After that, everything would have to be carried by pony or porter for the final 330 miles to K2. Even with a pukka British transport officer accompanying them for

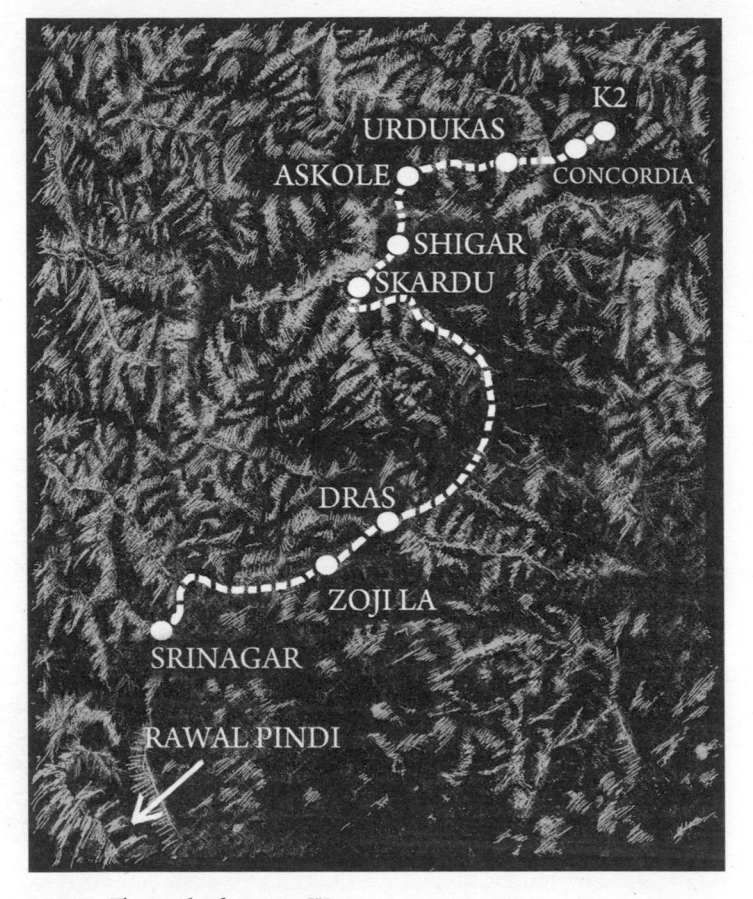

Map 2 The overland route to K2

the whole journey they still had a lot of problems with local porters. At Woyyil bridge, the end of the road, they were greeted with a huge scrum of pony men all offering up their nags while street sellers tried to flog trinkets. All around, petty thieves eyed up anything that might be spirited away unnoticed.

After a brief but intense burst of filming and photography, they left in a cloud of dust with twenty-five ponies, each carrying three loads. In addition to a newly hired shikari, or hunting guide, the aptly named Ghaffar Sheikh, they now also had both an expedition cook, Ahdoo, and that cook's own personal cook. As Bob Bates wryly noted in the expedition book, *Five Miles High*, 'In India every servant has his own servant.'[5] For Bates and Houston, who had grown up reading Rudyard Kipling, the great storyteller of British India, the whole trip had a magical quality. They were the stars of their very own *Boys' Own Adventure*, travelling through a land that didn't seem to have changed for centuries.

On the first march they made 17 miles, a good start. Each member of the team was allocated their own 'personal' Sherpa, or camp assistant. Initially the young Americans were a little embarrassed about this, but over the first week, one by one they fell into the role of 'sahib'. After a long day hiking it was hard to say no to a smiling face, who offered to put up your tent, unpack your sleeping bag, make you a cup of tea and even help to take your boots off.

On 16 May, after three days on the trail, they reached the fabled and much-anticipated Zoji La, the 11,230 ft pass across the Western Himalayas that connects Kashmir to Baltistan and had been for centuries an important stage on Oriental trade routes. During the winter and spring it was impassable, and even in May caravans had been known to wait for weeks before they could cross.

Fortunately, the Zoji La looked safe enough but there was a high risk of avalanches during the day. So they waited until just after midnight to make their way up a steep path flanked by tall black cliffs, illuminated by burning torches and uncertain moonlight. As Bob Bates crunched through the snow and stared at long caravans on their way to India from Tibet, laden with tea and precious rugs, he felt himself being transported back in history. The feeling continued on the following day when, in the Drass valley, they passed a boulder where almost eighty years earlier the British surveyor Henry Haversham Godwin-Austen had carved his initials, 'H.H.G.-A. 1861-2-3'.

Like his predecessors on Eckenstein's and Abruzzi's expeditions, Bob Bates was very struck at how different the landscape of Baltistan was from that of Kashmir. Instead of lush valleys and picturesque lakes, they found themselves hiking through claustrophobic valleys above which loomed huge peaks. The monotony was only broken by occasional Balti villages clinging to the hillsides, invariably surrounded by apricot groves. Bob was fascinated by their irrigation systems, formed of hundreds of yards of ditches and channels, dug by hand into the rock. The paths between villages were equally spectacular feats of manual engineering, zig-zagging their way along the same rock walls, sometimes at river level, sometimes hundreds of feet above the fast flowing water.

As the days rolled on, Charlie Houston, the expedition doctor as well as its leader, had to cope with a litany of blisters, pulled tendons and bruises, but the only serious incident occurred when a pony fell in the river and its load floated off downstream. Their cook Ahdoo made such a scene that for a few panicky moments Bob Bates thought that they might have lost all their precious stoves, but, as it turned out, the box contained his personal bedding – a big loss for the cook but not such a trauma for the other members of the expedition. They breathed a sigh of relief, and carefully checked that the vital pieces of equipment were spread around the pony train from then on.

Balti villages invariably looked much more charming from a distance than close up, where the smells usually made a stronger impression than the sights. In spite of their subsistence lifestyle, villagers were invariably very welcoming and generous, and curious to see the strange foreigners in their midst. Charlie Houston was frequently called upon to open up his medicine chest and run an impromptu clinic. Eye infections were commonplace and there was a shocking number of people with huge goitres on their necks, a common ailment in mountain regions caused by lack of iodine.

After almost two weeks Houston's party finally reached Skardu, the capital of Baltistan. It was the halfway point of their journey and the last town connected to the outside world by telegraph, so they took a few days off. Bob Bates filed an article for the London *Times*, and Charlie Houston busied himself writing letters. Their transport officer, Norman Streatfeild, shopped for tea and flour and collected a massive chest, filled with 75 lbs of coins to pay the large number of porters they would need for the next stage. Bob Bates was amused to be offered cast-offs from the French Hidden Peak expedition in the bazaar, but disappointed that there was no local beer on offer.

Forty-eight restful hours later, Houston's caravan rode and marched out of Skardu to begin the final approach march to K2. There would be little luxury ahead. Task number one was to get themselves and their horses across the roaring Indus, the vast river at places 12 miles wide, which originates in Tibet and then flows all the way down through Kashmir to Karachi before draining into the Arabian Sea. The only option was to float across on a large rickety-looking barge, of a type said to have been first used in the era of Alexander the Great. Their Balti steersman paused to pray before they set off at a furious pace across the racing current. When it reached the opposite bank, the barge was half a mile below its starting point.

At Yuno, the second village, they said goodbye to their ponies. From now on all their gear would have to be carried by human porters alone so they would need many more. The only problem was that the Yuno men they tried to hire refused to accept the official rate and demanded their wages be doubled. Eckenstein and Abruzzi had got on very well with their Balti porters, but thirty years later there was a more defiant mood in the air. The British Empire, on which the sun was never supposed to set, was looking a little shaky. Mahatma Gandhi's civil disobedience campaigns might not have reached directly into Baltistan, but as Houston quickly found out, the local men were simply unwilling to 'kowtow' to Westerners, whether or not they were accompanied by a British liaison officer.

What started as a trade dispute quickly developed into a tense, if slightly comical confrontation, with sixty unhappy Baltis advancing on the American camp to demand higher wages while Pasang Kikuli and his Sherpas unsheathed their ice-axes and a kukri, one of the famous crescent-shaped Nepalese knives, and begged to be allowed to take the locals on. When a stray stone hit one of the American tents, Paul Petzoldt threw it back and the Yuno men ran off, threatening to return fully armed.

Charlie Houston was not convinced that it would end in bloodshed but he didn't want their equipment to be damaged, or to find his expedition plagued by delays for the rest of the journey. Streatfeild was willing to raise the porters' wages a little but, as an official transport officer, he did not want to set a bad precedent by giving in completely. So rather than face another confrontation, he and Bob Bates offered to return to Skardu, to get help from local officials. The only way to get back quickly was to brave the torrid waters of the Shigar river on an even more primitive-looking raft than the ferry across the Indus. Luckily, Bates had done plenty of backwoods rafting in Alaska, and was completely unfazed. Captain Streatfeild was equally game so together they set off, accompanied by cheers from their fellow climbers.

Back in Skardu, Bates and Streatfeild were offered omelettes and sympathy. More importantly, they left the following morning accompanied by a policeman with orders to compel the Yuno men to work for the sahibs and arrest the ringleaders of the strike. Two days later, they rode back into camp, just in time to celebrate Bill House's twenty-fifth birthday with plates of rice and small mugs of rum. Next morning Charlie tried to get everyone off early, but in spite of the presence of the policeman, who as Charlie noted carried 'an impressive paper and an even more impressive club', Streatfeild could only muster forty-four porters. They were forced to leave twenty-four loads behind, to be carried up as soon as willing shoulders were located.

The march to the next village, Folio, entailed a total climb of 6000 ft, along paths flanked by soaring peaks. The headman greeted them as the first white men to pass through in twenty-five years. Charlie Houston was taken to a village elder with a very severe case of the eye infection trachoma who begged to have his swollen eyelids cut off. He advised the old man against such a drastic course of action but there was little else that he could do other than trim his eyelashes and offer him some painkillers. There was illness in their own ranks too, with Paul Petzoldt running a high fever, brought on, or so Charlie thought, by carrying a heavy load during the day.

By the time they reached Askole, the final village before K2, Petzoldt's temperature had risen to 40° C and he was unable to walk. Charlie prescribed aspirin and stayed up all night tending to him, but the fever refused to break. Petzoldt could not possibly carry on to K2 and there was no certainty how long he would take to recover – if at all. Later in America, after talking to specialists, Charlie concluded that Petzoldt was probably suffering from Dengue fever, but right now the third-year medical student was stumped.

There was no alternative: he and Charlie would have to stay behind while Bob Bates and the others continued to K2. If Petzoldt recovered quickly, they would try to catch up. If he didn't – that didn't bear thinking about. Charlie took the decision with good grace, but he felt desperately low. After spending so many months organising the expedition, he might never even see K2. To keep his mind off the issue, Charlie busied himself with an endless stream of patients, whose ailments ranged from stomach pains that had afflicted them for fifteen years to the biggest goitres he had seen so far.

On the morning of 6 June Bob and the others left Askole with fifty newly recruited porters. Over the last three weeks they had covered almost 270 miles, but the final 60 miles to K2 base camp would take them over the toughest terrain yet and require them to ascend a further 7000 ft. The landscape wasn't the only problem: barely a day's march from Askole, for the second time in fewer weeks, they were faced with a porter strike and demands for more money. Not wanting a rerun of their extra trip down to Skardu, Streatfeild refused their demands and, fortunately for him, the resolve of the Askole men was weaker than that of the Yuno porters. After securing a modest pay rise, they got back on the trail.

Three days out of Askole, Bob Bates finally caught sight of the Baltoro glacier. Their 39-mile 'highway to K2' looked anything but comfortable – riven by freezing cold streams, covered in broken rocks of all sizes, there was no easy way to travel up it. The Baltoro, as Bob later wrote, reminded him of a huge reptile, looming down on them. Their porters were so intimidated that they huddled together and prayed before climbing up the steep moraines that lead up to the top surface. Apart from the skeletons of three dead ibexes, there was no sign of life and, initially, no vegetation. The only sound was the rattle of rockfalls from the nearby slopes, and the rumble of huge boulders, which for no apparent reason seemed to detach themselves from the glacier and the slopes of the surrounding mountains and hurtle down toward them. Just like Filippo de Filippi in 1909, the young Americans were amazed to see the strange 'ice ships' that rose up in the middle of the glacier looking like a cross between a giant fang and a sail.

Halfway up the Baltoro, they camped at Urdukas, the green oasis opposite the Trango towers, a spectacular group of peaks that seem to rise vertically above the glacier. At 13,200 ft, it was a shock and welcome relief to find slopes peppered with small alpine flowers.

They spent the afternoon lazing on the grass until Pasang Kikuli spotted something on the glacier below. All day they had been looking out for ibex and the even more elusive snow leopard, but the creatures below appeared to have two legs rather than four. Dick Burdsall dug out his binoculars and zeroed in on them: to his amazement, it was Charlie Houston and Paul Petzoldt, resplendent in a red plaid shirt. His 6 ft frame looked distinctly undernourished, but when he reached them he insisted that he was now on the road to recovery, and to prove it quickly downed several mugs of tea and a fistful of crackers and cheese before enquiring what was for dinner that night.

That year the only other large expedition in the Karakoram was a British party attempting Masherbrum, the 25,659 ft peak further up the glacier. The climbers included T. Graham Brown, a veteran climber who Charlie Houston had first met in the Alps as a teenager, eleven years earlier. As they headed down the glacier, Charlie looked forward to seeing Masherbrum, but thankfully he had no plans to drop in on base camp. The British were having a torrid time, tormented by atrocious weather and frostbite. It would not have been a morale-boosting visit.

After six days of hard trekking, on 11 June they finally arrived at Concordia, the amazing natural amphitheatre where the Baltoro glacier collided with the Godwin-Austen and Vigne glaciers. All around them rose the giant mountains that had so impressed Aleister Crowley – Mitre Peak, Chogolisa, Golden Throne, the Gasherbrum massif, Broad Peak... The only trouble was it was such a cloudy day that they could see none of their summits.

Their first encounter with K2 was brief. As they marched up the Godwin-Austen glacier, suddenly for a few fleeting minutes the high clouds parted revealing the summit. As Bob Bates later wrote, his first impression was sheer wonder:

> *It was like something from another world, something ethereal seen in a dream.*[6]

Bates' reverie was short-lived. Before long the clouds rolled in and their altitude-induced headaches started.

They were now higher than any peak in Europe, and most of Alaska's giants, and they hadn't even set foot on K2. Their base camp at 16,600 ft was a small cluster of tents in a hollow, a few hundred feet further up the Godwin-Austen glacier. It was not exactly a luxurious spot, but at least it was protected from the wind and appeared to be safe from the huge avalanches that poured down the adjacent mountains, scattering tons of rock and snow with reckless abandon.

Not surprisingly, the Askole porters were very keen to get away, but equally predictably, they found it impossible not to haggle for a little extra baksheesh. Bob Bates ensured that a few 'faithfuls' received generous tips, but he was parsimonious with anyone who had caused trouble. Just before they left, Streatfeild arranged for the porters to return in forty-five days. To ensure punctuality, he handed their headman the same number of stones and told him to throw one away each day and come back when they were finished. Then at around 5.00 p.m. the Askole men departed, leaving the Americans and their Sherpas feeling 'very much alone'.[7]

As Charlie took stock, he was pleased with how the first half of the expedition had gone. They had travelled almost halfway around the world, without any major mishap. His team seemed to have bonded well, and though Petzoldt's mystery illness remained a cause for concern, he seemed to have recovered and everyone else looked fit and healthy.

They now had just over six weeks to make a thorough reconnaissance of the mountain and, if possible, climb it. Having familiarised

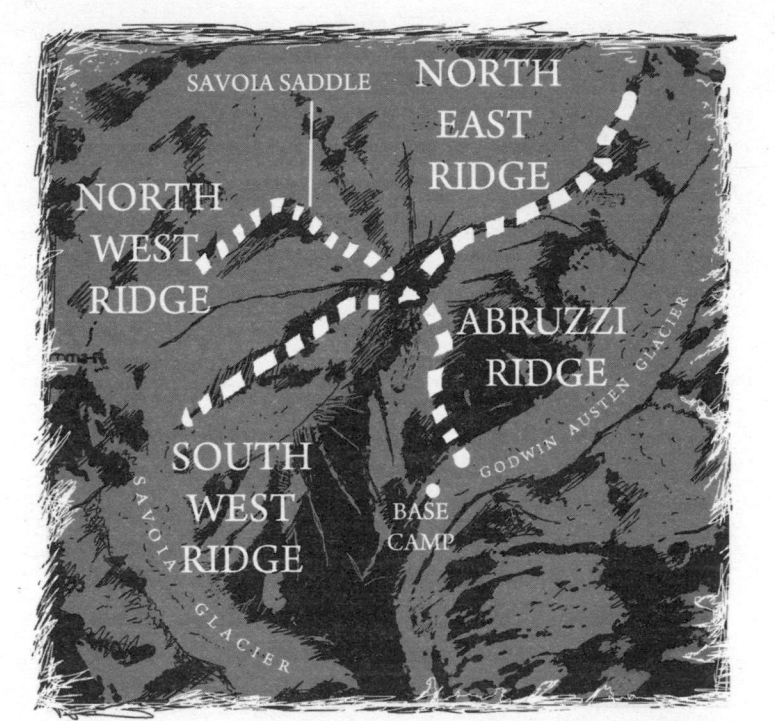

Map 3 The ridges around K2

themselves with the narrative of the Abruzzi expedition and Sella's photographs, Charlie and Bob had concluded that there were four ridges worth inspecting. None of them looked like easy climbs, but there was no question of attempting any of K2's huge faces: like Abruzzi and Eckenstein, they judged these far too avalanche-prone even to attempt.

Of those options, they decided that the north west ridge was the best option. Abruzzi had been pessimistic, but a detailed examination of Sella's photographs showed that the rock strata sloped upwards, making it easier to find handholds and therefore to climb. To add to its attractions, the north west ridge started at 22,000 ft so there was only 6000 ft of climbing to the summit. Getting to the start, however, required a 3000 ft ascent up a steep pass christened the Savoia Saddle by the Abruzzi party, in honour of the Duke's family, the Royal House of Savoy. As the Italians had accomplished this twice in 1909, Bates and Houston didn't think it would be too much of a problem.

On 14 June the whole team set off en masse toward their first target. They carried light packs to take things gently, but it still wasn't easy. The Savoia glacier, which ran along the western flank of K2, was heavily crevassed and it was very easy to break through the thin snow bridges that provided the way across. The only flat ground big enough to take their tents was in the middle of a labyrinth of cracks and chasms, making for a distinctly unsafe campsite. After helping to put up their shelters and snatching a quick lunch, Bob Bates and Norman Streatfeild said their goodbyes and headed back to base camp on the eastern side of the mountain with all the Sherpas, leaving the others to begin the reconnaissance proper.

It did not go well. Petzoldt's fever returned, confining him to his tent. Charlie and the others ventured out onto the glacier, but within thirty minutes it began to snow. Impatient to get some momentum going, they carried on for another two hours before they were forced to turn back in the face of a blizzard.

The next day was better. The weather cleared and Petzoldt declared himself recovered and raring to go, so they moved camp to a safer site, higher up the glacier. Above, perhaps just a few hours away, lay the Savoia Saddle, their staircase to the north west ridge. That night, the temperature plummeted to −17° C, but snug inside their tents with their primus stoves purring and endless cups of tea flowing, no one felt too bad.

Bill House hoped that if the next few days were successful, they might be able to set up an advance base camp at the top of the Saddle. However, his optimism was misplaced. On the following morning, he ventured up toward the pass, only to find the slopes that had looked climbable at a distance included sections inclined at 55–60°, making them virtually impossible to ascend.[8] To make things worse, underneath a thin covering of snow, there was solid green ice, which could only be climbed by chopping hundreds of steps. Even if they could get up the Saddle, it was obvious that this route would never be safe for their Sherpa porters, especially when they hadn't brought any crampons for them.

When they reconvened a day later at base camp no one had any good news. Petzoldt had taken a look at the west ridge but it didn't look climbable. Likewise, according to Bates, the south east ridge looked very steep. He and Streatfeild had also hiked further up the Godwin-Austen glacier to take a look at the final option – the north east ridge – but by the time they reached it the weather had deteriorated so much that it was not even visible.

Their first week had given them a harsh reality check. The mountain was steeper, the nights colder and the weather worse than anyone had expected. But though down, they were far from out. If the north west side of the mountain wouldn't go, they would turn their full attention to the eastern flank. And so on 21 June they headed for the foot of the south east ridge, in search of a tent that Bates had cached a few days earlier. In honour of the Duke and his 1909 expedition they christened it 'the Abruzzi ridge'. By early afternoon they were safely installed in the tent, and happy enough to send their Sherpas back.

Throughout the expedition, everyone was amazed by Paul Petzoldt's prodigious appetite and that night was no exception. The mainstay of their rations were Bob's tins of cunningly disguised Danish pemmican. Usually it was mixed with water and eaten as a kind of thick soup. The trouble was that pemmican soup rarely left diners feeling satisfied so it had to be bulked out with copious crackers. Bob Bates, their parsimonious quartermaster, reckoned on 3.5 oz per man but Petzoldt disagreed, and to prove his point, he and Bill House ate a whole pound of pemmican between them – on top of their regular portion. Bates took their competitive eating display with good grace, and rounded off the meal by regaling everyone with his favourite Alaskan ballads and a long reading from Charles Dickens' *Pickwick Papers*.

Fuelled by their night of gastronomic excess, on the following morning Petzoldt and House climbed up a spur on the other side of the glacier to get a better view of the south east ridge. From what they could see, its first 7000 ft was really a series of rock buttresses interrupted by steep ice couloirs. At around 25,000 ft, it ended in a long, flatter shoulder. Above that lay the summit cone, so high that for much of the time it was hidden by cloud.

It didn't look easy but the only way to find out properly was to take a much closer look. Bill House and Charlie Houston went on up. After about 1000 ft, they stopped at the first flat area and found some old pieces of wood, the last remains of packing cases carried up by Abruzzi's porters in 1909. Charlie's delight at finding these relics was tempered by the knowledge that Abruzzi's crack team of Alpine guides had declared the remainder of the ridge unclimbable. He soon discovered why: the ground was relentlessly steep and they could not see any possible sites for further camps.

In the thirty years since the Abruzzi expedition, a new approach to climbing big mountains had emerged during the repeated British expeditions to Everest. No one, apart from the odd crank (or vision-ary) such as Aleister Crowley, still believed that it was possible to rush a big mountain; instead the idea was to 'lay siege to a mountain' and ascend in stages, gradually acclimatising to the altitude.[9] Charlie Houston anticipated having at least nine camps on K2 and probably ten, each roughly 1000 ft or a half-day's climbing apart. If there were no reasonably flat areas available, the alternative was to hack ledges into the ice, or build tent platforms of loose rocks. This, however, was an exhausting prospect at high altitude.

On the night of 23 June the mood at base camp was subdued. Paul Petzoldt's fever had returned yet again and Charlie Houston was worried that he would not be able to continue. Earlier in the day, Petzoldt had suffered a partial collapse on the way down to base camp after negotiating a difficult ice cliff. Everyone was so depressed that they raided the expedition's prized bottle of Demerara rum and even the invariably cheerful Sherpas caught the mood.

Next day, instead of trying the Abruzzi route again, Charlie split the party, sending Bob Bates back round to the west side of the mountain to take a second look at the north west ridge, while he attempted to reach the north east ridge that had frustrated the Eckenstein party in 1902. Both teams returned to base camp empty-handed and despondent.

When Charlie wrote to his parents on 27 June, he had nothing but bad news:

> *I must tell you that this is a bigger, harder mountain than any of us realized before – and it will take a better party than ours a much longer time than we have left, in order to get anywhere at all.*[10]

On 28 June they held a council of war. Everyone agreed that there was no point in trying to ascend the Savoia Saddle again. It was embarrassing to give up on the pass that Abruzzi's team had climbed twice, but it was possible that in the intervening two decades the glacier had shifted making the slope leading up to it much steeper. Theoretically, they could go all the way round the mountain to take a look at its northern side, but they had promised Indian government officials that they wouldn't cross the border into Chinese territory, and anyway, Francis Younghusband's description of an 'inconceivably high mountain… clothed in fourteen to sixteen thousand feet of solid ice' hardly sounded like a better bet.

So the debate returned to the eastern options. Charlie Houston wanted to take another crack at the north east ridge but Bill House maintained they should try the south east, 'Abruzzi ridge', again. It still looked like the most obvious route to the summit and, even if they couldn't find any flat areas to place their camps, there was still a month left, enough time to hack out a whole series of tent platforms if needed. Bob Bates and Streatfeild didn't hold out much hope for either option.

Finally, a plan was agreed: first they would stock a camp at the foot of the Abruzzi ridge and then try their damnedest to force a way up. If they got nowhere, they would then move en masse to the north east ridge, and if they got nowhere on that they would accept that this year at least K2 would not be climbed.

As if to endorse their plans, or perhaps to mess with their heads a little bit more, they were gifted with several days of perfect weather, which allowed them to ferry countless loads up the glacier and set up advance base at the foot of the Abruzzi. Then, just when everything seemed to be going well, on 1 July disaster struck – in an unexpected manner. They had left a 4-gallon tin of gasoline under a large rock to keep it out of the sun. True to their intention, the tin stayed nice and cool. The rock, however, didn't. After a few hours, the ice holding it in place melted and the rock fell over, crushing the tin and spilling their precious fuel into the snow.

Three weeks into the reconnaissance, this was a major problem. The only way to get more fuel would be to go all the way back to Skardu and that was out of the question. They had just enough to get by, as long as they eked out their gasoline, but there was now no margin for error. Mountaineers, like armies, march on their stomachs, and without fuel they would be able neither to cook nor to melt water to drink, an even more serious problem.

There was just one possibility. Remembering the 1936 expedition to nearby Hidden Peak, Captain Streatfeild told them that, before leaving, the French had cached some gasoline at their former base camp. Probably any supply dumps would have been looted, but there was a slim chance that it might still be there. If not, Streatfeild suggested sending some Sherpas down to Askole to get firewood. It would be no use on the mountain itself, but it would keep the home fires burning at base camp.

Streatfeild set off with a small party of porters leaving Bill House and Paul Petzoldt to take a last stab at the Abruzzi ridge. Neither held out much hope, but this time they struck lucky when Petzoldt noticed a small flat area of snow on the other side of a rocky crest at around 19,300 ft. It wasn't huge, but there was enough space for three tents.

That night the mood at advance base was totally different. For the first time in almost three weeks they had made progress. There was still plenty of work to do, but having found their first site on an impossible-looking ridge, there were probably going to be others. Even if they couldn't get all the way to the summit that year, it would be achievement enough to make a thorough reconnaissance of the Abruzzi ridge, and maybe even reach the Shoulder.

The next few days seemed to justify their new-found optimism. On 3 July Bates and Houston carried up over a week's worth of supplies, and House and Petzoldt continued climbing to find a site for their third camp. Over the next week they gradually worked their way up the Abruzzi ridge, consolidating each camp and fixing permanent ropes on the most difficult sections.

Not that it was ever easy. The Abruzzi ridge's unremitting steepness made life distinctly unpleasant for both the lead climbers and those following in their wake. With so much loose rock on the mountain, it was impossible to prevent rockslides so everyone below the main climbers had to be constantly on their guard. And if that wasn't uncomfortable enough, the weather was beginning to turn.

On 6 July Petzoldt and House retreated to advance base when they sensed a storm brewing. It was a wise move: that night they were hit by the worst storm so far. The wind tore at their tents in violent gusts, making sleep impossible. By the morning it had abated, but they were all so exhausted that they decided to take a rest day – for everyone apart from the ever-industrious Charlie Houston, who insisted on going down to base camp to haul up yet more supplies. As if to prove his fitness, he made the round trip in a record three and a half hours.

On the following day, Streatfeild returned with the bad news that he had not found any gasoline and the good news that he had found some perfectly edible French delicacies to add to their larder. Though the storm confined them to camp, as Charlie Houston's diary revealed, their tails were up.

> On July 8, a furious wind that shook the tent canvas with the sound of gunfire kept us from getting higher... In the afternoon we mended clothes, read the Oxford Book of English Verse, and planned what food we should have when we met at our reunion next winter.[11]

Two days later they were back on the Abruzzi ridge; this time Houston partnered up with Petzoldt to take the lead. If the first 4000 ft had been difficult, now it became even trickier. At around 21,000 ft the ridge was blocked by an 80 ft pinnacle of rock, or gendarme, which took a lot of skill from Petzoldt to surmount. He brought Houston up and they continued climbing until they were stopped for a second time by the reddish coloured cliff just visible from the glacier below.

Petzoldt and Houston looked for a way around but they could not find a safe alternative so they carefully retraced their steps. After two weeks on the mountain Charlie had learned not to give in too quickly. The rock wall might look impassible at first glance, but rather than bang their heads against it or give up, they got on with establishing another camp and then went back down to hand over the challenge to the next pair, Bob Bates and Bill House.

They were happy to accept it and spent an afternoon examining the rock wall before returning on the morning of 14 July, armed with 400 ft of rope and a bag full of pitons. It was too cold to make an early start but by 10.00 a.m. they were at the foot of the cliff preparing to climb it. House took the lead, while Bates firmly anchored himself to a spike of rock close to the bottom and gradually paid out the rope.

The only way up was via a crack in the middle of the cliff; at the bottom it was narrow enough to find handholds and footholds on either side, but after around 20 ft the crack grew wider. As Bill House realised, there was no alternative but to wedge himself in, with his back to one side and his feet pressed against the other. Then slowly, painstakingly, he wormed his way up. After 40 ft of wiggling, wriggling and panting, he found a small ledge where he was able to rest, but when he tried to hammer a piton in for protection he found the rock too hard and the metal too soft. The piton simply crumpled.

As House wrote laconically in the expedition book, he was now 'pretty close' to his margin of safety. Bob Bates was holding him on what looked like a secure belay below, but no one was holding him from above. If he fell he would undoubtedly break his legs, or worse. Bob Bates called to him, worried that it was taking too long and warning him that he should come back down, but, as Bill realised, he had now reached a point where it was safer to continue than to turn around.

Fortunately, he made the right call. After another 15 ft the crack narrowed, and he was once again able to find footholds big enough to gain a good purchase. Roughly an hour and a half after starting, he finally hauled himself up onto a tiny ledge and was able to look down on Bob Bates below. This was a key moment in the expedition. In years to come, the crack would become known as 'House's Chimney', K2's equivalent of the 'Hillary Step' on Everest. Future generations of climbers would marvel at the skill, and guts, of the man who first climbed it. For now, though, Bill's most pressing issue was to bring Bates up. Even though he had the security of a rope above him, Bob cursed and complained and was only too glad to reach the top and congratulate his smiling partner.

They were now at 21,900 ft, around 1400 ft above the Duke of Abruzzi's high point and about 6500 ft from the summit. Down below they could see the dirty boulder-strewn surface of the Godwin-Austen glacier, snaking away into the distance. Above them they could see the next major problem – a long section of steep broken rock that they christened 'the Black Pyramid'. After identifying a site for their fifth camp and anchoring a rope to the top of the Chimney, they headed back down to the damp comforts of their tents below.

Over the next few days the endless relays up and down the mountain continued. Bob and Bill rigged an improvised rope-way and began hauling food up the Chimney leaving Charlie Houston and Paul Petzoldt to take back the lead and press on upwards. An unexpected highlight was the arrival of a large bundle of mail, which had come with the porters carrying wood from Askole. No one had ever expected to be reading letters from home in the middle of the Abruzzi ridge.

Bill House's first contact with America in three months prompted a bout of soul searching. Like everyone, he treasured letters from his friends and family and read them over and over again, but being reminded of home was a mixed blessing. Think too much about warm beds, hot food and, above all, the security of your familiar environment and you were liable to get depressed with your current lot.

Balancing that, Bill found news from the outside world an important corrective. It was easy to become obsessed with all the immediate problems at hand. On an expedition to a big mountain like K2, with all its challenges and hazards, a climber could forget that there was a bigger world out there, where other people were struggling with other sorts of problems, which in their own way could be just as daunting, or indeed far more daunting, than the question of how to get up a sheer rock face. And if other people could conquer seemingly insurmountable difficulties in their lives, then perhaps so could he.

It was a good moment to be having such positive thoughts for, as they all realised, the higher up they climbed, the harder the climbing was and the more they felt the altitude. Though there was no single feature quite so taxing as House's Chimney, the Black Pyramid was a dizzyingly steep labyrinth of broken rock, icy gullies and tall rock buttresses. And to add urgency to their work, the weather was becoming increasingly volatile.

On 17 July there was such a severe storm that Houston and Petzoldt were forced to turn back just a few hundred feet after their tent. When they arrived back in camp, their beards were iced up and their hands and toes were chilled to the bone. Their head Sherpa, Pasang Kikuli, had warm drinks for them and not quite so welcome words. This storm, he said, reminded him of one that he had experienced on Nanga Parbat in 1934, one of the most disastrous expeditions in Himalayan history.

On their way down from a failed attempt on Nanga Parbat, the world's ninth-highest mountain, an Austro-German team had been hit by terrible weather. Badly unprepared, three Europeans and six Sherpas had died, several of them starving to death in camps that had not been stocked with sufficient food. More recently, the 1936 French attempt on nearby Hidden Peak had been called off after relentless blizzards kept a French team trapped in their tents for two weeks.

The bad weather on K2 didn't last, but Charlie Houston was becoming more and more anxious. At some point, he was convinced, they too were bound to experience a prolonged period of storm and snow – but would they have enough food and fuel to tough it out when it came?

In spite of all his worries, Charlie pressed on. Two days later, he shook hands with Paul Petzoldt at 24,500 ft, the top of the Black Pyramid, and gazed in wonder at the other Karakoram giants arranged around them. Then, chancing their luck, they pressed their advantage and climbed on up through a tricky section of broken ice, until they finally stopped 300 ft below the Shoulder, the climax of the Abruzzi ridge and one of the few points on K2 where the angle eased off a little.

In front of them lay what looked like a relatively easy snow slope leading to the final 2000 ft of the rocky summit cone. It was late in the day, so rather than pressing on and having to descend in failing light, they turned back early, thrilled at a magnificent day's climbing.

Down at Camp 6, Bill House and Bob Bates were excited to hear what they had achieved but the mood remained tense. It was 19 July, just over five weeks into the expedition, and there were just ten days before their porters were due to arrive at base camp to begin the long trip back to Skardu.

They had enough food to survive one prolonged storm but hardly any margin for error. Back in New York, the American Alpine Club had given Houston a directive:

> To complete the reconnaissance of the mountain's ridges, and
> weather permitting, to make an attack on the summit.[12]

In private, Fritz Wiessner had asked Henry Hall, the president of the club, to emphasise to Houston 'the importance of coming through without loss of life rather than a brilliant success through being reckless'.[13]

By Charlie Houston's calculation they needed at least two more camps before a summit bid. Each of those camps would require reserves of food and fuel, in case of bad weather. So far, in comparison to the Eckenstein expedition's experience in 1902, the weather had been comparatively good, but it did seem to be becoming increasingly unstable. Even if the clear skies continued for long enough to make a summit bid, Charlie Houston was worried that they might be hit by storms on the way down. They had managed to conquer what had seemed like impossible obstacles on the ascent, but the idea of having to climb down House's Chimney or the steep slopes of the Black Pyramid in a blizzard filled Charlie with dread.

If their objective was to make a thorough reconnaissance of K2, they had done their job admirably. Over the last month they had examined all the obvious ways up the mountain and discovered that the Abruzzi ridge was a viable route. Armed with their photographs, maps and detailed descriptions, Fritz Wiessner would be able to come out with the main American Alpine Club party and surely go all the way to the top. But were they happy simply to be Fritz Wiessner's reconnaissance party? Having put in so much hard work, could they give up now and let him take all the glory?

Charlie's solution was a compromise: there was not enough food and fuel to fully stock two more camps, but there was enough for one more. With three days' worth of food, two men could take a proper look at the summit pyramid and there was a slim chance that they might even get to the top. However, if there was any sign that bad weather was coming, they would be under strict orders to head straight back down.

It was a neat if cautious plan. The only problem was choosing which pair would make the summit attempt. Dick Burdsall was down below at Camp 1 with Norman Streatfeild, but Bill House and Bob Bates were in good condition and as keen to go on as Charlie and Paul Petzoldt. So far on the expedition they had shared out the lead climbing but there would only be room in Camp 7 for two men. So who would they be? In the end Bill House and Bob Bates stepped aside, acknowledging that Petzoldt and Houston had reconnoitred the route up to the Shoulder and were marginally better acclimatised. House and Bates would help them carry their gear up through the Black Pyramid, and then return to Camp 6. None of the Sherpas looked strong enough to go any higher, but Pasang Kikuli pleaded with them to let him help with the load carrying and eventually Charlie agreed.

On 20 July, the five men set out early but it took them until mid-afternoon to reach the top of the Black Pyramid. Above lay a steep ice slope leading up to the snows beneath the Shoulder. A day earlier Paul Petzoldt had chopped steps in the ice and put up a rope for security but the sun was so intense that it had melted the ice, leaving the pitons anchoring the rope to hang free. It would take a few hours to put everything back in place, so, rather than carry on and have to climb back down to Camp 6 in the dark, Bob Bates, Bill House and Pasang Kikuli put down their loads and said goodbye, leaving Charlie and Paul to continue alone.

A few hours later, they stopped and put up their seventh and final camp at 24,700 ft. It was a little lower than they had hoped but close enough to the summit cone to be optimistic about the following day. In the intense cold they assembled their stove, looking forward to hot food and drinks and a good night's sleep before their big day. And then something very odd happened.

As they searched through their packs, Paul and Charlie realised that somehow they had left their matches below. They had enough food, they had enough fuel, but without a flame they could cook nothing and nor could they melt water.

Two years earlier, in 1936, Charlie Houston had been high on Nanda Devi with the British climber Noel Odell, poised for an attempt on the summit when he ate a spoon of rancid corned beef and almost immediately began to vomit. He was so ill that Bill Tilman had to take his place on the summit team. Now for want of a match, would K2 also be lost?

Charlie and Paul emptied their rucksacks and rifled through their pockets in desperation. Petzoldt could find nothing, but after a frantic search Charlie dug out nine pocket-worn, miserable-looking matches. Four were Kashmiri safety matches, and five 'strike anywhere' phosphorous tips.

The first match fizzled and died. The second broke off at the head. But against the odds, the third ignited.

They immediately began to melt as much snow as they could to have enough water for the following morning. In order to stop their precious water refreezing, they wrapped the pot in spare clothing and tried to keep it warm with their feet. Charlie wondered if forgetting the matches was a sign that the altitude was getting to him, but, whatever the reason, all he could do was pray for good weather and that at least one of the remaining matches would light on the following morning.

He was in luck – just. Once again it took three matches to get their stove alight. Outside the air was still, but even though they were sporting four Shetland wool jumpers underneath their wind-suits, as soon as they left the tent they felt very cold. Up above, the slopes alternated between hard icy crust and deep powder snow. The higher they climbed, the deeper the drifts they had to wade through, slowing their progress. Paul Petzoldt didn't seem to be suffering too much, but for the first time on the expedition Charlie really began to feel the altitude.

By 1.00 p.m. the rocky slopes of the summit cone at 26,000 ft were tantalisingly close, just a few hundred yards of snow and ice slope separating them from K2's final obstacle. From what they could see, the main hazard was a huge hanging glacier just below the top, which periodically disgorged enormous lumps of ice onto the snowfield below.

The last stage was not going to be easy but it looked as if there was a possible route upwards. First they had to cross the gently angled snow slope in front of them but, as Charlie soon discovered, it was much more taxing than he had hoped. The air was so thin that every five steps he had to stop to regain his breath. He pushed himself as hard as he could and made it all the way over to the rocks but by then he had reached the limit of his physical endurance. After a few brief minutes of rest, Charlie turned round and hauled himself back down the slope to the point where he had stopped just half an hour earlier.

A year later when he came to write his account of the climb, he tried to capture his almost religious feelings at this moment:

> *I felt that all my previous life had reached a climax in these hours of intense struggle against nature… in those minutes at 26,000 feet on K2, I reached depths of feeling which I can never reach again.*[14]

While Charlie was enjoying his moment of epiphany, Paul Petzoldt had started work on the summit cone. After checking out a possible campsite at the foot, he climbed a further 150 ft up a narrow gully edged with rocks until he too stopped, feeling very tired and conscious that it was too risky to carry on alone. Pausing only to take a quick self-portrait, using the tip of his ice-axe to depress the shutter of his camera, he then descended and climbed back down to Charlie, who was still prostrate in the snow.

It was 4.00 p.m. and the 1938 American Alpine Club expedition to K2 had just reached its climax at around 26,150 ft, just over 2100 ft short of the summit. With no time to lose, they descended carefully to their tent, while all around them the surrounding mountains glowed warm in the evening light.

Next morning, out of matches, they forced down an early breakfast of crackers, jam and cold water before descending to Bates, House and Pasang Kikuli, who were waiting for them at Camp 6. Charlie and Paul didn't pause too long to tell their story. With an ominous-looking dark ring around the sun and cirrus clouds on the horizon, everyone was in a hurry to get down. They did not stop until they reached Camp 4 underneath House's Chimney. Finally, they could relax and celebrate with a long-forgotten expedition luxury – a tin of kippered herrings.

On the following afternoon just before they said goodbye to K2, it gave them one last frisson. As they were climbing down an icy gully below their third camp, a huge boulder suddenly came hurtling toward them. Fortunately, Pasang Kikuli spotted it in time to warn everyone to take cover as it smashed into another rock and splintered. He later said that a Yeti had warned him to duck.

After a welcome reunion with Streatfeild and Burdsall at base camp, they washed for the first time in several weeks in their portable rubber bath. Then without any more ado, at dawn on 26 July, forty-four days after their arrival, they left the Godwin-Austen glacier and made a rapid march down to Askole before crunching on to Skardu. It had been an exhilarating experience and though they hadn't reached the summit, as a reconnaissance it could not have been more successful. When Bob Bates sent his latest dispatch back to *The Times*, it appeared under the headline: 'A Conquest on K2'.

Back home Charlie wrote a long article for the *American Alpine Journal* and took stock of the expedition. Early on, he had come under fire for taking such a small party but their experience seemed to have proved him correct. He was equally pleased with Pasang Kikuli and the Sherpas, who had shown their value on a mountain hundreds of miles away from their usual stomping ground. As for the decision not to make an all-out attack on the summit, he maintained that it was the correct one:

The risk would have been unjustifiable and very poor mountaineering.[15]

It was a moment, however, that would haunt him and which he would chew over many times in years to come. A full fifty years later he came back to the events, in an article in which he compared contemporary standards to those of the 1930s:

Could we have gone further? In today's world, certainly. Should we have tried again? Bound by the standards and practices of that time, facing bad weather (it did storm), and very tired from five weeks of exploration and load carrying we were right to turn back. Others, years later, pushed the envelope further; some did great and heroic deeds, others died, needlessly, victims to ambition and the mind numbing effects of great altitude. We lived to climb again, for many years... in true mountaineering, the summit is not everything, it is only part.[16]

Bill House and Bob Bates agreed that Houston was right to pull back at the end and maintained this position for the rest of their lives. Paul Petzoldt wasn't so sure, but it took him another fifty years to speak out in public. At the Telluride Mountain Film Festival in the late 1990s, Petzoldt appeared on a K2 panel with Charlie Houston. When asked about their decision not to go all out for the top, Paul blamed poor organisation, arguing that they should have taken more supplies and been better prepared for the summit attack. Charlie Houston did not rebut him directly but he was clearly hurt and angry.[17]

The concept of 'acceptable risk' was, of course, at the heart of the argument. Could they and should they have tried just a little bit harder? Or would it have been reckless to continue? In the article quoted above, Charlie Houston framed the question as a comparison between the climbing ethics of the 1930s and the 1980s, but at the time there was another, much more contemporary context into which the argument sat: the debate between young European climbers and the old guard of the British Alpine Club.

In the summer of 1938 the most important event in world mountaineering was not the latest expedition to K2 or Everest or Nanga Parbat – the really important story was the attempt on the north face of the Eiger in Switzerland by a young Austro-German team. To many in the mountaineering community in Britain and the United States, their approach was almost heretical and went against the codes of behaviour that had been built up over the years.

When mountaineering emerged as a sport in the 1850s in the European Alps, the first generation of climbers had believed that the faces of great mountains were too avalanche-prone to be climbed safely. Instead they tried for the summit via the sharp ridges that lay between them.

This remained common practice until the late 1920s when a new generation of European climbers arrived who were hungry for new challenges. All the main ridges had been climbed many times over, so they began to tackle the freezing cold, so-called unclimbable north faces of the big Alpine peaks. The north face of the Matterhorn was climbed in 1931 by two German brothers, Toni and Franz Schmid, and this was followed by attempts on the Cima Grande and several other peaks, the most famous of which was the Eiger, in Switzerland's Bernese Oberland.

The 5900 ft north face of the Eiger, known as the 'Nordwand', was and still is considered one of the greatest climbing challenges in the Alps – 6000 ft of treacherous rock. In 1935 and 1936, over the course of two attempts, six young climbers from Austria and Germany died in awful circumstances. Three froze to death, and three were killed in an avalanche. This prompted a lot of soul-searching and controversy in the mountaineering world. Colonel Edward Strutt, the august president of Britain's Alpine Club, denounced the fascination with north faces as 'an obsession for the mentally deranged', while others dismissed the young Europeans as 'suicide climbers'.

On 24 July 1938, while Houston's team was retreating down K2 after failing to reach the summit, Heinrich Harrer and three young

German and Austrian friends finally managed to climb the north face. On this occasion there were no casualties. It was a watershed moment in the history of mountaineering. The debates would go on but a new standard had been set and inevitably the same questions were soon being applied to K2. If the threshold of acceptable risk had now gone up in the Alps, should it also go up in the Himalayas and the Karakoram? More particularly, should Houston's party have tried harder in 1938? Some German mountaineers thought so, but Charlie and his friends in New York and London maintained that they had taken the best course. For the moment the debate was retrospective but would the next team from the American Alpine Club behave any differently?

Houston's 1938 team had done their job and prepared the way for an all-out attack. As Charlie Houston wrote in the *American Alpine Journal*:

> *Our purpose, reconnaissance, was completely accomplished and a way was found by which, with the smile of fortune, a second party may reach the summit.*[18]

The stage was now set for that party to pit their wits, and their lives, against K2. To add grist to the mill, they would be led by the most well-known German émigré in American mountaineering: Fritz Wiessner. Would he too play it safe and risk coming back empty handed? Or, like those young Europeans, would he raise the stakes and risk the consequences?

Chapter 3

A Climbing Party

It was 29 July and while Charlie Houston and his team were walking out from K2, 6500 miles away Fritz Wiessner was poised to climb North Twin, the third-highest peak in the Canadian Rockies. That summer he had organised a long trip through Alberta and British Columbia with Chappell Cranmer, a young student from Dartmouth College, one of America's most prestigious colleges. They had a great time, meeting up with various groups of friends on different mountains and climbing the three highest mountains in the Rockies. All in all it was the perfect trip for Fritz, who excelled at the technical side of climbing but also really enjoyed the social side too.

Fritz Wiessner was a lifelong and passionate climber. Born in 1900 in Dresden, Germany, into a comfortable middle-class family, his father was a painter and keen mountaineer, whose collection of books Fritz devoured at a young age. When he was just twelve, his father took him to the top of the Zugspitze, the highest peak in Germany. His mother disapproved, but over the next fifteen years the young Fritz became an avid climber, starting in Saxony, then moving on to south Bavaria and eventually the Alps and the Dolomites of north east Italy.

By the time Fritz left Germany in 1929, he was regarded as one of the best rock climbers in Europe. He was daring in his choice of targets, but always paid a lot of attention to safety and had a strong commitment to climbing mountains in 'good style', using the minimum of pitons and 'ironmongery'. When he arrived in the United States, he quickly made friends in the small American mountaineering world, joining the American Alpine Club in 1932 and going on to make an amazing series of climbs over the next decade. He led the first ascent of Mount Waddington, Canada's unclimbed 'Mystery Mountain', made a pioneering 'free ascent' of the sheer Devil's Tower in Wyoming, using just one piton for protection, and made several other first ascents of new routes in the Teton mountains of Wyoming and New York State's Shawangunks, today two of America's most popular climbing destinations.

K2, of course, was a completely different order of magnitude than any mountain in North America or Europe. Its base camp was 3000 ft higher than the summit of Mount Waddington and almost twice as high as the Zugspitze. Fritz, however, was optimistic by nature and confident in his own skills. The reports of Charlie Houston's successful reconnaissance convinced him that there was a real chance he might climb K2, but almost immediately, in autumn 1938, his follow-up expedition was hit by an unexpected snag.

On 2 November Ellis Fisher, the treasurer of the American Alpine Club, wrote to Fritz to tell him that the authorities in British India had given permission to a Polish team to make an attempt in 1939 and that he would have to wait until 1940. For a few anxious weeks, Fritz put his preparations on hold before news came through that the Polish expedition had been cancelled. Breathing a huge sigh of relief, Fritz began contacting prospective team members. He knew that none of the 1938 party had the time or the money to go out for a second year in a row, but he had already sounded out three of America's strongest climbers and skiers: Sterling Hendricks, Alfred Lindley and Roger Whitney. If they all signed up, he would stand a very good chance.

Unfortunately, however, Fritz's dream team turned out to be just that: Hendricks backed out because of the cost, Lindley's wife had a miscarriage, and Roger Whitney broke his leg skiing. The only experienced man available was his old friend Bestor Robinson, a gangly Californian lawyer who was one of the pioneers of rock climbing in Yosemite National Park in California.

It was a big problem. Fritz didn't want an extensive team, but he couldn't climb K2 with Robinson alone. And nor could two men pay for the expedition. Though 1939 was once again nominally an

American Alpine Club expedition, the members would have to fund it themselves. Fritz had budgeted his expedition at $15,000, $6000 more than Charlie Houston's reconnaissance, and was planning to go to Europe shortly to buy the best climbing equipment available.

The only solution was to widen the net. Fritz had been very impressed by Chappell Cranmer in 1938 and had met a couple of other Dartmouth students, George Sheldon and Jack Durrance, who seemed to have a lot of potential. Durrance was a part-time mountain guide, and the twenty-year-old Sheldon a close friend and climbing partner of Cranmer. In the end Durrance couldn't raise the cash, but Sheldon and Cranmer could and were both signed up.

At the other end of the age scale, Fritz approached Tony Cromwell, a forty-six-year-old New Yorker. Cromwell was old money, a dapper, bespectacled gentleman climber, who had enough time and dollars to indulge his passion for mountaineering. Fritz had first talked to him about K2 back in 1938 and he'd been part of Fritz's original team, but no one really thought of Tony Cromwell as an exceptional mountaineer. His entry in the American Alpine Club's yearbook contained the longest list of ascents of any member, but almost all of them had been led by professional guides and Tony had no experience of long expeditions. He agreed to go to K2 and act as Fritz's deputy and treasurer, but he warned him that he probably would not go above 21,500 ft, a full 7000 ft lower than the summit.

Fritz's other choice, Dudley Wolfe, was better known as a transatlantic yachtsman than a mountaineer. At forty-two, Wolfe was four years younger than Cromwell, but he was several boats and a penthouse richer, the heir to a huge fortune. Dudley was a keen skier and had until recently been married to Alice Damrosch, the daughter of the famous conductor Walter Damrosch and a former manager of the US women's ski team. He was relatively new to the sport, but splitting his time between Europe and America, Dudley had chalked up several seasons of guided climbing in the Alps. He agreed to join almost immediately.

The lack of experience in Fritz's team did not go unnoticed at the American Alpine Club. The Dartmouth students, Chappell Cranmer and George Sheldon, had only been climbing for a few years and, though older and more experienced, neither Tony Cromwell nor Dudley Wolfe were considered in the same league as Bob Bates or Dick Burdsall. It didn't make any sense for the main team to be inferior to the reconnaissance party. So Bill House, one of the success stories of the 1938 expedition, came up with a suggestion: why not take the 'Wyoming cowboy' Paul Petzoldt? Unlike the other members of the reconnaissance team who were all back in the USA by the end of the summer, Petzoldt had stayed out in India and might welcome a second crack at K2.

But Fritz was not keen. He had never forgiven Petzoldt for an incident in the Tetons a few years earlier when he had gazumped him on a new route, and he said that he had heard bad things about Petzoldt's business dealings. Henry Hall, the president of the American Alpine Club, pressed Fritz to reconsider. There were very few other options available and if Petzoldt had almost reached the summit with Charlie Houston in 1938, then maybe he could go all the way in 1939.[1] However, it was not to be. Even if Henry Hall could have persuaded Fritz, Paul Petzoldt, like so many other potential candidates, was shortly to become unavailable.

In one of the more bizarre episodes of K2 history, Petzoldt had become involved with two elderly Americans, whom he met in Srinagar in August 1938. Mr and Mrs Johnson were unlikely devotees of a Sikh sect, whose guru promised a fast track to nirvana for anyone who was willing to follow him and hand over their wealth. A retired doctor from California, Mr Johnson ran a clinic and TB sanatorium in a village close to the sect's headquarters. Mrs Johnson worked as his nurse and ran her own small business selling herbal cosmetics.

The Johnsons took an instant shine to the young American climber. They offered him a job and even agreed to pay for his wife to come over from the US. He was intrigued and agreed to join them. In spite of his image as a rough, tough climbing cowboy, Petzoldt was very interested in politics and philosophy and liked to describe himself as 'half a scholar'.[2] Besides which he was running out of cash and couldn't quite work out how to pay his way back to the US. Before long, the mountain guide from the Grand Teton National Park was part-timing as Dr Johnson's anaesthetist and even helping him perform operations.

When a few months later Petzoldt's wife, Bernice, arrived, things went from strange to stranger. She never settled into communal life and became convinced that Mrs Johnson was trying to poison her because she refused to take the sect seriously. The tension came to a climax one night in January 1939 when, after a dinner table argument, Mrs Johnson pulled out a shotgun and threatened Petzoldt. In the scuffle that followed he disarmed her, but in the process, he accidentally knocked her husband over. The hapless Mr Johnson hit his head on a paving stone and died a few hours later.

The leaders of the sect were desperate to avoid a scandal and offered to get a manslaughter charge against Petzoldt reduced to a charge of assault, if he agreed to keep Mrs Johnson out of the picture and lie about what really happened. Under extreme pressure, Petzoldt initially agreed to play along but, after talking to the US consul in Karachi, he changed his mind and engaged an Indian defence lawyer.

When the case came to trial in March 1939 Petzoldt was acquitted but the peculiar circumstances of Mr Johnson's death and the sensational reporting that ensued did nothing for his reputation. Rumours circulated that he was persona non grata in India and would be rearrested if he ever tried to go back. Having climbed higher than anyone else on K2, he could have been a real asset to Fritz, but after the court case there was never any serious chance that he might return to K2. Fritz would just have to make do.

If he had any private misgivings, Fritz did not make them public. Aged thirty-eight, he felt at the top of his game and had the self-belief and the climbing skills to take on K2. Even if his American teammates were not as experienced as he might have liked, he had engaged the well-known Sherpa Pasang Kikuli, the sirdar or head Sherpa on Houston's 1938 team, and eight other Sherpas. With Bestor Robinson, Chappell Cranmer and Pasang Kikuli, he had a powerful core team that could go all the way.

So in March he headed for Britain to meet his last recruit, Dudley Wolfe, who had recently travelled to Europe, and to buy equipment for the expedition. Dudley had already been on his own personal shopping spree back in America, decking himself out with the best gloves money could buy, several pairs of monogrammed slippers and a brace of cameras for the expedition movie. As they toured the climbing shops of London, buying up tents, stoves and sundry equipment, Dudley Wolfe's chequebook came in very handy. Occasionally he wondered if he wasn't being treated like a cash cow, but Dudley was rich enough to be generous and thrilled to be involved in such a great adventure. After ten days, Fritz left for Germany, promising to meet again in Italy where they would rendezvous with the rest of the team who were then on their way over to Europe by ship.

Unfortunately, unknown to Fritz, another prospective team member had dropped out. Bestor Robinson, the gangly lawyer from California, who was the only member of the party considered a serious mountaineer, had changed his mind at the last minute, sending the high-ups in the American Alpine Club into a tail-spin. Even if Chappell Cranmer turned out to be as strong as hoped, Fritz clearly needed more than one good climber on an expedition to the world's second-highest mountain.

So Ellis Fisher, the club's treasurer, got in touch with Jack Durrance, the Dartmouth student who had talked to Wiessner about K2 a few months earlier. Aged twenty-six, he was older than his friends and fellow Dartmouth College climbers, Cranmer and George Sheldon, and had worked for the last few summers as a mountain guide in the Tetons. He wasn't quite in Bestor Robinson's class yet, but he had a good reputation and looked destined for great things.

Jack Durrance had an unusual background, which was in many ways the inverse of Fritz Wiessner's. He was born in America but had gone to school in Germany, after his parents separated. In the early 1930s he had taken a job with an engineering firm in Munich. When they switched to arms production, Jack was sidelined and eventually denounced as a foreign spy and sacked. He returned to the United States in 1935 and enrolled at Dartmouth College and, following in Charlie Houston's footsteps, was planning to go on to medical school.

Tall and handsome with a mop of black hair and movie-star looks, Jack had a reputation as a ladykiller and a party guy, but he was also a rather sensitive man who was fascinated by botany and would later become a well-known iris breeder. Though a lot less famous than his younger brother, Dick Durrance, an Olympic skier, Jack was a solid climber and a founding member of Dartmouth's mountaineering club. He did not have enough money to pay his own way to K2 but, faced with a personnel crisis, the American Alpine Club now offered to put up most of the cash. Jack borrowed the remaining money from friends and signed up eagerly.

Three days later, he found himself in Ellis Fisher's New York apartment. Jack had a bag full of books on the Karakoram and a sore arm from a hastily arranged typhoid vaccination. Fisher had arranged for Charlie Houston to come for dinner, hoping that he might offer some tips to K2's latest suitor, but it quickly became obvious that Charlie was not at all optimistic about Wiessner's expedition and left early. Ellis Fisher took Jack down to the Port of New York, and showed him around the ship that would take him to Europe. Just before midnight, it steamed off into the moonlight.

The following few days were no less hectic. After a rapid but stomach-churning voyage across the Atlantic he arrived in Cherbourg on 27 March and then took a train to Switzerland. He met some old friends, tried and failed to buy a new pair of climbing boots and then took another train to Genoa on the Italian coast hoping to join Fritz and the others for the long voyage out to India.

When he came aboard the SS *Conte Biancamano*, Jack was thrilled to discover that everyone had been upgraded to First Class, courtesy of Dudley Wolfe. No one else had arrived yet, so he stole half an hour's rest before he shaved and washed. Then, just as he was relaxing in his cabin, a bellboy arrived with news that he had a visitor.

Jack assumed it was Fritz, but when he got up on deck he discovered that it wasn't his leader or any of the other Americans. In fact, his visitor was none other than the world's greatest living mountain photographer, Vittorio Sella, the seventy-eight-year-old veteran of the 1909 K2 expedition. The Duke of Abruzzi had been dead for six years, but Sella was still going strong and had recently been contacted by Wiessner, with a request for enlargements of his K2 photographs.

Jack barely had time to say hello when up the gangplank marched Fritz Wiessner and Dudley Wolfe. No one had told Fritz that Jack Durrance had been sent out as a replacement for Bestor Robinson. When Jack explained what was going on, Fritz looked disappointed and distinctly put out. It was a very embarrassing moment for both men but fortunately Sella was oblivious to the tension. He told Fritz how excited he was at the thought of another K2 expedition and advised him to take another look at the north east ridge, which he maintained was more sheltered than the route that Houston's party took. Then, after writing a good luck message in Jack's diary, Sella made a tearful exit. Shortly afterwards the SS *Conte Biancamano* weighed anchor and sailed for Naples where the remaining three members of the team were waiting to climb on board.

After the initial awkwardness the rest of the voyage went smoothly. Jack already knew his college mates, Chappell Cranmer and George Sheldon, of course, and found Tony Cromwell charming and affable. He was rather surprised at the inclusion of Dudley Wolfe, who didn't look like a typical climber, but he was a cheerful and easy-going travelling companion and the team soon bonded.

No matter how much they enjoyed each other's company, they could not ignore the disturbing global events coming to a head around them. It was the late spring of 1939. While they were heading off to do battle with K2, Europe was getting ready for war. All over the Continent, Fascism was on the rise. Franco's army had just taken Madrid, Hitler's forces had recently occupied Prague and Mussolini was just about to invade Albania. As the SS *Conte Biancamano* sailed across the Indian Ocean, its salons resounded to 'Vienna, Vienna, there's nowhere quite like you'. There were 800 Austrian Jews on board, heading for Shanghai to escape Nazi persecution.

The most intriguing passenger was Hjalmar Schacht, the German economist known as 'Hitler's banker'. Before long he was chatting to Wiessner and Jack Durrance, who spoke fluent German. Schacht was on his way to India with his nephew; apparently it was a holiday but no one was quite sure what to make of him. There were rumours that he was a spy, on a mission to check on Britain's colonial possessions.

Others said that he was now in disgrace, after taking part in a recent attempted coup. Durrance and Wiessner never found out, but Schacht was good company and was generous with his champagne and his conversation.

When seven years earlier Fritz had sailed to India with the 1932 Nanga Parbat expedition, the whole team used to start the day with an hour of exercise. This voyage was entirely different. The preferred tipple was 1931 Chianti and, as Jack Durrance wrote in his diary, they spent most of their time hopping 'from one entertainment to the other'. The elder members of the party – Wolfe, Wiessner and Cromwell – were not quite so keen to party as the Dartmouth boys, but, as film shot by Wolfe shows, they all had a great time: swimming, playing deck sports and generally enjoying the First Class life.

When after three weeks they reached Bombay they had the customary uncomfortable journey to Rawalpindi, but once they reached Srinagar in Kashmir, the high life recommenced. In 1938 Houston's party spent most of their time packing, and only had a few hours for sightseeing before setting off to K2, but Wiessner had planned a whole week's acclimatisation before the long march in to the mountain.

For the first few days, they stayed with Major Kenneth Hadow, a British officer whose family had long ties to Kashmir. Hadow was the great-nephew of Douglas Hadow, the young British mountaineer who in 1865 famously fell off the Hörnli ridge on the Matterhorn, pulling three other men to their deaths and ending the first 'Golden Age' of mountaineering. Hadow had become friends with Fritz after the Nanga Parbat expedition and, as everyone soon discovered, was a very generous host with a beautiful estate.

Even Tony Cromwell, who had lived a life of wealth and privilege, was surprised by all the servants and flunkies at their beck and call. In an article written on their return, Tony admitted that occasionally he had to pinch himself to check that it was all real. Europe might be on the brink of war and the sun going down on the British Empire, but in Kashmir the Union Jacks were still flying high and the gin and tonics were flowing by the gallon.[3]

After a few days of relaxation, they travelled up to the Gulmarg hill station in the mountains above Srinagar with two British women whom they had recently befriended. Naturally they travelled in style, taking a butler, a cook, a sweeper and three other servants. The ski-lodge was brand new and boasted its own caretaker and several assistants, but it wasn't all fun and games. For four days they worked hard to acclimatise and improve their fitness on the surrounding mountains, which soared to 12,500 ft. Dudley Wolfe showed himself to be a much more impressive skier than anyone had expected and they all exercised hard, during the day at least.

When they returned to Srinagar they found their British transport officer, George Trench, waiting for them along with Pasang Kikuli and eight Sherpas from Darjeeling. Tall and thin with a dainty moustache, Trench was a twenty-two-year-old artillery lieutenant in the 21st Mountain Regiment, then stationed in Peshawar close to the border with Afghanistan. The last-minute replacement for a local man who could not accompany them, Trench had limited mountaineering experience. Of more concern to Fritz, he was not familiar with any of the local dialects of Baltistan so he would not be able to offer much help liaising with their porters. Nevertheless he was charming and energetic and quickly bonded with the Anglophile Tony Cromwell.

Jack Durrance was fascinated to meet the famous Pasang Kikuli and his band of Sherpas. With their stocky build and smiling faces, they were just how he expected them to be. Pasang Kikuli, the tough-looking veteran of both British and German expeditions, was particularly impressive, and clearly commanded the respect of the others.

As Fritz took stock, he was quietly pleased. It had been a blow to lose Bestor Robinson, but the expedition had started well. The Sherpas looked very impressive, the expedition's equipment had arrived unscathed, his team had bonded and, according to a postcard that Fritz sent back to Ellis Fisher at the American Alpine Club, they were 'an exceptionally congenial' party. All that remained now was to negotiate the 330-mile trek to K2 base camp and the 12,000 ft ascent to its summit.

*

The approach march to K2 followed the same route as Houston's: a short journey through Kashmir, followed by a less comfortable march across Baltistan. It turned out to be pleasantly uneventful. They crossed the Zoji La pass just past midnight on 4 May, and then made their way past a series of villages that looked like, as Jack Durrance wrote, 'Marco Polo had just been there'.

The most memorable moments came between Askole and base camp when they had to cross several very dangerous-looking rope bridges. They were made from willow bark and were usually composed of long supporting strands on either side of a lower central strand that acted like a tightrope. The flanks were protected by a woven lattice also made from bark, but they rarely looked strong enough to hold a falling man.

Invariably, the worst rope bridges were suspended over the most ferocious torrents and required a strong stomach and steady nerve. Even Fritz found them uncomfortable and intimidating. When budding author George Sheldon wrote about them later, he was a marvel of understatement:

> These bridges are truly remarkable and not at all as pleasant
> and solid to cross as, say, the George Washington bridge.[4]

When their porters informed them that the bridges were only replaced when they broke, it only added to the fear they inspired.

Even though he had not started his medical training proper, Jack Durrance found himself playing the role of visiting doctor, doling out medicine at the same kind of impromptu village clinics that Charlie Houston had a year earlier. He dispensed castor oil for cases both of constipation and diarrhoea, and found that for the Balti porters headache pills seemed to be effective for more or less everything.

Amongst the Americans there was the usual litany of sprains, blisters and swollen ankles, but perhaps the most uncomfortable person of all was Durrance himself. Just a few days into the trek, his sleeping bag became infested with fleas, which tormented him for most of the approach march and only died off when he got to high altitude.

Wealthy Dudley Wolfe was more used to mahogany cabins and luxury apartments than roughing it on the trail. He tried to remain cheerful, though he admitted in a letter home that he had expected to be spending more time in government bungalows than camping on rocky ground.

The team bonding continued with members giving each other nicknames: Fritz was christened 'Baby Face' by the Americans, and 'Bara Sahib' or 'the big boss' by the Sherpas. Forty-six-year-old Tony Cromwell was known to everyone as 'Pop Sahib'. There were occasional practical jokes, and bouts of competitive marching, but as Fritz reported to Ellis Fisher in a letter of 8 May 1939, his boys were coming on well:

> *One word suffices to make them do their duty and work hard. I feel quite certain they will do well on the mountain, and that I will have no difficulties whatsoever in the running of a careful, efficient and co-ordinated climb.*

After twelve days on the trail they reached Skardu in mid-May, and then four days later arrived at Askole, the final village before K2. As befitting their last night in 'Baltistani civilisation' they celebrated with a large meal and a brace of Tony Cromwell's specially made rum cocktails. After hearing about Charlie Houston's troubles in 1938, Wiessner was slightly wary of hiring local porters, but nevertheless a week later they left Askole with 120 new recruits.

The first stages had all gone smoothly, but trouble awaited. When they reached Urdukas, the shock of green in the middle of the Baltoro glacier, the weather suddenly turned. For two days it snowed constantly. George Sheldon and Jack Durrance tried to jolly the porters along with cigarettes and jokes, but none of them had been provided with extra-cold weather clothing and unsurprisingly they refused to leave their makeshift shelters. Fritz was forced to experience the agony of waiting: every day's delay meant more food consumed and more to find. They were just a few miles from K2, but it might as well have been several hundred if they could not get their men out from under their tarpaulins and back on the glacier.

Fortunately, when the snow stopped the Baltis agreed to carry on but before long there was a new problem: the Americans had not brought enough pairs of snow goggles to equip every porter. Anyone who ventured onto the glacier without them risked a very painful bout of snow-blindness. Ever resourceful, Jack Durrance knocked up some makeshift glasses out of cardboard and spare lenses for his ski mask, but several men had to turn back and abandon their loads on the glacier.

Finally, on 31 May, after a journey from New York of almost two and a half months, Fritz and his team reached Concordia and got their first sight of K2. For Jack Durrance it was the 'greatest thrill of the trip'. For Fritz Wiessner it was even more special, as he recorded in his diary a few days later:

> Everything that I have learned in my long years in the mountains, whatever of strength, energy, endurance, instinct they have given me, is dedicated to this – cool and deliberate, but with a warm heart.[5]

They established base camp on Houston's old site, and on 1 June Fritz and Tony Cromwell set off early for the north east ridge. Fritz knew that ultimately they would probably take the 1938 route up the south east 'Abruzzi' ridge, but just in case Vittorio Sella was right about the northern route, he wanted to take a closer look. The others stayed back to organise base camp. If they were hoping for a few days' relaxation, things turned out very differently.

It all started when the last Askole porters had been paid off and had left camp. After putting away the expedition cashbox, Jack went to visit Chappell Cranmer, his fellow Dartmouth student and the youngest member of the team. That morning 'Chap' had not been feeling so well and had retired to his tent. Initially, Jack hadn't taken much notice – he was just too busy and after all they were now at 16,500 ft so a touch of altitude sickness was not unexpected. But as soon as he raised the flap of his college mate's tent, Jack realised that this was something much more serious.

Cranmer had a deep rattling cough and was bringing up mouth-fuls of foul-smelling green liquid. Jack had never seen anything like it. He spent the whole afternoon rubbing Cranmer's chest to loosen the phlegm but his patient only deteriorated. When he took a few minutes off to grab some supper, Cranmer took a turn for the worse and called Jack back in. For two hours, he gave him artificial respiration while the others watched in shock. At any moment it looked as if Cranmer might die.

The crisis passed, but only just. It was impossible to give any medicine orally, so Jack decided to give Cranmer an injection of codeine. With young George Sheldon's help he dissolved a tablet in boiling water but there were so many bubbles in the solution that he worried it might do more harm than good. Instead he painted Cranmer's arm with iodine and pretended to give him the jab, hoping that psychological first aid might prove a safer bet than doing it for real. Cranmer's condition eventually stabilised but he continued to cough up alarming quantities of putrid fluid and he lost control of his bowels three times.

A year earlier, Charlie Houston had spent three anxious days at Askole tending the sick Paul Petzoldt, wondering if he would pull through. That was nerve wracking but at least he had three years of medical school behind him. Jack Durrance had nothing but instinct and the few tips he had picked up on his undergraduate pre-med course. Decades later, reviewing his subsequent career as a doctor, he told an interviewer that Cranmer was the sickest patient he had ever dealt with.

Fritz Wiessner had no idea about any of this until he returned two days later. The reconnaissance had gone smoothly; they were able to get a good look at K2's north east ridge and rule it out as a potential route. Fritz was all set to take on the Abruzzi ridge but when he got back to camp he was shocked by what he found:

> *Everyone was terribly depressed, poor Chap had become ter-ribly ill, he was near death and just had passed the crisis, my best man seems to be out now for some time.*[6]

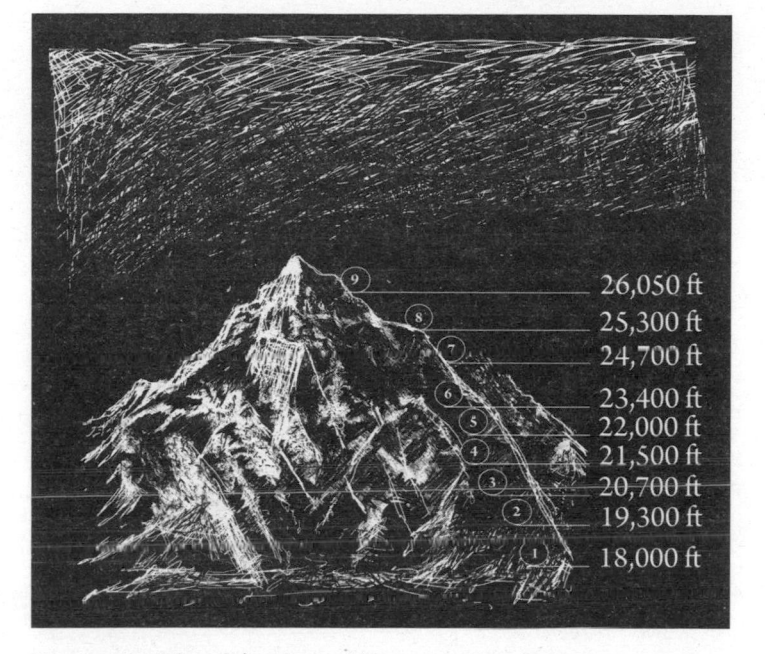

26,050 ft
25,300 ft
24,700 ft
23,400 ft
22,000 ft
21,500 ft
20,700 ft
19,300 ft
18,000 ft

Map 4   Fritz Wiessner's camps on K2

It was a major blow, but there was no alternative but to press on and hope that Cranmer would recover quickly enough to play a role.

From now on Fritz planned to follow Houston's route up the Abruzzi ridge, using the campsites identified in 1938, until they reached the Shoulder, the long plateau at 25,000 ft below the final summit cone. After that he wasn't absolutely sure but he estimated that he would need two more light camps. Like Houston, Fritz was very concerned about the weather and the danger of getting trapped in a storm, so he had brought extra supplies and equipment to ensure a wide margin of error. All the main camps would be stocked with sufficient food, tents and sleeping bags for a stay of several days in an emergency. To carry up this amount of material would require a lot of time and effort but at least all the exploratory work had already been done. The Askole porters were due back in mid-July for the return match, so they had roughly six weeks to get to the summit and back.

On Monday 5 June Fritz, Jack Durrance and George Sheldon set out from base camp for Camp 1 at the foot of the Abruzzi ridge. The sahibs carried 35 lbs each, the Sherpas 50. For three days in a row, Fritz led them up and down from base camp, building up a large cache of gear and food until finally on the night of 8 June they were ready to sleep at Camp 1 for the first time.

Over the next two weeks they moved on up the ridge, setting up further camps and hauling up hundreds of pounds of supplies and equipment. It was hard, relentless work but equipped with Charlie Houston's maps they made steady progress. Chappell Cranmer remained at base camp, slowly recovering. The others tried to get used to the vicissitudes of K2's weather and the discomfort of climbing at high altitude.

For each man it was slightly different. Though his friend Cranmer was still confined to his tent, George Sheldon was full of energy and keen to impress. Fritz Wiessner adjusted slowly but rarely had any really bad periods. Jack Durrance had a much more complex reaction. On good days he relished the thrill of climbing on one of the highest mountains on earth, in the company of Pasang Kikuli, one of the greatest living Sherpas. On bad days, his diary told a very different story.

> *There is no expression to describe how awful I felt physically today – back ached, short winded, and despondent spirits. Fritz did the lion's share of our step kicking, I the whale's share of our freezing.*[7]

Although Dudley Wolfe was by far the heaviest man on the team, he coped surprisingly well, even when carrying heavy loads, and did not seem to be too affected by the thin air. When George Sheldon wrote a progress letter to the American Alpine Club, he joked, 'Dudley is up on the mountain and you can't get him to come down.' Dudley's enthusiasm, however, wasn't quite matched by his mountaineering technique. In the Alps, he had always climbed with guides and was not very confident with his rope-work or belaying and was very sensitive to criticism. Two days after Sheldon's letter, Jack Durrance recorded 'a minor emotional blow up from Dudley' after someone dared to criticise him.

As on every expedition, regular deliveries of mail were the best escape from the tedium and hardships of everyday life. On 16 June a post runner arrived with several newspapers and over sixty letters. Jack Durrance received more than ten, 'mostly from women' as George Sheldon noted enviously. Sadly, however, Jack didn't get what he wanted most: new footwear.

It had been such a rush getting away from Dartmouth College that he hadn't had time to buy any heavy-duty mountaineering boots and the pair he'd ordered from Switzerland still hadn't turned up after two months. Jack confidently expected to be on the summit team, but he knew that he would not get very high with the lightweight boots he had with him.

By contrast, Tony Cromwell, the well-to-do New Yorker, was perfectly kitted out but he still had reservations about K2. He arrived in good enough shape and, after their first reconnaissance trip to the north east ridge, told Fritz that he might even try for the summit, but he was not a very effective deputy. When Fritz put him in charge of establishing their fourth camp, Tony singularly failed in his mission.

Part of the problem was that Fritz had decided not to put up any tents between Camp 2 at 19,300 ft and Camp 4 at 21,500 ft. There was so much loose rock in between that he thought it better to treat Houston's third camp at 20,700 ft as a supply dump. It was a smart move in one sense – no one wanted to lie in a tent and be bombarded by stones from above – but the downside was a long climb of over 2000 ft between Camps 2 and 4, which was tough for even a strong mountaineer.

In 1938 almost all the climbers on Houston's reconnaissance had some previous experience; they were used to carrying heavy loads and were not intimidated by unknown ground. Right until the end, when collectively they chose the summit team, the lead climbing had been shared out. 1939 was very different. As the weeks went by a clear pattern emerged: Fritz did all the pioneering, the others followed in his wake. When Fritz was in camp, his organisational skills and the sheer force of his personality gave everyone a boost, but if he was too far in front, or dealing with administrative matters at base camp, little was achieved.

After two weeks on the mountain, Fritz was becoming more realistic about the limitations of his team. As he confided to his diary, on 17 July, his men were not quite the happy bunch that he had praised earlier. His deputy leader, Tony Cromwell, did not like to take responsibility and 'cannot stand up under pressure of things being tough'. Jack Durrance was 'very helpful in the camps and the only really efficient man' but without proper boots he had problems with his toes. Dudley Wolfe was trying his best 'but he is somewhat insufficient and for that reason the others do not care to go with him on a rope'.[8] George Sheldon was going well but there was still no sign that his friend Chappell Cranmer was about to rejoin the climbing team. Fritz considered appointing Jack as his deputy in place of Cromwell but for the moment he left things as they were.

On 21 June Fritz led the way to Camp 4, an important milestone on the expedition. It was a difficult stage over an exposed route, but he managed it in fine style. Above lay House's Chimney – according to Houston, the trickiest bit of climbing on K2. As there was only room in their tents for three Sherpas and three sahibs, Jack Durrance went back down, leaving Dudley and George Sheldon to help set up camp.

Fritz was looking forward to the challenge but in the end he was given something much more testing: a huge storm. For eight days Camp 4 was savaged by high winds and freezing temperatures. Fritz had survived similar storms on Nanga Parbat in 1932, but the others had never experienced anything like this. When the expedition chronicler George Sheldon wrote an article about their attempt on K2 six months later, the strange mixture of terror and monotony was still vivid in his mind:

> We would lie in our sleeping bags swathed in several sets of underwear, wind-suits, boots, gloves and hats. At any moment we expected to be blown into nearby Tibet. We had nothing to read except the labels on the food cans. A meal became an event of tremendous importance... the eternal banging and

cracking of the tent, in the seventy-mile-an-hour gale, made
us virtually psychopathic cases.[9]

Some 2000 ft lower, Jack Durrance and Tony Cromwell were pinned down by the same storm at Camp 2 but at least they had volumes of Goethe and Tennyson to keep them company. Unsurprisingly, their thoughts frequently turned to what they would do after the expedition. Both were looking forward to a few more days of R & R in Srinagar, but even in the middle of the terrible weather Jack Durrance was plotting a stopover in Europe to do a few days' climbing in the Dolomites.

After almost a week, during a brief lull in the storm a Sherpa came up from base camp with some great news for frozen-footed Jack:

What was more than Xmas to me, my expedition boots
arrived. Now weather permitting and all other things being
equal I may be able to go higher. Proud as a puppy over my
boots – but the wind does not share my joy and blows on.
Reading, writing, 'chewing the rag' our favourite sports.[10]

A day later the storm abated. A rather miserable-looking George Sheldon came down accompanied by two Sherpas. At the beginning of the expedition, the twenty-year-old geology student had been one of the most competitive climbers on the team, ever rushing ahead to impress Fritz, but after more than a week trapped in a storm, he didn't look or sound good and several of his toes and fingers showed signs of frostbite.

Fritz stayed high and, supported by the head Sherpa, Pasang Kikuli, made the next big breakthrough: this year's first ascent of House's Chimney. It was, he later wrote, 'a very impressive pitch, I take my hat off to Bill House'. It took two hours and a lot of work to climb it, further increasing his admiration for his old climbing partner and one of the stalwarts of the 1938 reconnaissance. They found several ropes left over from the previous year, but rather than risk using them, they put up fresh lines.

Fritz was one of those mountaineers who acclimatised slowly but steadily. After a month on the mountain he was now feeling better than ever. The others, however, were not made from the same mettle; as the expedition went on, and the climbing became more demanding they found it increasingly hard to cope, much to Fritz's frustration:

> It is terrible if Tony and Jack just sit at [Camp] 2 and work only as far as the dumps at 3 instead of pushing through to the higher camp. I am terribly disappointed and write a note to the two, which I hope will wake them and make them see reality.[11]

When on 2 July Fritz's note was carried down by a Sherpa, Jack and Tony were more irritated than chastised. Fritz didn't seem to realise that they too had been held back by the storm. More than that, there was a growing sense of disconnect between Fritz's spearhead party and men lower down the mountain. Jack Durrance still felt that he and the others were working hard, for the good of the team, but as he wrote in his diary, it was no fun being 'puppets' on Fritz's trip.[12]

After the inactivity of the previous two weeks, everyone was glad to be moving again but a few days later on 5 July, on the way back from an exhausting trip to Camp 3 with a large cache of supplies, the usually very cautious Tony Cromwell slipped and fell almost 50 ft. He didn't break anything but he emerged more despondent than ever, his badly bruised ribs making load carrying yet harder. George Sheldon, twenty-six years Cromwell's junior, was still struggling. With his frozen toes showing no sign of improvement, Tony took a rare executive decision and sent George back down to base camp to recuperate. George left intending to return, but Jack Durrance's medical notes paint a picture of a young man close to his limit:

> George Sheldon has suddenly developed swollen feet due to his touch of frostbite... During my own sleepless nights I have heard him cough and groan and curse, and he looks haggard and used up... His spirit is determined to stay aloft and help

as much as he can, but all his reactions are slow, inaccurate
to a degree and upon occasion clumsy, the effect of altitude.[13]

Higher up, Fritz and the Sherpas continued to make good progress, finding a safe route through the loose rock and tricky pitches of the Black Pyramid, the difficult stretch of broken rock at around 24,000 ft, and almost reaching the end of the Abruzzi ridge. Dudley Wolfe did not assist them, preferring to stay at Camp 5 to meet the resupply party. But though he waited patiently for several days, they didn't come.

Communication, or the lack of it, was becoming a real problem. Prior to the expedition, they had thought about taking walkie-talkies, but in the late 1930s portable radios were still a rarity. Even if they had found some, Fritz did not approve. Throughout his climbing career, he disliked using any so-called artificial aids and more generally disliked technology. He never climbed with oxygen, and even when he was doing very tough rock climbing always used the minimum of pitons.

From the point of view of sporting ethics, his insistence on doing things the natural way might have been admirable, but on a big 'siege' type expedition like this, communication between camps was particularly important. In theory they could communicate using smoke signals, but in practice the only way for the top camps to keep in touch with the lower ones was either via hand-delivered notes or by going up or down in person.

The pattern established early on showed no signs of changing: Fritz forged ahead doing all of the lead climbing and a lot of the load carrying; Dudley Wolfe moved up the mountain in his wake and never contemplated going down; and the others stayed behind at the lower camps, making more or less half-hearted attempts to keep supplies moving. The tension came to a head on 9 July, when lack of food forced Fritz to interrupt his attack on the summit and descend to Camp 2 to find out why resupply was taking so long. Dudley Wolfe predictably chose to stay high, so Fritz went down alone. His arrival and the good news of his progress above was a morale boost for the others, but five weeks into the climb they needed more than a metaphorical shot in the arm. K2 had taken its toll and, as Jack Durrance admitted to his diary, the team was now sorely depleted:

> *Pop sahib [Cromwell] declares he is now used up and no good above Camp 4. George Sheldon is an invalid with frost bitten toes at base camp. Chap Cranmer is still too weak to visit 1 and 2, so that Fritz, Dudley and I are the only ones left. As it stands, Fritz and I are to attempt the top when weather breaks. We don't expect to leave until August.*[14]

Fritz also recognised that there were problems but he was still feeling good and crucially the weather was holding. Even if Cromwell and Sheldon were out of the picture, he was sure that K2 was within his grasp. All he had to do was galvanise his troops for one final big carry up the Abruzzi ridge making a dash for the summit. Then they could sail back to America with an amazing story to tell and enter the history books as the first men to climb one of the world's truly high peaks. If things did not go quite so smoothly and there was no summit attempt before 23 July, when their porters were due, Fritz would split the party, sending Tony Cromwell out with the bulk of their equipment, while he and Jack stayed to finish the job.

On 11 July, at 8.30 a.m., everyone roped up for that final push. Sheldon's frostbite was so bad that he couldn't accompany them, but he loaned his boots to George Trench, their British transport officer, who had come up from base camp. Having now spent almost six weeks on K2, Trench was determined to set a personal record by climbing House's Chimney, before beginning preparations for their departure.

On the following afternoon they reached Camp 5. When Jack shook hands with Dudley Wolfe, he was shocked to realise that it was twenty-one days since he had last encountered 'the hermit of K2'. Over the last couple of weeks, Jack had spent a lot of time thinking about Dudley. A summer season mountain guide, Jack was used to assessing clients, and the higher Dudley got the more Jack worried about him. When in the Alps, Dudley could afford to hire the best guides in Europe, but his wealth meant nothing here. The very fact that he had reached Camp 6 proved that Dudley had strength and determination but the problem was that he didn't seem to have a reverse gear. Fritz went up and down regularly, Jack and Tony ferried loads between the lower camps, but Dudley always preferred to stay put than to descend, even when it meant spending a lot of time alone. Whether he didn't have the inclination or the technique to climb down mountains as well as up, it was impossible to tell, but Jack suspected the latter.

That evening Cromwell and Trench descended leaving Jack and Dudley to share a tent. When he learned that Dudley was planning to continue to the next camp at 24,700 ft, Jack decided it was time to confront the issue head-on. He warned Dudley that he simply wasn't good enough to go any higher. The climbing was only going to get tougher so it was crazy to carry on if he did not have the skill to climb back down.

Not surprisingly, Dudley wasn't very pleased to hear Jack's comments. As far as he was concerned, he was doing fine. He had reached 23,400 ft – why couldn't he go all the way? It was Tony and the young Dartmouth boys, Jack included, who couldn't take the strain. Next morning Dudley told Fritz about their conversation and asked what to do. He knew that others didn't rate him, but perhaps, Dudley suggested, it was all just jealousy? They might be better technical climbers, but on K2 that didn't seem to mean very much.

It was a very strange situation. Fritz obviously knew that Dudley didn't have much mountaineering experience but he had two qualities the others lacked. In the first instance, he was very enthusiastic and actually seemed to want to get to the summit. In the second, he didn't seem troubled by the altitude. It would be very hard to say no to him when he was going so strong, especially when everyone else was falling by the wayside.

Events of the following day seemed to confirm Dudley's position. As they made their way up toward Camp 7, Jack Durrance found it harder and harder to breathe. Every step was a struggle. When he got about a third of the way up at around 24,000 ft, he realised that he just couldn't climb any further. Fritz sent Jack down with an escort of three Sherpas and Pasang Kikuli, who was suffering from frostbite, and told him to return the next day when he felt better. If for any reason he could not make it, he was to send a party of Sherpas back up with more supplies.

Jack made it down and survived House's Chimney but back at Camp 4 he had his worst night so far; his heartbeat was completely irregular and he had real difficulty breathing. He was so scared that he insisted that one of the Sherpas should sleep next to him.

When later Jack reviewed the events and tried to make sense of his collapse, he couldn't quite work out what had gone wrong. Was it simply the effects of the altitude and bad weather? Or had he been ground down by the general chaos of the expedition? He had not slept well for many weeks and was sure that the effort he had put in to help George Trench get up House's Chimney and the heavy pack that he had carried up to Camp 6 had not done him any good. The fact that he rarely had enough advance warning of Fritz's plans, his lack of acclimatisation, his worries about being chosen for the summit team had all contributed to his general feeling of stress and anxiety; but as to what caused him to collapse at that particular moment – the truth was that he simply didn't know. The only thing he was sure of was that he had reached his limit and had to get down to a lower altitude – and get down fast. So next morning, Jack got the Sherpas up at 5.00 a.m., intending to make a speedy getaway. Nothing happened quickly at high altitude, however, and it took over three hours to break camp.

Up above everything seemed to be proceeding according to plan. Fritz sent a Sherpa down with the good news that Camp 7 had been established at 24,700 ft and that everything was going well. Privately, however, he was desperately frustrated. The only American who was able to keep up with him was Dudley Wolfe, the least competent climber. It was amazing that he had managed to get this far, but try as he might Dudley would never get to the summit. With Jack Durrance out of action for the foreseeable future, he would probably have to make his attempt with just one Sherpa in support. If that Sherpa had been an experienced man like Pasang Kikuli, Fritz would not have been worried, but Kikuli showed no signs of returning, so he would probably have to take the less experienced Pasang Lama. As he wrote in his diary on 13 July:

A sad state of affairs. Here I am, head of a group whose climbing strength is nil by now, while the mountain shows an opening for the first time.

Fritz's assessment was bleak, but realistic. When Jack reached Camp 2, on 12 July, after a long and gruelling descent, he found Tony Cromwell and George Trench all played out. Apart from a brief burst of enthusiasm when he first arrived at base camp at the beginning of June, Tony Cromwell had never really felt confident about getting anywhere on K2 and it was obvious now that he could not do any more climbing. There was no good news from base camp either; Chappell Cranmer had not recovered from the mystery illness that had kept him a virtual prisoner in his tent and George Sheldon's frostbite still hadn't cleared up. Just as many had predicted back in America, Fritz's inexperienced team had imploded. They had tried their best, but K2 had just been too hard for them.

Jack Durrance, however, wasn't quite ready to give up. He was still reeling from his collapse a few days earlier, but instead of retreating to base camp, he decided to stay at Camp 2 to recuperate and liaise with the Sherpas stationed higher up the mountain. His tent mate, the head Sherpa Pasang Kikuli, was also keen to return to Fritz but for the moment his frostbite was just too painful for him to go back up. Instead Tse Tendrup, one of the most experienced men, was left in charge of the four-strong support party tasked with keeping Fritz resupplied. Tendrup, a tough-looking Tibetan, had served on both the 1936 French expedition to Hidden Peak and the 1938 reconnaissance. He was a good solid deputy for Pasang Kikuli – or so everyone thought.

As they languished in their tent Jack was fascinated to hear Pasang Kikuli's stories about life in Darjeeling and his previous expeditions to K2 and other Himalayan giants, but he could sense the head Sherpa's frustration. A year earlier on the K2 reconnaissance expedition, Pasang Kikuli had begged Charlie Houston to let him climb up to his final camp, but now here he was, made a virtual invalid. As for Fritz Wiessner, in spite of his irritation at the others, he just kept on going. On 14 July, accompanied by Dudley Wolfe and Pasang Lama, he set up Camp 8 at 25,300 ft, a full 600 ft higher than Houston's last camp. Dudley Wolfe was still ploughing on, the summit was almost in sight and there was no reason why he couldn't reach it, with or without Durrance. All that Jack and the others had to do was keep the Sherpas busy, the supply lines moving and the camps well stocked in case of any problems on their return.

The weather as usual wasn't quite ready to endorse Fritz's plans. For two days he was confined to his tent by another powerful storm but luckily this time it didn't last. On the morning of 17 July Fritz left camp with Dudley and Pasang Lama. A year earlier Charlie Houston and Paul Petzoldt had broken the same trail, but their final day felt more like an epilogue than the climax of a story. Fritz planned to write a very different narrative. If they could put up a final camp on the shoulder of K2, and if the summit cone was as easy as Petzoldt had predicted, then there was a very real chance they might climb their way into the history books.

First, though, there was an awkward piece of climbing just above Camp 8: a huge crevasse, or bergschrund, had opened up just below the Shoulder. It was full of soft snow; getting across felt more like swimming than climbing. It took Fritz almost two hours to force his way through and Pasang a further hour. Dudley Wolfe, however, found it impossible. He might have been strong and determined, but he was just too heavy and did not have the technique to get through the soft fluffy snow without sinking. After floundering in vain, he turned back for Camp 8 to wait for reinforcements. With a bit of luck he hoped the snow might firm up over the next few days and he would come up with the next party.

Fritz and Pasang Lama were now on their own. Above them lay 600 ft of relatively easy-looking snow which led up to the rocky summit pyramid. They were exhausted but the skies were clear and the weather looked set for several more days. All the other Americans on his party had fallen away but Fritz had no doubts about continuing.

K2 was his mountain and he would climb it.

Chapter 4

HIGH AMBITION

In 1929, the year that Fritz Wiessner arrived in New York, the race began to construct the highest building in America. The First World War had let loose the bulls of the US stock market and there was no sign they would be back in their pens anytime soon. The first contender, appropriately enough, was 40 Wall Street, right in the heart of America's financial centre. Originally it was planned to be 840 ft high but when its owners heard that a few miles uptown the automotive magnate Walter Chrysler had commissioned a rival, destined to be 80 ft taller, they asked the architects to add an extra three storeys.

In May 1930, 40 Wall Street officially opened and was crowned Manhattan's, and ergo the world's, tallest building. Its title, however, was short-lived. Just a few weeks later, the Chrysler Building opened on Lexington Avenue. In terms of bricks and mortar, it was a few feet shorter than 40 Wall Street but just before its inauguration, amid great secrecy, a 125 ft steel spire was erected on top of the final storey, making it a total of 1046 ft tall.

The Chrysler Building held the title for longer than its predecessor, but only just. On 1 May 1931 the ribbon was cut on the Empire State Building; its ultra-modern design included an airship terminal and mooring mast on the 103rd floor, which helped it to come in at 1454 ft, easily trouncing all rivals for the next thirty-nine years. Of course the great irony was that by the time the race reached its climax, America was in the grip of the Great Depression. For many years, whole floors of the Empire State Building lay empty, a potent symbol of capitalism's hubris.

When Fritz Wiessner made his first business trip to America, he had harboured no plans to stay permanently. He just wanted to set up some deals and make a little money in the land of opportunity before returning home to Germany. With hundreds of thousands unemployed, it wasn't the perfect moment, but Fritz had soon fallen for what he called America's 'easy-going ways'. By the mid-1930s he had decided to take up US citizenship, in spite of resistance from his family. His ski wax business had taken more time to get off the ground than he had initially hoped, but over the last decade he had steadily built up a network of contacts and, with skiing becoming ever more popular in the United States, was optimistic that everything would soon come good.

For an immigrant with no ties of family or friendship to his new home, climbing had been a good way to get to know people. It was still very much a minority sport but its devotees were passionate and committed. They also tended to be rich. In later years, some of Fritz's critics would claim that he deliberately set out to make connections with men like Dudley Wolfe and Rand Herron, whom he had taken on the Nanga Parbat expedition in 1932, because of their wealth. To claim this, however, would be to miss one of Fritz's most defining traits: his real desire to bring in new climbers and to increase the popularity of the sport. If his latest expedition succeeded, it would undoubtedly bring him fame and would give an Empire State Building-sized boost to the American Alpine Club, and American mountaineering in general. However, as New York's architects had learned the hard way, any ambitious endeavour carried huge risks.

Now he was a few thousand feet from the top and about to go beyond the high point achieved on the 1938 reconnaissance. Before striking out for the summit, though, Fritz needed to put up one more camp. A year earlier Paul Petzoldt had spotted a natural platform at the foot of the summit cone which looked an ideal position for a small camp, but after spending so much time wading through the soft snows below, both Fritz and Pasang Lama were too exhausted to reach it.

Instead, they pitched their tent in the lee of a large boulder and settled in for the night. Next morning they moved to where Petzoldt had suggested. For added protection, they built a wall of stones around its perimeter. Fritz was in no hurry. For now, there were no threatening clouds on the horizon and the weather looked set for at least a few good days. He would take things steadily and carefully; as he wrote in his diary when he first saw K2, now was the time to be 'cool and deliberate'.

Down at base camp, there was a much greater sense of urgency, though directed toward a very different goal. In less than a week the Askole porters were coming to carry their equipment off the mountain. It had taken 120 men to get them to base camp, but only 23 would be needed for the return journey.[1] There was a lot to organise for deputy leader Tony Cromwell, if they were going to leave on time. He had George Trench, the transport officer, to help him but George Sheldon and Chapell Cranmer's minds were elsewhere.

Chappell Cranmer had never recovered from his dramatic illness at the beginning of June, but he wanted to leave the Karakoram feeling that he had achieved something. So he and Sheldon had decided to make a brief geology field trip down the Baltoro glacier before the long journey back to Dartmouth College. Sheldon's frostbitten feet were still a problem but he too was looking forward to getting away from base camp and the demands of 'Herr Wiessner'.

On 18 July Cranmer and Sheldon waved goodbye to Cromwell and Trench and slowly made their way back down the glacier. At the same time, Jack Durrance and Pasang Kikuli began recovering the valuable sleeping bags and spare tents from the four lower camps in preparation for the expedition's departure. If they were going to get away on schedule and not delay the porters at base camp, they needed to start packing straight away.

Jack sorted out the spare equipment at Camp 2 and sent Pasang Kikuli up to Camp 4 to collect what was there. When he arrived, he had a surprising encounter with Tendrup, the Sherpa who was supposed to be in charge of keeping the upper camps resupplied with food and fuel. He had descended with another Sherpa, Kitar, against orders. Why wasn't he higher up the mountain, Pasang Kikuli demanded?

Tendrup complained that it was very uncomfortable and cramped, but promised that he would go back up straight away. Pasang Kikuli collected the spare equipment and then waited for Tendrup and Kitar to start back up, before descending to Jack at Camp 2. There was so much to carry back down to base camp that they had to leave several tents still standing and abandon a lot of food. When Jack weighed their loads, he discovered that they had salvaged over 230 lbs of gear.

Although everyone was now focused on leaving K2, they were still eager to know how the summit party was getting on. Fritz had not sent down any notes for several days, so what was happening? Would the expedition end in triumph, or would they go home defeated? There was no way to tell but, with the good weather continuing, it looked as if Fritz stood a fair chance. On the morning of 19 July, he prepared to take it.

The day began with a crucial decision: should he and his Sherpa, Pasang Lama, go right or left? The most obvious route to the summit was via a steep icy gully, or couloir, that led to the easy-looking snow slopes of the final ridge. The only problem was the menacing glacier that overhung it, looking as if it might collapse at any minute. There was a lot of avalanche debris at the foot of the couloir, suggesting that the mass of ice above was distinctly unstable. Although the gully offered a fast route upwards, it also looked like a particularly dangerous one.

The alternative was to head up the steep rock slopes to the left. This was by far the harder option from a climbing point of view but at least there was no obvious risk of avalanche. It didn't take long for Fritz to make a decision: he would avoid the couloir and hope that the rocks weren't quite as difficult as they looked. Fritz had been tackling impossible-seeming rock pitches since his teenage years, so why change the habit of a lifetime?

Fritz led the way up, with Pasang Lama belaying him carefully. To his amazement it was warm enough to take his gloves off. In the far distance, Fritz could see Nanga Parbat, the Himalayan peak he had attempted and failed to climb in 1932; closer at hand lay Chogolisa, with its icy summit, and Masherbrum, the 'K1' of Montgomerie's survey, almost a century ago.

Up they climbed, slowly and methodically, until after about nine hours Fritz stopped at 27,500 ft, roughly 800 ft from the top.[2] Ahead lay a 60 ft traverse leading to the final snow slopes of the summit ridge.

The difficult climbing was almost over, he thought, the rest should be easy. Fritz got ready to lead them across, but instead of paying the rope out, Pasang Lama held it tight.

'No, Sahib, tomorrow.'

Fritz couldn't quite believe it: come back tomorrow when they were so close to their goal? But Pasang Lama was adamant: it was too late. The evil spirits that lived on top of the mountain would soon emerge, so they simply could not carry on.

Over the last few days, Pasang Lama had shown himself to be a confident climber and a good companion, but now at a crucial moment in the expedition his nerves were beginning to show. Fritz tried to persuade him: the sky was clear and they could look forward to a moonlit night. It would take just three or four hours to get to the top and a few more to get back. The remainder of their route looked relatively easy. Surely it made more sense to keep on going than to turn back now and have to climb down over those difficult rocks that they had struggled with all day? The alternative, to carry on to the summit and then climb down the steep rocks at dawn, would be much safer.

Pasang Lama, however, did not want to know. His leader might have had a great day, but he had spent most of it standing on a series of narrow perches, belaying Fritz. He didn't have the same high-quality boots as his sahib and wasn't used to climbing at night.

Years later, when Pasang Lama became famous in his own right for making the first ascent of Cho Oyu, the world's sixth-highest mountain, with the Swiss climber Herbert Tichy, he was interviewed by the Austrian mountaineer Kurt Maix. When asked about Fritz Wiessner, Pasang Lama's smile disappeared. He told Maix that his former leader was simply crazy. 'Climb, climb, climb,' he remembered, 'and say when dark, we at the summit. I never see someone climb like he… maybe he could see with his fingertips. I say I go no further'.[3]

For a moment, Fritz thought about leaving Pasang Lama and simply carrying on alone. There were precedents in the Himalayas: in 1924 Edward Norton had left Howard Somervell at 28,000 ft on Everest, while he continued toward the summit. Nine years later, Frank Smythe had been equally happy to let the young Eric Shipton descend Everest alone while he made his solo bid for the top. But this was different. Norton and Smythe were both confident that their partners could get down under their own steam, but Fritz was not so certain. They had just climbed some of the most difficult slopes ever attempted at high altitude, and though Pasang Lama had been a perfect partner, it was inconceivable that he would be able to reach Camp 9 by himself. Unable to persuade him to change his mind, Fritz was forced to turn back. It was a decision that would haunt him for the rest of his life.

As he predicted, climbing down over difficult slopes in the dark was both dangerous and time-consuming. At one stage, Pasang got his rope tangled up and inadvertently sent the two pairs of crampons attached to his rucksack tumbling down the mountain, never to be seen again.

It was 2.30 a.m. by the time they reached their tent, far too late to stand any chance of returning on the following day. So instead, Pasang stayed in his sleeping bag, while Fritz enjoyed a spell of sunbathing. It was so warm at Camp 9 that he was able to lie naked for several hours. If nothing else, he would return to America with a world record for high-altitude tanning. And Fritz wasn't the only one enjoying the weather.

Down at base camp, Jack Durrance was celebrating his twenty-seventh birthday with a bar of Yardley soap and his first bath in nine weeks. His underwear was so filthy that he virtually had to cut it off; the flesh underneath didn't look much better. Over the last two months he had lost roughly 25 lbs and was very much looking forward to the restaurants and bars of Srinagar.

After six weeks on a steep, invariably cold mountain, Jack could at last revel in the simple pleasure of walking on a hard, relatively flat surface. The fact that he could dry off in the sun while reading a stack of mail was a treat beyond all expectation. Pasang Kikuli had gone up to Camp 1 to salvage some of the expedition's abandoned food and Tony Cromwell and George Trench were almost ready to leave.

All that remained was for Fritz to make a triumphant return and everyone could start for home. Over the last few days, Jack had spent a lot of time wondering how Fritz and Dudley were getting on but there was still no news. If absolutely necessary, Jack had come up with a plan B, in which Cromwell and Trench would set off with the main body of porters, leaving him to wait for Fritz and Dudley, but everyone hoped it wouldn't come to that. All he could do was wait and watch and hope for some signs of movement above.

That night when Jack scanned the Abruzzi ridge with his binoculars, he did not see the smoke signals that Fritz had promised if he reached the summit. However, on the following day he noticed that the tents at Camp 6 were partially collapsed. The summit party must be coming down and would probably reach base camp within the next two days. Then they could go home. Hurrah!

But Jack was wrong.

The tents had been collapsed not by the summit party, but by Tse Tendrup and the three Sherpas, who were supposed to be hard at work keeping Fritz resupplied. For the last seven days they had been alone on the mountain. Apart from briefly encountering Pasang Kikuli at Camp 4, they had not had any contact with any one of the sahibs, above or below. They had been left with orders to keep the supply chain running, but the bad weather and their reluctance to climb unsupervised had scotched that plan. And one thing was now abundantly clear to Tse Tendrup: Fritz, Bara Sahib, 'the big boss', was dead.

Tendrup had never actually climbed as far as Camp 8 where he assumed his leader was based, but when he shouted up from just below, there was no reply. Therefore, he figured, there must have been an accident and Fritz, Dudley Wolfe and Pasang Lama must have perished. For Tendrup there was no alternative explanation and none of the other Sherpas in his party was prepared to climb to Camp 8 to check out his story.

After so many weeks on the mountain, the Sherpas, like the Americans, just wanted to go home. They would descend to base camp and give the remaining sahibs the sad news; along the route they would clear the remaining camps, just as they had seen Pasang Kikuli clearing Camp 4 a few days earlier. Who could say – they might even be allowed to keep some of the precious sleeping bags? Bara Sahib and the summit party were dead, they would not be needing them.

In fact, as the great American author Mark Twain might have quipped, reports of Fritz's death had been greatly exaggerated. On the same day that Tendrup and the others headed down the mountain to announce their leader's death, Fritz headed back up from his top camp to take a second crack at the summit.

This time, though, he decided to try the other route to the top. During his first attempt, he had taken a good look at the icy couloir, to the right of the rocks, and realised that it wasn't quite so dangerous after all. Unlike the route that he and Pasang Lama had tried two days earlier, the couloir seemed to offer a direct approach to the summit, which should prove much quicker.

On the morning of 21 July, two days after their first attempt, Fritz and Pasang Lama broke camp at 6.00 a.m. It was slower going than they had hoped. In order to get to the couloir, they had to traverse some loose scree slopes and then carefully climb a steep face, covered in a treacherous layer of snow and ice. By the time they reached the foot of the couloir it was 10.00 a.m. That wasn't their biggest problem, though.

As Fritz looked upwards he realised that without the crampons that Pasang Lama had lost two nights earlier, the task ahead would be very difficult. He began chopping footholds but in the thin air of 27,000 ft it was brutally hard work. Fritz estimated that he might have to cut 300 to 400 steps before they reached the summit slopes. It would be impossible to do this and return in a single day, so once again he would have to face Pasang Lama's reluctance to climb at night.

Fritz had expected that by now Dudley Wolfe or Jack Durrance, or at very least some of the Sherpas, would have come up to their top camp, Camp 9, but no one had made the trip. The only solution was to go back down to Camp 8, borrow some crampons and pick up more food and fuel. Pasang Lama was only too happy to descend – after two summit attempts he was utterly spent and asked Fritz if someone else could take his place for the next attempt.

When they set off to find Dudley the following morning, Pasang Lama's exhaustion quickly became apparent. Just above Dudley's camp, the Sherpa slipped and Fritz only just managed to hold onto him. It was about time that Fritz got some reinforcements, but when he reached Camp 8, he was sorely disappointed.

The first thing he noticed was that one of their tents was partially collapsed. Dudley Wolfe was standing outside the other, but he was on his own. Dudley's only news was that there wasn't any. He had spent the last six days alone and had neither heard nor seen anything from below. Jack Durrance hadn't made it, and nor had any of the Sherpas. Dudley's matches had run out, reducing him to drinking meltwater from the folds of the tent. Overjoyed though he was to see Fritz and Pasang and hear how close they had come to victory, Dudley was furious with the rest of the team.

After making Dudley his first hot meal for days, the three men started off down the ridge toward the next camp, Camp 7, where they assumed Jack and the other Sherpas were based. Even if they hadn't made it all the way to Dudley, somebody had to be there. The ground was steep and icy requiring a lot of care; Dudley's limitations soon became apparent.

He had never mastered the technique of down-climbing and was very nervous about descending while facing in to the mountain, though it was by far the safest method. Nor did he like kicking footholds in the snow. So Fritz went into the lead and began the arduous job of cutting steps. Then suddenly, when he was getting ready to hack out another one, Dudley stood on the rope that stretched between them and caused Fritz to fall off. Within seconds both Dudley and Pasang Lama had come off too and were sliding down K2, out of control.

According to the textbooks, in such a situation a climber should arrest their fall by digging the head of their ice-axe into the snow, but because he had just been cutting steps, Fritz was holding his axe at the wrong end. He managed to get hold of the head and was just about to dig in when there was another sharp pull, causing him once again to somersault through the air. Dudley and Pasang Lama were now in front of him and all three were heading for a sheer drop onto the Godwin-Austen glacier 9000 ft below. Fritz was convinced it was the end but he tried to arrest their fall again, and second time round managed somehow to bring them all to a halt.

Everyone was badly shaken. Dudley had lost his rucksack and, after his second slip of the day, Pasang Lama had damaged his ribs. Fritz was rattled but unhurt. It took so long to recover that by the time they reached the next camp, it was almost evening. There was no hot tea or warm soup, though, to greet them. Instead everything was in utter disarray. One tent had huge gashes in its canvas and a broken pole, the other was almost full of snow. The food they had struggled so hard to carry up was scattered all around, and when they finally managed to excavate the one usable tent, they realised that all the sleeping bags and air mattresses had been taken away.

Fritz just couldn't understand what was happening. Like Charlie Houston he had been very concerned about being caught on K2 in a big storm, so he had brought enough supplies to ensure that all the main camps had enough reserves of food and fuel for a party to hold out for several days. As well as provisions, the four principal camps were all supposed to have spare sleeping bags and mattresses, in order to allow climbers to move quickly up and down the mountain without having to carry a lot of personal gear.

Now, at the very moment when the expedition was reaching its climax, the whole system seemed to have fallen apart. Fritz had left his sleeping bag at his top camp and Dudley had lost his, during the fall. All they had left to share between them was Pasang's small, Sherpa-size bag. After two summit attempts and five days in the 'death zone' this was no way to spend a bitterly cold night. What were his teammates trying to do? In his diary entry that night, Fritz did not mince his words:

> *What had been going on during the days when we were high –*
> *sabotage? We could not understand… It was obvious to us*
> *that nobody had been at 7 for many days or cared about the*
> *3 men above. To the hell with them!*[4]

Down at base camp, they were equally perplexed but not quite so angry. The Askole porters had just arrived and almost everything was packed and ready to go – but where was Fritz? For the third night in a row, Jack stood out on the glacier staring up at the Abruzzi ridge, searching for the smoke signal that would indicate the summit party was on its way down. At 9.00 p.m. he even lit a signal fire of his own, hoping that it would prompt a response, but there was no reply.

Once again, Jack Durrance and Tony Cromwell reformulated their plans. They couldn't leave without Fritz and would have to wait another day. First thing tomorrow, they would send head Sherpa Pasang Kikuli up to Camp 2 to collect some abandoned food and make contact with the returning climbers. If for some reason he didn't, then on 23 July George Trench would leave with most of the Askole porters and Jack and Tony would climb back up the ridge in search of Fritz. No one wanted to split the party but the Askole porters couldn't stay at base camp for more than a few days without running out of food.

The events the following day had the quality of a French farce, but there was nothing to laugh about. At 5.30 a.m. Pasang Kikuli and another Sherpa, Dawa, set off from base camp for Camp 2. The weather was good and if everything went smoothly they were hoping to be back by lunchtime with some much needed supplies and their missing expedition leader. There was only one flaw in the plan: Fritz wasn't anywhere near Camp 2. He was still at Camp 7.

There might have been blue skies above base camp, but at 24,700 ft K2 was covered in cloud and so cold and unsettled that no one could leave their tent until 10.00 a.m., four and a half hours after Pasang Kikuli left base camp. Fritz still wanted to collect crampons and supplies to make another attempt, but after a freezing night his priority was to get another sleeping bag. After his fall, there was blood in Pasang Lama's urine so unsurprisingly he was desperate to return to base camp and be relieved of his role on the summit team. In spite of their awful night, Dudley Wolfe wasn't so sure. He told Fritz that he didn't want to miss out on his next attempt, so rather than go down with Pasang, he would remain at Camp 7. Fritz promised to return in a few days and immediately send up Jack Durrance and a party of Sherpas with supplies. It was a fateful decision, and would be endlessly debated in years to come.

A few thousand feet further down the mountain, Tendrup and his party of Sherpas were also descending, carrying the sleeping bags that they had taken from Camps 6 and 7, but remarkably they neither saw Fritz above nor Pasang Kikuli below and didn't reach base camp until early evening. Not surprisingly, when Tendrup told everyone that the entire summit party had disappeared and were undoubtedly dead, it prompted considerable alarm. Jack Durrance, however, wasn't quite convinced; in his diary he described Tendrup's men as 'a weather-worn lot, worried with a guilty conscience for having quit the mountain without orders or contact with "Bara Sahib" since July 14th!'[5]

By the time Tendrup had told his story, Fritz and Pasang had reached Camp 2 and were close to desperation. Fritz just couldn't believe it: not a single Sherpa or sahib on the mountain. No sleeping bags or air mattresses at Camps 6, 5, 4 or 3. At Camp 2, one tent was completely empty, the other half full of food but nothing to keep them warm. All that he and Pasang Lama could do was take down the empty tent and use it as a rough blanket. Fritz was furious: this wasn't just sabotage – it was attempted murder.

On the afternoon of 24 July Fritz was finally reunited with the rest of his team, but not in circumstances anyone had envisaged. Jack had stayed at base camp to finalise the loads for the departing porters and Tony had gone up the glacier to get a better view of the Abruzzi ridge. He found no evidence of any accident and was on his way back when suddenly he spotted two forlorn-looking figures half walking, half staggering down from Camp 1. It was Fritz and Pasang Lama.

Tony rushed over but Fritz had barely got over the shock of meeting his teammates when he turned on him. Though he could only speak in a harsh whisper, he accused Tony in no uncertain terms of abandoning the summit party. Dudley Wolfe, he hissed, was furious and law-suits would follow. Fritz's reaction was understandable but this was not what Tony expected to hear. As far as he was concerned he had done his duty: he had organised their departure, sorted out the Askole porters and waited at base camp for Fritz. It was Fritz who had abandoned the men below him, not the other way round.

Back at base camp, the priority was to prepare warm food. As each party told their story, the narrative of the previous week became a little clearer. Jack explained that after collapsing on the way up to Camp 7, he had gone to recuperate at Camp 2 and then returned to base camp several days later with all the spare equipment to prepare for the march out. He was unhappy that he hadn't been able to stay high but both he and Tony had thought that Tendrup, Pasang Kikuli's deputy, and his party of three Sherpas were in contact with Fritz. No one at base camp had any idea what was going on above them, and no one realised that any of the camps above Camp 4 had been stripped of their sleeping bags. The sahibs had not given the orders – all that had been done on Tse Tendrup's own initiative.

When he calmed down, Fritz told them how he had come very close to the summit on 19 July and was determined to go back up to take another crack at it. The weather still hadn't broken and, after a couple of days of rest, there was still time, he insisted, to make a third attempt. There was none of the cool deliberation in Fritz's diary entry that night, but the passion was still there:

> *The mountain is far away.*
>
> *The weather is the best we had so far.*
>
> *Will it be possible for me to go up after a rest with some Sherpas and with Jack, if he is in shape, pick up Dudley and then call on the summit?*
>
> *7 days of good weather will be necessary. Maybe the Gods will be with me and let me have what is due to me?*

That night as he chewed over the extraordinary events of the day, Jack came to a very different conclusion. Pasang Lama was totally exhausted and had collapsed in his tent. Fritz looked utterly spent. It was obvious that no matter how much he wanted it, there would be no third attempt.

There was just one problem, but it was a big one: Dudley Wolfe, the 'hermit of K2'.

Chapter 5

THE FALL OUT

Dudley Wolfe had always been rich, but hadn't always been happy. There was something rootless about him, an unsettled quality that expressed itself in a life of almost constant motion. If he wasn't yachting he was skiing, if he wasn't skiing he was climbing, if he wasn't climbing he was driving or shopping or big-game hunting.

He is sometimes referred to as a 'Great Gatsby' figure, but there was nothing self-made about Dudley Wolfe. He was born wealthy, the second in a family of four. His father, or so Dudley Wolfe Snr liked to claim, was a blue-blooded English aristocrat; his mother, the bona fide heiress to a vast American fortune made in real estate and railroads.

Dudley attended the best schools but struggled academically. He preferred sport, initially American football and wrestling. He was built big: 5 ft 10 in and 180 lbs when he was happy with his weight, 220 lbs when he wasn't. When the First World War broke out he tried to enlist but didn't get into the US Army because of his flat feet and poor eyesight. Undaunted, he tried to join the French Foreign Legion; when they told him the waiting list was too long, he opted for the Red Cross ambulance corps instead.

En route to Europe Dudley stopped off in England where by chance he met a long-lost uncle who revealed that, though his mother was genuinely rich, his father was in fact the son of a Jewish tobacconist from the distinctly unaristocratic East End of London. It was a disturbing moment, but Dudley continued to the Western Front, where his elder brother, Clifford, was also fighting.

The three Wolfe boys, Clifford, Dudley and Grafton, all had wild streaks in their youth, but in the 1920s Dudley's big brother Clifford changed path and became involved in the family business. Dudley made an effort and worked briefly in real estate, but, like his younger brother, Grafton, he was more interested in yachting than clinching land deals. By the early 1930s he was the proud owner of a schooner and a racing cutter and a member of some of America's and Britain's most famous yachting clubs.

Then came love and marriage. Dudley was a good catch for Alice Damrosch, a New York socialite, the daughter of the renowned conductor Walter Damrosch. She was a handsome, outdoors type of girl and an accomplished skier. Dudley was her second husband, but for a few years at least they were happy, spending a lot of time at her house in the Austrian Alps, where Dudley learned first to ski and then to climb. The lessons, however, were more successful than the marriage, and after four years Alice and Dudley agreed to an amicable divorce.

It was through one of Alice's friends, Betty Woolsey, that Dudley first got to know Fritz Wiessner. Though he had no expedition experience and had never climbed without guides, he signed up for K2 almost immediately. The two men hit it off straight away. For Dudley, Fritz meant excitement and adventure and the opportunity to prove himself in another sphere; for Fritz, Dudley meant genuine enthusiasm and financial support for the expedition. He knew that Dudley was a novice, but as always, Fritz was keen to get new people into the sport. As he told the American mountaineer David Dornan many years later:

> He was a very strong, tough man with a splendid physique
> who looked like a very good prospect for high altitude work.
> He was not an elegant climber, but on the big peaks it isn't
> really necessary to have top-notch technicians.[1]

As the expedition progressed, Dudley had become increasingly exasperated at all the negative comments from Tony Cromwell and the Dartmouth boys about his climbing technique. He knew that his rope-work and belaying technique weren't as good as everyone else's, but then again, none of them coped as well with the altitude as he did. If a mountaineer of Fritz Wiessner's stature had faith in him, that was good enough for Dudley.

The problem was, the higher he got, the more isolated he became. It was now 25 July, two days since Fritz and Pasang Lama had disappeared down the mountain. They had promised to send Sherpas back up with more supplies but so far no one had come. Dudley had spent seven of the last eight days alone. There wasn't much to do in the tiny camp, perched on the rocks at 24,700 ft, except sit and wait and hope the others wouldn't take much longer. He didn't even have his precious cameras or his diary – both had been lost in the fall.

Meanwhile, 8000 ft below, base camp was the busiest it had been for weeks. Tony Cromwell and George Trench were preparing to leave with twenty-two of the thirty Askole porters who had turned up.[2] Tony had offered to stay but he looked so unhappy that even Fritz felt sorry for him. Tendrup, the Sherpa who had brought down the premature tale of Fritz's death, was also going back in disgrace. 'Nobody wants to see him any more,' wrote Fritz in his diary.

Shortly after Tony left, Jack Durrance and three Sherpas – Dawa, Phinsoo and Kitar – headed in the opposite direction, back up the mountain. For Fritz it marked the first stage in his next attempt on the summit. If everything went according to plan, Jack and the Sherpas would meet Dudley, climb back up and restock Camp 8. After a few days' rest, Fritz would follow and make what he hoped would be his third and final attempt.

Jack Durrance, however, saw it entirely differently. Pasang Lama was crocked, Pasang Kikuli was still suffering from frostbite and Fritz was a shadow of the man who had led them up the mountain. There would be no more attempts on K2. It was a rescue mission pure and simple and he wasn't even sure how far he would get.

At first it went well. Jack surprised himself by racing up the scree slope below Camp 1 faster than his three Sherpas. By 3.00 p.m. he was at Camp 2, repitching the tent that Fritz and Pasang had used as a blanket a few nights earlier and brewing up soup and cocoa. Jack slept well and roused everyone at dawn to climb the next 2200 ft to Camp 4.

By the time he got there, he wasn't feeling so positive. The ascent from Camp 2 to Camp 4 had been very difficult, with plenty of loose rock to negotiate and avoid. The weather was warming up, melting the ice that held stones and boulders in place. They reached Camp 4 at midday but it was clear to Jack that neither he nor his Sherpa Dawa were in any state to continue. Dawa had been a very solid climber so far on the expedition, but he had developed severe chest pains and a very sore throat and clearly needed to go back down.

Jack had already gone higher than he expected to and did not think there was any chance that he would be able to reach Dudley at Camp 7. So on the following day, he descended with Dawa leaving Kitar and Phinsoo at Camp 4 to wait for Fritz and Pasang Kikuli to come up and complete the rescue mission.

If only it had been so simple. When Jack reached base camp, Fritz seemed to have deteriorated. His throat was still very painful and he could barely raise his voice above a whisper. After spending a day staring at his emaciated legs and comparing frostbite injuries with Pasang Lama, he had finally accepted that there was no chance of a third attempt this year and he was not even sure that he was capable of reaching Dudley.

Fortunately, Pasang Kikuli felt differently. He told Fritz and Jack not to worry. His frostbite had abated and he was sure that he could rescue their comrade without the assistance of any sahibs. He would take his last fit Sherpa, Tsering, up to Camp 4, collect Kitar and Phinsoo, and then fetch Dudley.

In theory, this went against the protocols established by the British in the Himalayas. The unofficial rules stated that Sherpas always had to have a 'sahib' with them and that it wasn't safe to let them climb alone. They were essentially seen as high-altitude load carriers, whose job was to follow their Western masters and carry supplies. In practice, even on British expeditions, things weren't nearly so clear cut.

Some Sherpas were considered very good mountaineers in their own right and respected as such. On this expedition there had been several occasions when Sherpas had been left alone and expected to move up and down K2 independently. This hadn't always worked, as witnessed by Tendrup's behaviour, but Pasang Kikuli was in a different league. Jack sensed that he had been feeling guilty about his frostbite and the fact that he hadn't been able to do more on the expedition so far. This was his chance to prove himself and enhance his reputation.

At 6.00 a.m. on 28 July Pasang Kikuli and Tsering left base camp promising to return with Dudley Wolfe and the other Sherpas in three days. It was an optimistic boast, but next morning as Fritz and Jack scanned the Abruzzi ridge through powerful binoculars, it looked as if he might be able to do it. Just below Camp 7, they spotted three figures climbing steadily. It was Pasang Kikuli and two of his Sherpas, Tsering and Kitar. On the previous day, Pasang Kikuli and Tsering had climbed 7000 ft in a single push – an unprecedented feat at high altitude.

It was an astonishing achievement, but a slightly unsettling one. Fritz and Jack had now become bystanders. All they could do was watch and hope that Pasang Kikuli would succeed – and endlessly discuss how they had got themselves into this awful position.

High on the Abruzzi ridge, the expedition's problems were going from bad to worse. Pasang Kikuli and his two Sherpas did succeed in reaching Camp 7 but they were not prepared for the sight, or the smell, that greeted them. Dudley Wolfe was lying in his sleeping bag, and it was obvious that he had not been out of his tent for several days. He had fouled his bedding and the food that lay around him was contaminated with urine and excrement. He was conscious, and the Sherpas even managed to persuade him to go outside the tent, but he refused to come down with them. Even a note from Fritz and a pile of mail from home didn't make a difference. Tomorrow, Dudley said, tomorrow I will be ready. The Sherpas tidied up the adjacent tent, but they had not expected to have to stay at Camp 7 and had left their sleeping bags below. After making Dudley some tea, they left him alone promising to come back the following day.

This was not how sahibs were supposed to behave; clearly it was not going to be so easy to rescue Dudley Wolfe. Pasang Kikuli, however, felt he could not return empty-handed. He was a sirdar, a head Sherpa, and had a name to live up to. Though he did not know it yet, he had just been given a 'Tiger' badge by the Himalayan Club, the organisation that managed the hiring of Sherpas. It was their highest honour, awarded to Pasang Kikuli for his sterling work on Charlie Houston's K2 reconnaissance expedition of 1938. For any Sherpa, reputation was crucial – make a name for yourself for reliability, and work would come flowing in. But fail to deliver on your promises... not so good.

A powerful snowstorm began that night and didn't let up for twenty-four hours, forcing Pasang Kikuli to wait for another day before returning to collect Dudley. When he left, on the morning of 31 July, he took Phinsoo and Kitar again, leaving Tsering behind with instructions to prepare tea for their return. If they could not persuade Dudley to come voluntarily, Pasang Kikuli said, they would drag him down. And if they couldn't drag him down, they would get him to sign a chit acknowledging that they had done their best and that he was staying at Camp 7 entirely of his own accord.

Down at base camp Fritz and Jack continued their vigil, staring up at the drama unfolding above. Fritz's voice had come back, just in time for him to worry aloud. When on 29 July he spotted three figures go up to Dudley's camp and then three come back down, he grew very anxious. Why had only three come down? Was Dudley so sick that he couldn't move? Fritz calmed down later that evening when Pasang Kikuli did not light a distress signal, but it only showed how desperate he had become. The *absence* of a smoke signal – was that all he had to be pleased about?

On 1 August Fritz's diary entry was terse and to the point:

No activities above

No Fire Signal

Weather windy and clear

At 7.30 the following morning, Jack Durrance spotted a single figure coming out of Camp 6. The tension grew. Just one Sherpa descending? Had the others stayed up with Dudley? Five hours later, Tsering reached base camp having more or less run down the mountain. Once he calmed down, he told Jack and Fritz how Pasang Kikuli had found Dudley in a terrible state and how worried he had been. Two days after that first encounter, Tsering continued, Pasang Kikuli had gone back up with Kitar and Phinsoo to try to get Dudley down for the second time, but neither his sirdar, nor his sahib, nor the other two Sherpas had come back. Tsering had then waited for a whole day before retreating to base camp.

Fritz refused to assume the worst. Pasang Kikuli and the others were such good Sherpas with such good technique that it was impossible to think anything could have gone wrong. They must have stayed up with Dudley to await reinforcements. So on 3 August Fritz set off on the expedition's third rescue attempt. The only Sherpas fit to accompany him were Dawa and Tsering, but neither were at anywhere near their best.

Jack Durrance offered to join them but Fritz told him to stay back with the exhausted Pasang Lama, now the last Sherpa at base camp. Food was running so short that the final eight Askole porters had been sent home with instructions to return as soon as possible with more supplies. Jack sent a note with them for Tony Cromwell, informing him of recent developments. He signed off with their usual goodbye, 'Berg Heil' (Good Climbing!), but by then it had a very hollow ring.

When Jack went out on the glacier that night he saw none of the promised smoke signals that were supposed to indicate how Fritz was getting on. With some trepidation, he inspected the glacier below the Abruzzi ridge, but he found that nothing new had come down the mountain. Try as he might, he just couldn't shake off a feeling of dread, as he noted in his diary:

> *Nothing seems to have any other logical answer from data on hand and observation taken than disaster. Which as yet I completely refuse to accept.*

The weather just kept on getting worse. On 5 and 6 August it snowed hard. Sometimes the ridge above was visible, sometimes it was obscured by snow and clouds. Jack thought he noticed that one of the tents at Camp 5 had been repitched, but once again his eyes deceived him. None of the rescuers had got nearly that high: Fritz and his two Sherpas were 3000 ft below, at Camp 2, sheltering in their tents from yet another storm.

After two days of drifting snow and howling winds, Fritz was forced to give up. He climbed down to base camp for the last time on the afternoon of 7 August, as he recorded in his diary, 'feeling desperately low'. Next morning, Jack went out on the glacier to check for avalanche debris or any indication of what was going on above, but once again he was none the wiser:

> No sign, nothing. Thus, in a snow squall which had blown up the Godwin Austen Glacier, ended the last ritual on behalf of our comrades who have been lost, what actual fate no one knows. With head bowed I made an attempt at singing.

More snow was on its way, and there was nothing else they could do to help the missing men. Whether Dudley, Pasang Kikuli, Phinsoo and Kitar had died together or separately, there was no way to tell, but there was no question in anyone's mind that they must now surely be dead. With expedition stores just about to run out completely, Fritz and Jack packaged up Dudley's remaining possessions and began the long walk out from K2, leaving almost 300 lbs of gear to be collected at some later stage. As they looked back from Concordia, K2 was shrouded in clouds.

Meanwhile, 7000 miles away in America, none of their friends at the American Alpine Club had any idea what was happening. In the last official expedition letter, written on 14 June but not received until many weeks later, George Sheldon had written that the worst calamity so far was a large rip in Tony Cromwell's trousers. Dudley Wolfe was high on the mountain 'going darn well' and their biggest burden was the large bundles of love letters that they periodically had to carry up to Jack Durrance. George had finished on an ebullient note:

By the time you get this report the summit will either have fallen or the mountain will be smiling serenely at a party of departing figures who dared challenge but weren't good enough. We hope and will certainly try to make the former prevail. At any rate, believe it or not, it won't be long before we start our march back, and then it won't be any time before we are back ogling at the New York World's Fair. What an anti-climax!

In the intervening weeks there had been a couple of reports about the expedition in the *Times of India*, but by the summer of 1939 international newspaper editors had more pressing issues to cover than the fate of the latest American K2 expedition. The world was not yet at war, but the beasts were prowling and the tanks massing, and it was obvious to most observers that it soon would be.

In Srinagar the endless round of cocktail parties continued as if the British residents were oblivious to developments around them. A few months earlier, the young bucks of the American K2 party had captured hearts, and several women were eagerly awaiting their return. But when the first members reached town in mid-August, they weren't quite the happy party that everyone remembered. Three men were missing, including the leader Fritz Wiessner and the chief heartbreaker Jack Durrance, and the new arrivals did not look quite so carefree.

When they finally arrived at the end of the month, the discord within the team came out in the open. Tony Cromwell had neither forgiven Fritz nor forgotten their confrontation on the Godwin-Austen glacier when he had been threatened with legal action for dereliction of duty. Now his principal concern was to read the draft report that Jack and Fritz had written on the way back.

He was not pleased. As far as Tony was concerned it was a whitewash, totally exonerating Fritz from his failings as the expedition leader. The two men argued and, when they got back to Srinagar, Tony made it plain to everyone that he thought Fritz was fundamentally responsible for what had gone wrong. Trench, the young British transport officer, took Cromwell's side and was openly rude to his former leader.

Fritz and Jack went back to the house of Major Hadow, with whom they had stayed on the way out, and started work on a revised version but Cromwell could not be appeased. He refused to allow Fritz onto his houseboat, declined an invitation to a farewell team dinner and, when he departed a few days later, welcomed Jack Durrance to his leaving party but pointedly did not invite Fritz.

More significantly, Tony got his retaliation in first, sending two letters back to America with his version of the expedition. The first was an official report chronologically listing the events and the various camps on the mountain. Unlike Fritz's timeline, Tony's claimed (mistakenly) that the fall between Camps 7 and 8, involving Fritz, Dudley and Pasang Lama, had taken place *before* the summit attempt and that Fritz had left an injured Dudley Wolfe ill in camp, while he and Pasang Lama had continued up. The second letter, to Ellis Fisher, the treasurer of the American Alpine Club, was even more inflammatory, virtually accusing Fritz of murder. Trench, likewise, wrote to Fisher, detailing Fritz's failures of leadership on the mountain.

When Jack Durrance heard about the letters, he was appalled and immediately informed Fritz. Though he too had grown very weary of Fritz's assertive style and thought his leader had made serious mistakes on the mountain, Jack did not approve of Cromwell's behaviour and recognised the huge pressure Fritz was under.

Fritz had been ill for much of the journey back from K2 and still looked exhausted. When Jack told Major Hadow about the letters that Tony and George Trench had written, Hadow was so shocked that he complained to the senior British official in Kashmir, the grandly titled Lieutenant Colonel Denholm de Montalte Stuart Fraser. Hadow and Fraser both dismissed Cromwell's accusations outright and tried unsuccessfully to get Trench to come back to Srinagar to retract his letter.

On 1 September Fritz and Jack went to Fraser's office to get an official death certificate for Dudley Wolfe. On the same evening they heard that German troops had invaded Poland, prompting Britain to declare war on Germany for the second time in twenty-five years. Fritz grew even more gloomy: not only was he the leader of an expedition that had ended in the death of four men, but now his birthplace was at war with the very Empire that was now hosting him. In a letter to Dudley's former wife, Alice Damrosch, Fritz was candid about how he felt:

> *The whole story of the happenings seems still like a nightmare. I am also so depressed about the fact that I could not take a more active hand in the rescue attempts, and that we were forced to leave the mountain without knowing the exact cause of the accident and could not recover the deceased. I have never been hit so hard in my life, first to lose the summit which seemed in my hands, the terrible realization of Dudley and the Sherpas' death and now a war.*[3]

British officials, if anything, went out of their way to make Fritz feel more comfortable. He was invited to join the Himalayan Club, and Major Hadow even organised another skiing trip. Pasang Lama, who had made a rapid return to his home in Darjeeling, wrote to Fritz to say that his whole town was in mourning for the deaths of Dudley and the three Sherpas on K2. Pasang Lama even offered to accompany Fritz on a return trip to K2 in 1940, to recover the bodies and make another attempt on the summit. It was all very kind but nothing could distract Fritz from his troubles.

On 4 September he and Jack Durrance met the American consul, Edward Groth, and spent several hours retelling the story of the expedition. Groth was very sympathetic to the two weary Americans and agreed that Tony Cromwell's accusations were, as he wrote in a later report, 'unfounded and unjust'. As far as he was concerned Fritz was 'an excellent climber and a good leader' and could not be held responsible for what went wrong, though he did wonder if national differences in behaviour and temperament hadn't prompted the breakdown of the expedition:

> *Though on paper and by law, Wiessner is an American citizen he is still in many respects largely German in his outlook and actions... With his German background, also owing to the*

fact that he possesses a large share of German bluntness (a national characteristic which was apparently unknown to all but one of his colleagues and fellow-expedition-members) it is not remarkable that there should have been a clash of temperaments... he is very forceful in giving commands and totally unaware that the abrupt blunt manner in which the order may have been given might have wounded the feelings of his associates, who in this instance, being Americans, naturally had a different attitude and outlook in matters of this sort.

Fritz for his part might have been Germanic in manner, but he had no doubts about his allegiance: against his parents' wishes, he had decided to become an American citizen and had acknowledged the fact that one day he might have to fight against his homeland. It was not a great prospect, though.

To add to his growing list of problems, Fritz was informed that the ship he and Jack were supposed to be taking back to Italy had been cancelled. Even if they could find an alternative, getting from Europe to America might prove even more complicated with hostilities already under way. Jack decided to head east and return via the Pacific; Fritz headed west, flying to North Africa before taking a boat back to America.

It was an awful journey. Fritz was stopped at Bombay and interrogated by the local police, who had been told that he was a German spy. They released him but he missed his ship and was forced to make a rapid and unplanned trip to Karachi and then Alexandria, where he finally boarded a ship to New York. Ironically, one of the other Americans on the passenger list was none other than Tony Cromwell, his former friend now turned arch-enemy.

When Fritz finally reached New York almost two months later, he was in an even worse state. Having survived two and a half months on the world's deadliest mountain, he had injured his back on the voyage across the Atlantic so badly that he needed to spend several weeks at an orthopaedic hospital. It wasn't long before he got his first visit from not one but two teams investigating the events on K2.

The first was an American Alpine Club committee who had been asked to prepare a report on the expedition. After the letters from Cromwell and Trench, officials at the club felt they had no alternative but to act. Though no one believed the latest set of rumours – that Fritz had deliberately abandoned Dudley in order to avoid repaying money owed to him – it was clear that something had gone badly wrong and, because this was an 'official' American Alpine Club expedition, they had to be seen to act.

Though they were later accused of being biased against Fritz, the investigative committee included three of his friends: Bill House, Bestor Robinson and Terris Moore, another well-known Harvard mountaineer. The others – committee chairman, Walter Wood, and the club treasurer, Ellis Fisher – were all experienced members of the American Alpine Club. Charlie Houston was invited to take part but declined to do so.

While the committee interviewed members of the team and looked at their diaries and records, a second and potentially more serious investigation was taking place. It was instigated by Clifford Smith, Dudley Wolfe's elder brother. Clifford had been deeply shocked by all the rumours, and was determined to get to the bottom of what had happened, even if it meant paying for an attorney and a stenographer to take formal depositions, which might be used later in a courtroom.

Clifford interviewed Fritz in his hospital bed, just a few days after he returned to New York. He had read Fritz's revised final report as well as Cromwell's version and wanted to know why Fritz had left an ill Dudley Wolfe to fend for himself. Fritz explained that Cromwell had got it wrong, that when he left him at Camp 7 Dudley had been in good health. Cromwell wasn't lying, Fritz said, he was just mistaken.

When Clifford moved on to Cromwell himself, he heard a very different story to what he had expected. There were no more accusations of foul play by the expedition leader; instead Tony insisted that there had been no tension in the team at all and accepted that he had been wrong about the timing of the fall between Camps 7 and 8.

Whether prompted by guilt, or embarrassment, or the fear that there really might be a law case, Tony Cromwell and other members of the expedition were now battening down the hatches and saying nothing. When Clifford interviewed George Sheldon and Chappell Cranmer, they were equally unforthcoming and played down any criticism, even though Cromwell had convinced both of them that it was principally Fritz's fault.[4]

The only team member to speak out was Jack Durrance, who told Clifford that the blame should be shared between Dudley and Fritz:

> *I think Dudley's ambition got away with him. I don't think he should have attempted to climb it. He was always guided. He never guided a rope himself. He was always taken up – and Wiessner did it. I think it was a frightful mistake.*[5]

In the end, after several frustrating weeks, Clifford Smith's investigation fizzled out. There were no law-suits or criminal investigations, just a plaintive letter to the American Alpine Club asking them to contact the family if at some point in the future another team found Dudley's remains.

The club's committee felt under more pressure to 'do something', though what that should be was, if anything, more complicated. No one really wanted to sit in judgment on what had obviously been a difficult and divided expedition. As Henry Hall, the club president, wrote to Ellis Fisher:

> *I have the same desire behind the whole thing as you have – to protect the good name of the Club, if necessary at the expense of individuals… Above all this whole thing mustn't be allowed to start dissension.*[6]

As the committee deliberated, inevitably they compared the 1938 and 1939 expeditions. The first had pulled back at the moment of truth; the second had pushed harder and come within a hair's width of success – only to end in disaster. As one of the committee members, Bill House, revealed many years later, much of the debate was again framed as an argument between the British 'safety first' mentality and the German 'the summit justifies the risks' approach.

This was unfair on Fritz. He never claimed to be a champion of German 'Nordwand' tactics and if anything considered himself to be a very careful climber who paid a lot of attention to rope technique and safety. His approach on K2 had been very steady and methodical and he saw a lot of parallels between his desire to always climb with the minimum of pitons and other 'artificial aids', and the British obsession with 'fair-play'.[7]

On the other hand there were unavoidable questions about his leadership. One American and three Sherpas were missing, presumed dead, and his deputy leader clearly held Fritz responsible. Two fundamental criticisms were levelled at Fritz: firstly, that he had knowingly taken a weak team and should therefore have behaved more cautiously; and secondly, that when things started to go wrong he should have pulled back. In particular should he have allowed Dudley Wolfe to go so high, knowing his limitations?

Fritz was adamant that the responsibility for the tragedy lay not with him but with his team. They had failed to support the summit party and crucially had stripped all the camps of their vital sleeping bags. If they had followed orders, kept the camps well stocked and the Sherpas moving up and down the mountain, no one would have died and they might even have returned successful. The chief culprit, he said, was Jack Durrance.

This was a strange turn of events. The American Alpine Club's investigation had been precipitated by Tony Cromwell's accusations, but instead of turning his fire on his deputy, or on Tse Tendrup, the disgraced Sherpa who had given Fritz up for dead and stripped the upper camps on his own initiative, Fritz pointed the finger at the man who had nursed him on the way out from K2 and supported him in Srinagar, when the rest of the team had deserted him. So why did Fritz turn against Jack?

The answer was surprising but compelling: while in hospital in New York, Fritz had found a note in his mountaineering gear, left by

Jack several weeks earlier at Camp 2, in which he congratulated Fritz for climbing K2 and informed him that he had just ordered the sleeping bags to be removed from the lower camps. This was the decision, Fritz now insisted, which had caused the disaster and Jack's note clearly identified him as the man who had made it.[8]

The members of the American Alpine Club committee were split. No one blamed Tse Tendrup; even if he had both failed to do his duty and stripped the upper camps, it was not really his fault. He was a Sherpa and, according to the prevailing wisdom of the day, should have been better supervised. Nor did anyone blame Tony Cromwell, or really try to ascertain his role in the events. The fact that he had made all the allegations against Fritz, and that as the expedition's deputy leader should have been on top of all the logistical issues, was quietly forgotten. No, there were only two men who could really be held responsible: Fritz Wiessner or Jack Durrance. But which one?

In part, the committee agreed with Fritz that stripping the camps was both reckless and incomprehensible and that Jack Durrance was to blame. Jack's only real defence, committee member Bill House wrote years later, was that at the time he was suffering from some kind of mental breakdown, caused by exposure to high altitude. Crucially, though, the committee also felt that Fritz had made a fundamental mistake in overestimating the capabilities of his team and agreed with Jack that Dudley Wolfe should never have been allowed to go so high.[9]

Neither of these conclusions, however, were going to dampen the flames of controversy and as the months went by the pressure grew to kill the report altogether. When Fritz got hold of an advance copy, he wrote to Walter Wood, the chairman of the committee, arguing that it was unjust and inaccurate. He took particular umbrage at the vague criticisms of the 'weak human administration' of the expedition, and circulated the report to his friends. They in turn wrote to the club, threatening to publish a counter report if the official one was sent out to members.

The scenario that club president Henry Hall had foreseen, that the K2 controversy would tear the club apart, was happening right in front of his eyes, and the consequence was inevitable: the report that had taken so many months to compile was shelved. Instead of publishing it in full, in July 1940 ordinary members of the club were sent a one-page summary and a chart showing the various members' movements on the mountain. Anyone contemplating a similar expedition in the future was welcome to read the report but it would never be circulated in full.

The end of the affair left no one happy. Fritz felt that the damage to his reputation had been done and resigned from the club on Boxing Day 1940. Whatever he had said to Clifford Smith, Tony Cromwell was still very angry with his former friend and leader and resigned at more or less the same time, claiming that the club should have thrown Fritz out much earlier. Jack Durrance backed away from the confrontation. He showed Chappell Cranmer his expedition diary, poured his heart out to Charlie Houston, but he refused to take Fritz on publicly, in spite of all the criticisms that had been made against him.

Unlike 1938, there was no expedition book. George Sheldon wrote a long piece for the *Saturday Evening Post* and Chappell Cranmer collaborated with Fritz on an article in the *American Alpine Journal*. Both accounts studiously avoided the most controversial issues. In 1955 a much more complete version of the story appeared in a small German book that Fritz co-authored with Franz Grassler, *K2: Tragödien und Sieg am zweithöchsten Berg der Erde* (Tragedy and Victory on the Second Highest Mountain in the World), but though most of it later appeared as a long article in the American magazine *Appalachia*, it was never published in its entirety in the United States.

The *Appalachia* article ran with an editorial note inviting anyone who disagreed with Fritz's version of the expedition to write in with comments. Neither Tony Cromwell nor Jack Durrance nor any other member of the team took up the offer. The controversy never quite went away, though. When in 1955 the British geographer Kenneth Mason wrote his celebrated history of Himalayan mountaineering, *Abode of Snow*, he was utterly scathing with regard to Fritz's leadership of the 1939 expedition, summing it up with a much quoted line:

> It is very difficult to record in temperate language, the folly of this enterprise.

By the mid-1960s, however, opinions had begun to change. Unlike the other members of the team, Fritz had carried on climbing and continued to nurture and mentor young talent. His protégés recognised his incredible technical skill, and many came to see the 1939 K2 expedition as an amazing near miss, not a mismanaged fiasco.

Two stalwarts of the new generation of US climbers, Bill Putnam and Andy Kauffman, started a campaign to bring Fritz back into the American Alpine Club in order 'to rehabilitate the good name of American climbing'. Kauffman was one of the American team who made the first ascent of K2's neighbouring peak, Gasherbrum I, in 1959, and Bill Putnam was a well-known and well-liked climber, and a future president of the club. Tony Cromwell, who had by then rejoined, resigned for the second time, but the response from the vast majority of members was very favourable. In 1966 Fritz was made an honorary member, the highest award the club could bestow.

In the 1970s and 1980s there were several very positive articles about him in American climbing magazines, written by the latest generation of US climbers and mountaineering writers, including David Roberts, Ed Webster and Galen Rowell – all of whom had climbed with Fritz. When it came to the K2 expedition, they followed Fritz's line, arguing that it was Jack Durrance's incomprehensible decision to strip the camps that led to the expedition's unhappy climax. In Galen Rowell's 1977 book *In the Throne Room of the Mountain Gods*, he turned on Kenneth Mason and Wiessner's critics and systematically and eloquently repudiated their complaints about his leadership.

> *Leaders don't belong in the first summit team?* What about Maurice Herzog on Annapurna? *Sherpas must not move unsupervised over difficult terrain?* What about the repeated instances on many of the hallowed British attempts on Everest? *Mountain summits aren't worth risking lives for?* Only a rare windless night on May 22nd 1963 kept four Americans from perishing in an open bivouac near the top of Mount Everest. *The team was not strong enough to continue?* This party set up nine camps and stocked them

well enough to place many men on the summit. *Taking a climber of Wolfe's meagre experience on a big mountain was unprecedented?* Andrew Irvine, Mallory's famous companion on Mount Everest in 1924, was even less experienced but like Wolfe he outperformed those with better records.[10]

Then in the mid-1980s news came that his close friends, Andy Kauffman and Bill Putnam, were working on the first biography of Fritz, which would finally establish his credentials as one of the greatest climbers of the twentieth century. But that is not how it turned out; their book, *K2: The 1939 Tragedy*, was far from a Kenneth Mason-style all-out attack, but it was very critical of Fritz and his leadership of the 1939 expedition. So what happened? Why did two of Fritz's greatest champions appear to turn against him and reignite the controversy?

In the years since its publication this has prompted much speculation. In his 2009 history of K2, the American climber Ed Viesturs put forward the theory that it might have been another case of biographer's ennui: much like the American Lawrence Roger Thompson, who wrote a scathing biography of his former friend, the poet Robert Frost, after spending many years working closely with him, had Kauffman and Putnam simply grown tired of Fritz and his sometimes imperious manner?[11]

More recently, in 2013, in an article for the American magazine *Ascent*, the respected mountaineering writer David Roberts suggested another possible explanation, after interviewing Fritz's daughter, Polly Wiessner. She recalled an incident in 1966 when she had gone climbing with her father and Andy Kauffman in the Swiss Alps. At the climax of a difficult ascent, Kauffman had appeared to lose his nerve and it had needed an act of heroism on her father's part to get everyone back down safely. Might this embarrassing incident have turned Kauffman against his former hero? Both Viesturs' and Roberts' explanations are possible, but the answer found in Andy Kauffman's papers, now lodged in the archives of the American Alpine Club in Colorado, is very different. It revolves around an argument between Fritz and his biographer over something that has been central to the history of K2 since the very first expedition by Eckenstein and Crowley in 1902, namely, the effect of high altitude on a climber's performance.

The story begins in the early 1980s when Fritz Wiessner started work on an English language version of his 1955 German book on K2.[12] It contained a slightly expanded section on the 1939 expedition and a new epilogue. Fritz was hoping to get it published in America and showed it to Andy Kauffman. Kauffman was very positive about it, and at around the same time began working with his friend Bill Putnam on what they hoped would be a definitive biography of Fritz.

Three years later, in the autumn of 1985, Kauffman had what he thought was a good first draft. Much of it dealt with Fritz's early climbs in Germany and the US, but there was a long section on the 1939 K2 expedition. Like all the other American writers who had recently covered the events, Kauffman and Putnam agreed that the main cause of the tragedy was Jack Durrance's decision to strip the camps but Kauffman added something new: a discussion of the role of altitude in the tragedy.

In the decades since 1939, a lot of research had been done into the impact of high altitude on both physical and mental processes. Kauffman calculated that Fritz had spent five days on K2 above 26,000 ft, in the 'death zone', and that Dudley Wolfe had spent at least seventeen days above 24,000 ft. Modern advice is to spend the minimum time possible at these heights and very few of today's climbers would willingly stay so high for so long. After talking to several physiologists, Kauffman had become convinced that some of the mistakes and bad decisions made on K2 in 1939 could be put down to high altitude's insidious effects. Might prolonged exposure to high altitude, he asked, explain why Dudley Wolfe had made the fateful decision to remain at Camp 7 and not descend with Fritz and Pasang Lama after their summit attempts? Might it explain why Fritz had agreed to let him stay and could Durrance's behaviour also be explained as the consequence of high-altitude cerebral oedema, a very dangerous condition in which fluid collects on the brain?

When Kauffman showed his manuscript to Fritz, he did not get the response he had hoped for. Fritz was very critical of what he read and threatened to withdraw co-operation. In particular, he utterly rejected Kauffman's altitude theory: individual climbers, he believed, coped with high altitude differently and he was absolutely sure that his decision-making had not been compromised. He was a slow acclimatiser, but at the climax of the expedition, Fritz insisted, he was in the shape of his life and would have been able to lead another summit attempt if he had been supported properly and if those camps had not been stripped of their sleeping bags. He did not want any excuses to be made for Jack Durrance's actions and still held him responsible for what had gone wrong.

Andy Kauffman was shocked. He tried to put it down to an old man's inevitable crotchetiness, but he was both hurt and taken aback. He thought about giving up, but having put so much time into the book, neither he nor Putnam was prepared to abandon the project.

Then a year later, something unexpected happened: Jack Durrance got in touch. Over the last forty years, he had kept well away from the K2 controversy and, apart from a brief lecture at an American Alpine Club event, had avoided comment on the expedition itself. When he made contact in December 1986, initially Kauffman was wary. He warned Jack that he was still a good friend of Fritz Wiessner's and that he and Putnam were writing a very positive biography. Jack was also tentative. A year earlier he had given an interview to David Roberts for an article about Fritz, but later he had changed his mind and refused to allow Roberts to use any quotes. Clearly he had now got to the point where he wanted his side of the story to be heard.

When he met Andy Kauffman a month later in Denver, it quickly became obvious that Jack had not changed his mind about Fritz. He maintained that Dudley Wolfe was incapable of looking after himself and should never have been allowed to climb high. After graduating from medical school, Jack had become a specialist in pulmonary medicine. He agreed with Kauffman that prolonged exposure to high altitude had affected Fritz's judgment and felt that his own collapse on the mountain was probably caused by a combination of pulmonary and cerebral oedema, fluid on the lungs and the brain. Forty years on from events, he admitted that he couldn't really remember anything that had happened between his collapse at 24,000 ft and his return to base camp, six days later.

Kauffman was far from convinced, but Jack did offer him something unexpected: access to his K2 diary. Dudley Wolfe's journal had been lost on the mountain and Kauffman had only ever seen a partial, typed-up copy of Fritz's diary, but Jack was prepared to hand over his original handwritten account, which ran from the moment he left the US in March 1939 to the point where he separated from Fritz in Srinagar in September of that year.

When it arrived, it was indeed a remarkable document, the record of Jack Durrance's transformation from a Dartmouth College party animal who spent much of the first half of his diary writing about the liquor he'd consumed and the women he'd met, to a much more reflective character, struggling to understand what he had just experienced on K2 and meditating on the lessons that might be learned. Contrary to what many people thought, the diary showed that Jack had gone into the expedition full of enthusiasm and had stuck it out to the end. As to the specifics of the K2 tragedy, there was one highly significant revelation: Jack Durrance had not ordered the camps to be stripped and the sleeping bags to be removed – Tony Cromwell, Fritz's deputy, had.

As the entry for 18 July 1939 revealed, Jack had been waiting at Camp 2 when 'up danced Dawa' with a note from Cromwell and Cranmer ordering him to collect and bring down all the valuable items from the lower camps. The subsequent stripping of the higher camps, as Jack's diary made clear, was carried out on Tendrup's own initiative and neither he nor Tony Cromwell had any idea what the Sherpas were up to until they returned to base camp. The central allegation made against Jack Durrance for so many decades – that he had been responsible for the disastrous decision to strip the camps – was simply wrong.

Their access to Jack Durrance's diary prompted Kauffman and Putnam to change their focus from a general biography of Fritz to a much more detailed investigation of the 1939 expedition. They remained on speaking terms with their former mentor, but after 1985 co-operation effectively broke down. As rumours swirled that Fritz had a new biographer, they began speaking to the other surviving team members and collecting a mass of archival material.

Two years later, in 1988, Fritz died at the age of eighty-eight after a series of strokes. He was mourned as one of the greats of American mountaineering. In his *New York Times* obituary, his near miss in 1939 was hailed as 'perhaps his greatest feat'. In the *American Alpine Journal*, Hans Kraus called him a 'role model whose actions and spirit will continue to inspire mountaineers for generations to come'.

When four years later, in 1992, Kauffman and Putnam's book, *K2: The 1939 Tragedy*, finally appeared, Fritz was presented in a far less flattering light. Quoting heavily from Jack Durrance's diary and documents from the period, Kauffman and Putnam argued that, though a great climber, Fritz was not a great leader. They questioned his judgment on the mountain and argued that it was unjust for Fritz to blame Jack Durrance for what had gone wrong on K2.

While acknowledging Fritz's rejection of their thesis, Kauffman and Putnam continued to maintain that excessive exposure to altitude might have impacted on his thinking and, crucially, on what they called his 'fateful decision' to allow Dudley Wolfe to stay on his own at Camp 7 while he descended with Pasang Lama. The book was by no means a hatchet job, and a lot of their criticisms were formulated as rhetorical questions but, coming from two of Fritz's previous champions, it seemed particularly damning.

Not everyone was convinced, however. As critics such as British author and climber Jim Curran pointed out, Kauffman and Putnam strayed into the same anti-German stereotyping that Fritz had been subject to from his early days in the US. They did not go so far as to call him a Nazi, as some of his enemies had, but their description of him as an individual reared in the 'Teutonic' ethos, who preached a kind of 'Darwinian naturalism with its emphasis on survival of the fittest', echoed the typecasting that had dogged Fritz in the 1930s.

In an odd kind of way the story of the book and the reactions to it mirrored the original 1939 controversy, with Andy Kauffman becoming Fritz's chief detractor, while younger climbers and historians like Ed Webster and David Roberts took over the role that Putnam and Kauffman had played in the 1960s, fighting Fritz's corner.

The history of Kauffman and Putnam's book is, of course, a tangent to the larger story of the expedition, but it does hint at some bigger truths. Fritz's very negative reaction to Kauffman's first draft showed that, even forty years after the events and the bitter arguments that followed, he remained highly sensitive and had not changed his position on the causes and responsibility for what had gone wrong. Clearly it still mattered to him a lot and he was very concerned that he would be treated fairly in the first English language book about the events of 1939.

The other big, and very simple, truth is that so much of the controversy really revolved around judgments on Fritz's personality, and crucially his German roots. Those who liked him saw his 'Germanic bluntness' as something of no consequence. So what if sometimes he could be forceful and self-righteous, he was a very positive and dynamic figure who genuinely loved the sport of mountaineering and wanted to share that passion. If he had had a more responsible and supportive team in 1939, they believed the tragedy would not have occurred and that Fritz might even have reached the top.

To his detractors, however, Fritz's assertiveness was more than just superficial: it allowed him to overestimate his own powers and made him the kind of leader who could only rule by diktat rather than by consent. They felt his refusal to take any responsibility for what had gone wrong showed that he was blind to his own faults. Judging from the correspondence that he left in his personal archive, Andy Kauffman started off in the former camp and ended up firmly in the latter. By the time he finished his book he had lost faith in Fritz and always assumed the worst; if it hadn't been for his writing partner, Bill Putnam, the book's conclusions would probably have been even harsher.

Jack Durrance's actions are more puzzling. Why did he take so long to tell his side of the story? He could have responded straight away to the accusation that he was responsible for clearing the camps of their sleeping bags. So why didn't he? Did he think that Tony Cromwell would own up? Perhaps deep down, Jack felt guilty about the failure of the expedition, and his own poor performance at high altitude. If he did feel guilty about his role in the disaster, he was judging himself too harshly: his diary and his actions prove that he tried his best and played an honest if sometimes weak hand. There would be many more climbers to come who would be equally taxed by their first encounter with K2.

The other obvious fact is that if the events had happened ten years earlier, or ten years later, the whole controversy would not have been nearly so intense. When George Mallory and Sandy Irvine disappeared on Everest in 1924, no one blamed the expedition leaders, Edward Norton or Charles Bruce, for the decision to allow an inexperienced climber like Irvine to be one of the summit pair. There had, and would be, many more deaths in the Himalayas and the Karakoram in years to come, but the fact that the events on K2 were taking place in the summer of 1939, when the Allied powers were on the verge of war with Germany, made Fritz's background disproportionately important and the debate much fiercer.

Another two decades and several books later, the 1939 expedition still haunts American mountaineering and the arguments about Fritz's leadership have not gone away. Perhaps, though, the fairest assessment of the events came from Terris Moore, a leading climber of the 1930s, and one of the members of the American Alpine Club's investigative committee. In a letter to Andy Kauffman written in 1990, he argued that there really were two ways to look at the events of 1939: either to make the obvious criticisms of all the parties involved, or simply to acknowledge that the things that went wrong could have occurred on any mountaineering expedition. Fortunately, most of the time, most climbers survived the risks they took, but only 'by the grace of God'.[13]

Charlie Houston, however, was not so forgiving, neither in later life nor in 1939. Fritz's great rival for K2 and the soul of American mountaineering was furious about what had happened. On the 1938 reconnaissance, he had taken the cautious route, followed Fritz Wiessner's advice 'not to do anything reckless' and brought everyone back alive. Now four men were dead, including his favourite Sherpa, Pasang Kikuli, and all because of what he regarded as Fritz's poor leadership.

But there was something else: Fritz had *almost* reached the summit, but he had not quite made it. K2 remained one of the great prizes in mountaineering. Even if it was obvious that the war in Europe would not be over quickly and would probably get much worse, eventually it would end. When it did, K2 would still be there, ripe for the picking, Charlie Houston's very own 'mountain of destiny'.

Chapter 6

UNFINISHED
BUSINESS

War is not good for mountaineering, but it is good for mountaineering equipment. Tents, ropes, boots, cold-weather clothing, oxygen systems – all saw massive improvements during the 1940s as each side sought to give its troops an edge over the opposition. In the US, several members of the 1938 and 1939 K2 teams found themselves working for different branches of the military, helping to design and test specialist equipment for mountain troops and more general cold-weather gear for regular soldiers.

Fritz Wiessner acted as technical adviser to the US 10th Mountain Division and saw his ski wax business given a major boost when the army put in large orders. Bob Bates, Charlie Houston's great friend and climbing partner, worked for the Quartermaster Corps of the US Army, coming up with ideas for everything from survival suits for Arctic fliers to new-style pockets for general-issue field jackets. Anything that looked promising was field tested in Alaska or the far north of Canada. If it passed muster it was taken to the front line under Bob's watchful eye. Charlie Houston's role in the war might have initially appeared to have no direct connection with mountaineering but in fact it was closely linked. In 1941 he was commissioned as a naval lieutenant and sent to Pensacola Naval Air Station in Florida to be put in charge of high-altitude training for pilots. For the air force this was a life-or-death issue: if they were not prepared and properly equipped, pilots could black out long before their planes reached their ceiling heights. Charlie spent a lot of his time in and around naval decompression chambers, training new recruits when and how to use oxygen equipment and taking them through high-altitude simulations.

As Charlie knew only too well from his experience on K2 in 1938, spending periods of time at high altitude was also an occupational hazard for mountaineers. There was, however, very little detailed scientific research available on the subject and most 'evidence' was anecdotal. Like their aviation counterparts, in the 1920s and 1930s several British climbers had experimented with bottled oxygen on Everest, but at the time there was much debate about both its value and the sporting ethics of using an 'artificial aid'.

Charlie Houston wasn't sure about supplementary oxygen either. He liked to keep his mountaineering simple and natural; bottled oxygen might enable you to get higher but it added major logistical and financial complications to any expedition so he had never used it on any of his expeditions. Like Fritz Wiessner, he believed that the best way to deal with altitude was through gradual acclimatisation: rather than rushing a big mountain, the idea was to move up slowly in stages, and gradually get used to the lower pressure and the thinner air.

This approach obviously would not work for a pilot who might need to get from sea level to 10,000 ft in a matter of minutes, but could acclimatisation alone enable a climber to reach the top of a really big mountain like K2 or Everest? A number of pre-war British climbers had reached 28,000 ft on Everest and Fritz Wiessner had got almost as high on K2, but could anyone get all the way to either summit without supplementary oxgyen? The jury was still out, but many scientists doubted that it would be possible.

In the summer of 1946, just a few months after the war ended, Charlie persuaded the Naval Air Force to let him find out about the limits of acclimatisation by staging an experiment, code-named 'Operation Everest'. He recruited four naval volunteers and installed them in a large decompression chamber, equipped with a portable toilet, a bath and several medical test rigs. Over the next five weeks the pressure was gradually reduced to simulate increasing altitude.

When they weren't pedalling on their exercise bikes, the four human guinea pigs spent most of their time relaxing as best they could, while undergoing regular examinations. They were even allowed to smoke.

Charlie's experiment attracted a lot of press attention, but though it seemed like a post-war scientific curio, the stakes were high. It was known that exposure to high altitude could cause the heart and the pulmonary arteries to enlarge and *in extremis* cause massive bleeding. In a notorious experiment carried out in 1875, three pioneering French aviators, the famous balloonist Gaston Tissandier, and two assistants, Joseph Crocé-Spinelli and Théodore Sivel, had taken a balloon to over 28,000 ft to discover the impact of a rapid ascent on their bodies. Only Tissandier made it back alive. When the balloon hit the ground with a resounding crash, Crocé-Spinelli and Sivel's faces were black, their mouths haemorrhaging blood.

Charlie's volunteers' technological ascent was much more gradual, taking weeks rather than hours. The moment of truth came on day thirty-four when the decompression chamber was taken down to a pressure equivalent to the summit of Everest. At 26,700 ft one man requested supplementary oxygen; at 27,700 ft a second man followed suit. The other two volunteers carried on pedalling under their own steam and smiling for the cameras, albeit rather wanly, until finally they reached 29,000 ft. When a day later they were let out of the chamber, they were thinner and hairier but seemingly no worse for wear.

The results showed that it was possible to operate at 29,000 ft without any artificial oxygen but that acclimatisation was a very individual process – two men made it to the 'summit', two men didn't. Charlie was pleased with the results but he knew that surviving inside the controlled confines of a large naval decompression chamber was not quite the same thing as doing it for real in sub-zero temperatures and gale-force winds – the only way to find that out was to go climbing. And that's exactly what he planned to do.

By the end of the war Charlie and Bob Bates had already begun organising their return to K2 but, like the mountain itself, it was never going to be easy. In addition to the familiar challenges of raising money and putting a team together, there were new political complications in a post-war world where the old certainties were rapidly disappearing. When Bob Bates approached the British ambassador in the summer of 1946 hoping to obtain a permit for another expedition, his application was politely but firmly declined.

Britain might have emerged victorious, but it was clear that the Empire that had sustained it for centuries would not last much longer. In 1947 British India, the 'jewel in the crown' of its former Empire, gained its independence and split into two: the Dominions of India and Pakistan. Within a few months, the world's newest countries were at war and even when a ceasefire was announced it was obvious that for years to come the region would be very unstable.

The map of Central Asia was changing fast. For centuries, both Tibet and Nepal, the two countries either side of Everest, had been almost entirely closed to foreigners. In the 1920s and 1930s, the Lhasa government had reluctantly allowed a handful of British expeditions to attempt Everest from the northern, Tibetan side but no one had ever tried Everest from the southern, Nepalese side. Then in the decade after the war, everything began to change.

In autumn 1950, a resurgent China invaded Tibet and had absorbed it into the People's Republic. For the foreseeable future there would be no further attempts on Everest from the Tibetan side, by Western climbers at least. At roughly the same time, something even more unexpected happened: the Nepalese government opened the country's frontiers to the outside world. In the first half of the twentieth century, Nepal had maintained a policy of almost total isolation, but its leaders had now realised that it needed outside friends, to avoid being swallowed up by one of its huge neighbours, China or India.

One of the first Westerners to benefit from Nepal's new policy of openness was Charlie Houston. In 1948 his father, Oscar, secured permission to take a small trekking party to the Solu Khumbu, the mountainous region of northern Nepal where Everest and four of the world's highest peaks are found. Charlie was very happy to be invited, even more so when by chance he encountered his old friend, the famous British climber Bill Tilman, in Kathmandu.

Map 5 K2, 1953

Together they hiked into the heart of the Solu Khumbu, the home-land of the Sherpas, becoming in November 1950 the first Westerners to photograph the south side of Everest. They returned home unsure that it could be climbed from the Nepalese side but this was nevertheless a watershed moment in Everest's history.

Back in America, Charlie's friends suggested that he should use his diplomatic contacts to come back the following year to make a full-blown attempt to climb on the world's highest mountain. Britain's Alpine Club was already in talks with the American Alpine Club about a possible joint Everest expedition so it seemed like the ideal moment. Charlie, however, had other ideas; K2 was his mountain, not Everest, so better to use those diplomatic contacts to further that goal.

Before the Second World War, K2 had always played second fiddle to Everest. It was the mountain that Crowley and Abruzzi attempted because they knew they would never get permission to climb Everest. But Charlie Houston didn't see it that way: K2 was his *first*, not his second, choice. The fact that, on the map, it had now moved from India to newly created Pakistan meant a new layer of logistical complication, but the mountain itself had not changed and nor had his ambition to make the first ascent.

In spring 1952 Charlie's wish came true when his new friend Ava Warren, the US ambassador in Karachi, persuaded the Pakistani government to let him stage the third American expedition to K2. This time, Charlie was sure, he would succeed.

All round the world there was a sense that the long-awaited 'Golden Age of Himalayan mountaineering' was underway. In 1950 the French climber Maurice Herzog led the first ascent of one of the world's ten highest peaks, Annapurna, on the border of Nepal and India, and there was a veritable 'Race for Everest' with teams from Britain, Switzerland and France applying to the Nepalese government for permission to attempt the world's highest mountain.

Those wartime advances in cold-weather clothing and equipment were beginning to pay dividends but more importantly there was a new can-do, 'anything's possible' spirit and much greater public interest in mountaineering. Charlie Houston wanted to keep his K2 expedition low key and hated any feeling of national competition but he relished the opportunity to return to the Karakoram and take care of unfinished business.

His first and most important task was to select a team. Charlie believed that most of the problems on Fritz Wiessner's 1939 attempt could be put down to poor leadership and an inadequate team. The best chance of success, or so he was convinced, would come not from finding brilliant individuals but from assembling a group of climbers who worked well together. They would all have to be solid all-round climbers with expedition experience but he wasn't interested in what he called the 'prima donnas' of the mountaineering world.

After putting out a notice via the American Alpine Club, Charlie and Bob Bates talked to about twenty-five candidates before making their final selection. Several Americans who would later win fame for first ascents in the Himalayas were turned down in favour of men who felt more like team players. Fritz Wiessner was probably still the best climber in America and the only person to have climbed really high on K2, but there was no question of inviting him. Over the years, the bad blood between Charlie and Fritz had only grown more intense.

Charlie and Bob's final selection was very different from the mixed group that Fritz had to work with in 1939. There were no vast gaps in age or experience. All were relatively young, aged between twenty-five and thirty-five, all highly educated and all well practised in expeditionary mountaineering. Three of them, Bob Craig, Dee Molenaar and Pete Schoening, had gone to the University of Washington, in the Pacific Northwest, and had spent a lot of time climbing in the rugged Cascade range that runs through the heart of the state.

Seattle-based climber Dee Molenaar had trained as a geologist, but his real passion was photography and painting. His close friend Bob Craig was a square-jawed philosopher who would later direct the Aspen Institute for Humanistic Studies, one of America's first think tanks. Both had worked as guides on Mount Rainier, the Cascades' highest peak, and then as civilian advisers to the US Army's Mountain and Cold Weather Training Division. Pete Schoening was a chemical engineer and another very strong climber who had made first ascents in the remote Yukon mountains.

The tallest member of the team was George Bell, a lanky bespectacled physicist then working at Los Alamos in New Mexico on the first thermonuclear bombs. He was one of the most widely travelled of the group and had climbed in both the European Alps and the Andes.

Moving further north, the final member of the team, fresh-faced and handsome Art Gilkey, had gained most of his wilderness experience in Alaska, where he worked for two summers on research projects on the vast Juneau glacier. Another geologist by training, he was in the final stages of a PhD at Columbia University.

Individually they were all very strong, technically accomplished climbers, but, as Charlie and Bob had hoped, they were also strong team players who would remain firm friends long after the expedition.

Once he had his permit and his team, Charlie's next two hurdles were finance and equipment. Though in the US there was now much more public interest in mountaineering than there had been in the 1930s, there was still nothing like the funding available in Europe, where big newspapers and sometimes national governments were willing to put large sums of money into major Himalayan expeditions. Charlie budgeted his 1953 attempt at $25,000, almost three times the cost of 1938. He asked each member to contribute just over $1000 and hoped to raise the rest from gifts and loans, as well as income from press articles and a documentary for the US TV network NBC.[1]

When it came to equipment, there was some sponsorship from American companies like the sports clothing manufacturer Eddie Bauer, which supplied the expedition with fifty parkas free of charge, but most items had to be bought or borrowed. By the early 1950s Charlie had shaken off his Anglophilia; unlike 1938 when almost everything had come from England, this time most of their equipment was sourced in the US. Their contacts within the US Army enabled Charlie and Bob to obtain the latest thermally insulated 'Bunny Boots', which had just been introduced during the Korean War, as well as experimental tents and climbing packs.

As for food, Bob Bates was once again appointed expedition quartermaster. His high-altitude menu included dried meat bars and that expedition favourite, pemmican, supplemented with dehydrated fruit and vegetables, Italian panforte and, for the first time on a Himalayan expedition, baby food. Like most 'good ideas at the time', it turned out not to be and was rejected as unpalatable.

After drafting in friends and family for a couple of very busy weekends, they packed about a ton of food into heat-sealed bags, each containing enough for two men for a day. Together with 3.5 tons of climbing equipment, their rations were sent off by sea to Karachi in April 1953, soon to be followed by Bob Bates who went out in advance of the main party to deal with bureaucracy and logistics. Just before he left for Pakistan, Bob paid a visit to Fritz Wiessner, but apart from a rather half-hearted letter in which he asked for Fritz's 'blessing', Charlie Houston had no direct contact with him.[2]

In late May everyone converged on New York, the jumping-off point for the big adventure. Over the course of a very hectic two days they raided NBC Television's stores for 11,000 ft of film stock, requisitioned several cameras and tape recorders, sat down for a seventy-person send-off meal at the American Alpine Club and gave umpteen interviews to local and national journalists. Geology student Art Gilkey burned gallons of midnight oil to finish the latest instalment of his PhD while his new teammates Pete Schoening and Dee Molenaar bunked down in his small Manhattan flat, glad to be sleeping rather than studying.

When they all convened at Idlewild International Airport on 25 May, Charlie Houston was shocked to discover that, in spite of all the tons of equipment they had sent out in advance, they were still facing a huge bill for excess baggage. The only solution, with the airline's connivance, was to distribute a full 240 lbs of equipment and high-altitude clothing amongst their personal bags and coat pockets.

On the following morning they landed at London Airport and scanned the newspapers for any news of the latest Everest expedition. With four nations attempting 26,000 ft peaks, 1953 was fixing to be a big year in Himalayan history. A team from Japan was making the first attempt on Manaslu, the eighth-highest mountain in the world, while climbers from three other nations were attempting to conquer the mountains that had defeated them before the war: the British on Everest, the Germans on Nanga Parbat, and now the Americans on K2.

While Charlie's team settled in for the next stage of their aerial journey, Bob Bates was busy in Pakistan, shepherding their supplies and equipment through Pakistani customs. Like several other mountaineers of the early 1950s, he had become interested in the idea of using aircraft to parachute in their supplies to base camp, rather than employing large numbers of porters to carry them in. He approached the Pakistani Air Force and got a positive response, but though the commodores were keen, the politicians were not. When Bob met Foreign Secretary Akhtar Hussain, he warned him not to do anything that might antagonise Pakistan's Chinese neighbours, and most especially to give up any thought of flying in their supplies. As he explained, there was still a lot of uncertainty over the precise border between the two countries and Pakistan did not want to add China to its list of real or potential enemies.

On 27 May Bob was reunited with Charlie and the rest of the team at Karachi before they flew together to Rawalpindi, two days later. The contrast between 1938 and 1953 was striking: back then it took almost four weeks to get from New York to Rawalpindi but this time, travelling by plane rather than ship, they completed the same journey in just over three days.

Rawalpindi was the same bustling garrison city that Charlie remembered from 1938 but if anything it was even more crowded. Stick-thin refugees from the recent war with India thronged the streets and huddled under makeshift shelters, cobbled together out of old iron sheeting. The Seattle-based climbers Dee Molenaar and Bob Craig had both seen military service during the war, but neither had seen anything like the destitution visible on seemingly every corner.

Before Charlie and his team could leave town they had almost a week's worth of meetings to endure. Pakistan was just a few years old and everyone wanted to talk politics with their American guests. Even though it was Ramadan, there was an endless round of invitations and dinners.

On a less formal and more welcome note, they met the final two members of the team: Colonel Mohammad Ata-Ullah, their official Pakistani liaison officer, and Captain Tony Streather, a twenty-seven-year-old British soldier who had come out to look after expedition transport.

Streather looked every inch the pukka British sahib with a dainty moustache and smiling eyes. A career soldier, he had joined the army at the age of seventeen and had done most of his service on the North West Frontier. Though relatively new to mountaineering, he had accompanied a Norwegian team that made the first ascent of the 25,000 ft Tirich Mir in the Hindu Kush, and had even managed to reach the summit – on his very first mountaineering expedition. In 1952 he had been considered for the British Everest team, but though ultimately he was not chosen, he had by now been bitten by the mountaineering bug and told Charlie Houston that he very much wanted to be one of the climbers on K2. Having had such a good experience in 1938 with his last British liaison officer, Streatfeild, Charlie was happy to oblige.

Colonel Ata-Ullah was a very different character. Aged fifty, he was a senior doctor and Kashmir's Director of Health Services. He was 28 lbs overweight with dodgy knees and no experience whatsoever of climbing. Charlie's permit for K2 gave him no choice: he was required to take a Pakistani liaison officer and, in spite of his apparent lack of fitness, Ata-Ullah came highly recommended. For his part, when first approached, Ata-Ullah was surprised and slightly embarrassed to be asked but ultimately he turned out to be a very good candidate – a cultured and gentle man who quickly became an important part of the team.

A few days before they left Rawalpindi, Charlie heard that the British had indeed reached the summit of Everest. It was a bittersweet moment: he had many friends in Britain and wished John Hunt's team every success, but part of him hoped that this would be K2's year, not Everest's. His moment of regret was short-lived, though, and soon he and Bob were composing a congratulatory cable to the Alpine Club in London, the co-organiser of the British expedition.

After a week of good-willing and glad-handing, they eventually took off for their final destination. It was a hair-raising flight, piloted by two daredevil Poles who had flown for the RAF during the war. They took their passengers over 13,000 ft passes and past mountains that were thousands of feet higher. It was a cloudy day rendering K2 invisible, but they came within 10 miles of Nanga Parbat in the Himalayas, and even thought they could spot signs of the Austro-German team, then climbing its slopes.

Ninety draughty minutes later their Orient Airways plane landed on a dusty airstrip just below Skardu. Over the last few years the city's population had grown massively, swelled by thousands of refugees displaced by the partition of India and Pakistan. What in 1938 had resembled a medieval city now contained a modern hospital and a cinema. On the way into town, the Americans received a noisy reception from hundreds of children and their parents, who lined the road armed with banners asking their new American friends to help 'solve the Kashmir problem'.

In 1938 when Charlie and Bob had first gone to the Karakoram, K2 lay in the far north of a British protectorate, the princely state of Kashmir and Jammu, but when Indian independence came in 1947 and the country was divided on religious and ethnic lines, its ruler had been invited to choose whether to join Hindu India or Muslim Pakistan. Elsewhere in the former Empire, this had generally been a relatively easy choice but Kashmir was unusual in that it had a Hindu ruler and a largely Muslim population. While the raja vacillated, Muslim tribesmen invaded Kashmir from Pakistan, prompting him to appeal to India for military assistance. Because Kashmir was so strategically important, India was only too pleased to send in its troops, beginning a long conflict which split the region and remains unresolved to this day.

Though climbing K2 was of very little interest to the Indians and Pakistanis arguing over the division of Kashmir, the political problems between the two countries did have one important consequence for the expedition. Sherpas had played an important role in the American expeditions of 1938 and 1939, but with their hometown of Darjeeling just inside the Indian border they were considered Indian citizens and, as such, no longer welcome. Instead, Houston's party was joined by a squad of Hunza porters, specially recruited for high-altitude work. They were tough mountain men from north east Pakistan but only one of them had any expedition experience. However, the simple fact that they had just trekked for two weeks over very harsh terrain to meet the Americans was a good indication of their hardiness and enthusiasm.

The final stage, from Skardu to K2 base camp, looked much more familiar to Charlie Houston and Bob Bates than the first half of the journey. There were no cinemas or airstrips – in fact nothing seemed to have changed since 1938. They crossed the Indus in the same rickety barge that was said to have been used by Alexander the Great and then began the 125-mile trek across some of the most spectacular and unforgiving terrain on earth.

By the time they reached Askole, still the last village before K2, their caravan had swollen to almost 200 and the expedition accounts book was looking very busy. Though the landscape hadn't changed, the cost of hiring local porters had increased by 600 per cent since 1938. With over 3.5 tons of food and equipment to carry up the Baltoro glacier they had little choice but to pay up.[3]

Colonel Ata-Ullah was amused to see how the young Americans were initially reluctant to have a personal porter assigned to them and insisted on doing their own camp chores. Then, as had happened in 1938, after a few days on the march, they began behaving like 'indolent grand Moghuls',[4] who were only too happy to be looked after.

For Dee Molenaar, his first trip outside North America was a whirlwind of emotions. He'd been charmed by the civility of London, struck by the hostility of Germans at Frankfurt Airport and appalled by the poverty in Karachi and Rawalpindi. His fellow Seattle-based climber, the chemical engineer Pete Schoening, was fascinated to meet local people but quickly realised that he and the other Americans were as much on display as any of the picturesque locals were.

British transport officer Tony Streather's linguistic skills were very useful but he made the cardinal error of employing a contractor from Skardu to look after hiring and firing. There was never a problem recruiting porters, but they never seemed very happy and always complained a lot. A few days in, Tony discovered why: the Skardu contractor was taking half their wages. He was promptly sacked but their porter troubles continued with endless complaints and relentless petty pilfering. Tony Streather's high-altitude boots were stolen along with several pairs brought along for their Hunza porters. At one stage there were so many thefts that the Americans had to mount hourly watches to protect their equipment.

The first sight of their goal came on 19 June, when after fourteen days of hard trekking they arrived at Concordia, the huge rocky amphitheatre, and saw K2 looming down on them through the mist at the end of the Godwin-Austen glacier. Initially it was partially covered in cloud, but when the mountain deigned to appear it made a big impact on everyone, first-timers and veterans. Second time round, Charlie Houston was no less impressed:

> After 70 miles of walking up the Baltoro, you go round the corner – Wham!– Awesome is an overused word but it is awesome![5]

Charlie and Bob were very eager to get going quickly, so on the following morning they set off early, hoping to find the same site for their base camp that they had used in 1938. By lunchtime they had located it but it wasn't until many hours later that the last of their porters straggled into camp. It was freezing cold and the Askole men wanted to leave as soon as possible. By the time the last of them were paid off, the expedition cashbox was almost totally empty with just a few cents' worth of local currency remaining.

They were now on their own: seven Americans, one British officer, one Pakistani doctor and six Hunza high-altitude porters. They had just over fifty days before they were due to leave and seventy days' worth of food, theoretically a healthy margin in case anything went wrong. In 1938 it had taken just twenty-three days for Charlie Houston and Paul Petzoldt to get from the foot of the Abruzzi ridge to their high point of 26,000 ft, so with a bigger team, Charlie was confident that they had the time and the resources to go all the way to the top.

The big imponderable was the weather. On his first expedition Charlie had escaped lightly, but both the Eckenstein expedition of 1902 and the more recent 1939 Wiessner expedition had been plagued by storms. This year they had the advantage of a large radio receiver at base camp and regular weather reports to help them plan their movements, but if the storms came, they would just have to ride them out.

Charlie's plan was simple: over the next month his team would work its way up the Abruzzi ridge using the same campsites as 1938 and 1939. A scouting party of two men would identify the route while the others consolidated the camps behind. The lead climbing would be shared and they would change tent partners regularly in order to get to know each other. There would be no repetition of 1939: Charlie would not allow any camps to be stripped until everyone was off the mountain. Their main technological innovation was to bring handheld walkie-talkies; a new generation of rugged portable radios had been developed during the Second World War, which they hoped would enable good communication between camps.

Their immediate task was to get between 1200 and 2000 lbs of food and fuel to Camp 1 at 17,700 ft, but in the back of Charlie's mind there was a nagging sense of dread: how soon would they come upon the evidence of the 1939 tragedy? Would they find Dudley Wolfe's body at Camp 7 or would his remains be on the glacier below? And what of Charlie's favourite Sherpa, Pasang Kikuli, and his gallant comrades – would there be any indications of what had happened to them?

There was only one way to find out.

Chapter 7

TEAMWORK

At first Dee Molenaar hadn't thought it was for him. In 1953 he was working for the army as a climbing instructor; even if the military would grant him leave of absence, he wasn't sure that he could afford to go on an expedition to the Karakoram mountains. Everest, K2, the Himalayas – that kind of mountaineering cost big money and was for the 'upper echelons' on the East Coast. When his friend and fellow instructor Bob Craig had told him that the famous climber Charlie Houston wanted to interview potential team members in person, he was even less convinced. Getting from Seattle to New Hampshire was time-consuming and costly. Dee was all set to say no but Bob persisted and even persuaded Houston to enlist Dee on recommendation alone. His dad had loaned him some money and now here he was a few months later, staring up at the world's second-highest mountain.

After almost a month travelling, Dee's feelings were still a little mixed. It was a very happy team and there was no doubt that he was surrounded by fabulous mountains but K2 really did look high and dangerous, and even before he reached the Karakoram he had started to miss his wife Lee and his baby daughter Patti. Most of the others on the team had girlfriends or wives but he and Charlie were the only two with children, and the idea of being away from home for many months was painful.

Charlie Houston was also missing his family. By the spring of 1953 he had two sons and a daughter, and a busy medical practice in Exeter, New Hampshire. His wife, Dorcas, recognised how important climbing was to him and did not stand in his way, but Charlie was no longer quite the carefree single man that he had been in 1938.

For everyone on the team and their relatives back home, regular mail services were a lifeline. In addition to personal letters for friends and family, the team produced regular newsletters, distributed by Charlie's father and great support, Oscar. The fifth dispatch, written by Bob Craig, and datelined 18 June, the day they arrived at base camp, was full of excitement and made no mention of homesickness or the high-altitude headaches from which many of them were suffering:

> *We were on schedule, we were in good health, we were minus*
> *certain items of equipment but we were smack dab under K2*
> *and spirits were, and this morning continue to be, high.*

As they unpacked their gear, a few casualties became apparent: a large Cheddar cheese had been broken and crushed, and several chocolate bars had melted during transit and coated everything around them. On the plus side, they found several good luck messages and a few pin-up photographs, hidden inside the boxes that their friends had helped them pack a few months earlier in America.

On 21 June they celebrated the first of two expedition birthdays, Dee Molenaar's thirty-fifth, by chasing him round the camp and, with all due ceremony, tearing off the jeans that he had worn all the way up the Baltoro glacier. A few days later he got an opportunity for revenge, when the team's hair clippers were found and Dee took on the role of barber, dishing out regulation crew cuts.

Then it was time to start up the mountain.

Unlike Fritz Wiessner in 1939, Charlie Houston had elected not to do any skiing trips or training climbs prior to K2. Instead he hoped that the sheer slog of all the load carrying, up and down the Abruzzi ridge, would get everyone fit and acclimatised. Apart from a couple of bottles intended for medical emergencies, he had not brought any oxygen; the British might have brought tons of the stuff for their attempt on Everest, but Charlie didn't think it was necessary for K2, and anyway he didn't have the money or the manpower to fly out dozens of bottles and then carry them up the mountain.

Like the other big Himalayan 'sieges' of the period, getting to the summit would require a long slow build-up and the creation of eight or nine camps before they reached the point where the fittest members of the team would strike for the summit. They had left the US with almost 4 tons of gear and their first task was to hump about half of it to Camp 1, on the Godwin-Austen glacier, just below the Abruzzi ridge.

Houston intended to use the Hunza porters to help get supplies only as far as their second camp at 19,300 ft. After that, the Americans would have to do all their own carrying. The ground was too steep for inexperienced porters and Charlie knew from 1938 that when there were too many people on the mountain, anyone below would be subject to a constant bombardment of loose rocks.

Originally, their liaison officer, Colonel Ata-Ullah, was only supposed to go as far as base camp and then return to Skardu, but he enjoyed the approach march so much that he asked to stay for the duration. Bob Bates calculated that they had enough food to cope with one extra mouth and the deal was done: Ata-Ullah would man the radio and keep them in touch with the outside world as they made their way upwards. He was not the only stowaway. Though base camp was a miserably cold spot, miles from any trees or vegetation, a solitary squirrel had somehow managed to float in on a glacial stream one day, and was adopted as camp mascot.

While the others carried loads up and down to Camp 1, Bob Bates and Charlie Houston scouted ahead to locate the site of Camp 2. Both remembered a large flat area with space for several tents but, to their embarrassment, they just could not find it. They recognised features and cairns that had been put up to mark the route in 1938, but as for the site itself, they had no luck at all. When Bob and Charlie returned to base camp they looked a little sheepish and spent the evening arguing whether they should have changed path higher up or lower down.

On 28 June it was the day of reckoning. Charlie and Bob each took a party up their respective routes. A few hours later Charlie won the argument, arriving at Camp 2 after a long slog. As he emerged over the steep slopes below the platform where they would pitch their tents, Charlie wondered what they would find. Fourteen years earlier Fritz Wiessner had spent three days at the same spot, waiting for a storm to die down before continuing up the mountain to rescue Dudley Wolfe and the three missing Sherpas. The weather never improved and Wiessner had been forced to retreat. Would there be any clues as to what had happened next to the men he was forced to leave above?

Fortunately, there was nothing too harrowing: a couple of iced-up sleeping bags, a 5 lb tin of Ovaltine and a collapsed tent, which they repitched and used to house their Hunza porters. There were no skeletons or final notes. The 1939 mystery would be solved higher up, if at all.

Once Camp 2 had been established, the build-up of supplies continued in earnest. Bob Craig and Art Gilkey took over the lead and worked their way up to the next stage, Camp 3 at around 20,700 ft, 400 ft higher than Mount McKinley, the tallest peak in North America. Whereas Camp 2 was big enough for five tents, Camp 3 consisted of two narrow platforms built out of rocks scavenged nearby, just above a steep gully. In 1939 Fritz Wiessner had decided that this part of the Abruzzi ridge was so prone to rockfall that he hadn't bothered pitching any tents at all and instead turned his Camp 3 into a supply dump. That, however, had meant a long debilitating slog between Camps 2 and 4. This time Houston's team found a safer spot underneath some overhanging rocks and set up two tents.

Though Houston had not planned for the Hunza porters to go above Camp 2, they were so enthusiastic and did so well that he let them carry on for a further 1000 ft to the next site. After Camp 3,[1] though, the party split. The Hunzas stayed down at base camp with Ata-Ullah, who kept himself busy looking after the mail and communications with the outside world, while the Americans continued up alone.

At 21,500 ft they found more evidence of Wiessner's 1939 expedition. Inside two flattened tents at Camp 4, there were thermos flasks, stoves, containers of fuel and tins of jam, pemmican, powdered egg and another large tin of Ovaltine, which looked as if it had only just been opened. More disturbingly, there were several more iced-up sleeping bags. For a moment Bob Craig wondered about Fritz Wiessner's claim that all the camps had been stripped of their bags, until he realised that these were probably left behind by Jack Durrance or Pasang Kikuli, on their abortive attempts to rescue Dudley Wolfe.

After almost a month on the Abruzzi ridge they reached House's Chimney, the narrow crack in an almost vertical cliff at just under 22,000 ft that offered the first real test on K2. Though he had been up and down several times in 1938, Charlie Houston was both excited and nervous. The younger members of the team had noticed that at the beginning of the expedition he was carrying a few extra pounds and, though he'd lost them by now, Charlie hadn't done that much high-grade rock climbing in recent years. He was sure that he wanted to go first, but would he make it in fine style or would it all end in embarrassment? With George Bell and Dee Molenaar watching from below, Charlie wedged himself in and began to worm his way up.

He soon encountered several iced-up ropes, relics of 1938 and 1939, but there was no way to tell how securely they were attached so he didn't risk using them. The climbing was as hard and challenging as he expected, but after several stops to get his breath back, cunningly disguised as pauses to adjust pitons and blow his nose, he reached the top of the cliff with both relief and pride.

After bringing up Molenaar and Bell, Charlie made his way up a steep snow slope to Wiessner's Camp 5. In addition to the usual chaos of flattened tents and abandoned cooking equipment, they found a laundry bill for Dudley Wolfe, from a high-class dry-cleaner's in New York. Just what it was doing on K2 was anyone's guess, but, for sure, it had never been paid.

The ascent of House's Chimney had been one of their most productive days so far but there was another 6000 ft to go before the summit. As if to up the ante yet again, they heard over the radio from Ata-Ullah that the Austrian climber Hermann Buhl had just climbed Nanga Parbat, five weeks after Hillary and Tenzing's triumph on Everest. With their two biggest rivals both doing so well, Charlie felt under even more pressure to succeed on K2. His most immediate problem, however, was more mundane: how to perform his first dental extraction.

For over a month Bob Bates had been nursing a very sore tooth, damaged irreparably for the sake of good manners. At one village on the march in, he had been presented with 'the toughest chicken on earth'. Bob felt obliged to tuck in but, after chomping on a drumstick, he had badly cracked one of his molars. By early July Bob had an enormous abscess and the pain was so bad that he just had to do something about it.

Charlie radioed down to Ata-Ullah to locate his dental forceps from the expedition's medical stores and have them sent up to Camp 2. Then he and Bob descended. Watched over by Mohammad Ali, one of the Hunza porters who doubled as the local tooth doctor, Charlie dosed Bob Bates up with novocaine and prepared to pull the offending tooth. With Bob Craig playing nurse-cum-dental-chair, cradling the patient's head in his hands, and George Bell manning the cameras to record what was probably the world's highest-ever dental surgery, Charlie yanked the tooth out in one swift move, much to his and everyone's relief.

After a short course of antibiotics, Bob Bates was smiling again – but not for long. During June and the first part of July they had enjoyed good weather but everything had started to change. On 11 July high winds kept everyone awake all night and forty-eight hours later they were hit by a second storm, which confined them to the tents for three days. Bad weather on K2 was not unexpected but the sheer ferocity of their first big storm left everyone reeling.

Charlie Houston shared a tent with transport officer now turned team member Tony Streather at Camp 3 at 20,700 ft. It was a good opportunity to get to know each other but the circumstances were not exactly ideal. A veteran of several years spent patrolling the North West Frontier, Tony was no stranger to bad weather but even he was shocked by the strength of the wind.

On the first night Charlie dreamt that he was being crushed between two large blocks of ice. When he awoke in his sleeping bag he was not surprised to discover that there were no icebergs in the vicinity, but as he looked up at the sagging tent canvas above, he realised that a mass of snow had landed between the rear of their tent and the rocks behind. If it carried on accumulating, either the fabric would rip or the tent poles would snap. Even worse, the whole thing might be pushed off its narrow perch, sending them tumbling down the mountain. The only solution was to get up and clear it away, but with the storm raging and the snow drifting, it was a singularly unpleasant prospect. Reluctantly, Charlie did the first shift but the snow continued to fall so Tony had to repeat the task a few hours later.

Higher up, at Camp 4, Dee Molenaar was stuck in an equally small tent with the 6 ft 5 in George Bell. An accomplished artist, Dee had brought along a set of watercolours and a sketch pad. On 13 July he began his latest high-altitude artwork, not knowing whether the bad weather would continue long enough for him to complete it. Sure enough, the storm raged on well into the following day.

It blew so hard that Dee and George couldn't even get out of their tents to urinate. Fortunately, they had a peanut tin on hand to act as an improvised chamber pot, but, as Dee noted in his diary, while there was no embarrassment about tossing urine out of the front of the tent, 'defecation requires more guts'.

On 16 July the wind died down for long enough for the Americans to get back on the move, but the storm marked a turning point. Instead of the clear blue skies that marked the beginning of the expedition, the weather was increasingly turbulent. Charlie Houston still stuck to the theory that K2 was too far north to be affected by the monsoon but, whatever the cause, the snow was falling and it was becoming colder and colder.

He was already worried about their schedule. They had a reasonable margin when it came to supplies, but every day confined to their tents meant more rations consumed. With a sense of growing urgency, Charlie and the others returned to House's Chimney and began to haul up supplies to the top. In 1938 it had been a long tedious process, but this time they had a secret weapon: a five-piece aluminium A-frame winch, built by chemical engineer Pete Schoening back in Seattle. Once it was assembled, hauling loads became much quicker and easier.

With Camp 5 established at the top of the Chimney, they began working their way through the loose rock above. They were now above 22,000 ft and could feel the effects of the altitude much more keenly but at least they were on the move. When Charlie Houston wrote the ninth K2 newsletter on 18 July, he estimated that they would be ready to make an attempt on the summit in about two weeks, between 1 and 3 August. Morale, he reported, was high and there had been no major mishaps, other than a bizarre incident at Camp 3. An Alpine chough, a crow-like bird, had somehow flapped its way up to 20,000 ft and taken exception to Bob Craig's air mattress, which had been left outside his tent drying in the sun. By the time the yellow-billed bird departed, the mattress had so many holes that it was useless.

Their next milestone came on 20 July when they reached Wiessner's Camp 6 at 23,300 ft. They had found plenty of evidence of the 1939 expedition below, but nothing quite like the tableau they witnessed here under a large overhanging rock: the wind had shredded the tents and left them as mere skeletons, but lined up on the ground sheets were three neatly rolled-up sleeping bags and a small box, which contained a bundle of tea wrapped in a handkerchief. If it hadn't been for the ripped canvas and the ice that glued their sleeping bags to the spot, the Sherpas might have been there yesterday. Charlie Houston found the frozen scene deeply moving: fourteen years earlier, it had been Pasang Kikuli's last stop before he set off to rescue Dudley Wolfe, but as to his fate and that of the two Sherpas with him, there was still no indication.

As high above, Charlie and his team continued the painstaking work of putting up the final few camps, down at base camp, Ata-Ullah kept himself busy with occasional forays onto the Godwin-Austen glacier and long sessions listening to the radio. He and Charlie had a regular 6.00 p.m. walkie-talkie conference, and he tried to distract the men above with digests of the world news. There was plenty going on: in the Korean War it looked as if there might soon be a truce, and in Moscow big changes seemed to be afoot – Lavrentiy Beria, Stalin's infamous henchman, had just been arrested, a sign of the vicious power struggles going on in the Soviet Union, in the wake of the great dictator's death earlier in the year.

Politics and the outside world seemed more and more distant but there was also some more personal news from Ata-Ullah over the radio: at the end of the month, Charlie's wife, Dorcas, was going to fly out to meet him at Rawalpindi. They had already been apart for nine weeks; Charlie hoped that they would return from K2 in triumph, but as he gazed up at the cloudy skies, 'victory' was not the first thing in his thoughts.

As Ata-Ullah invariably added at the end of his weather reports, more storms and turbulence were on their way. On 23 July Charlie and his team were trapped in their tents for another two days, with the wind howling round them and no prospect of doing any climbing soon. When the weather improved, the climbing only became harder. Above Camp 6 lay the steep slopes of the Black Pyramid, almost 1000 ft of dark granite, polished by centuries of avalanches and rockfalls. It was broken only by narrow gullies choked with snow and rock slabs coated with treacherous layers of ice.

On 27 July they made their first foray. For Charlie Houston, this was mountaineering at its most challenging and rewarding, but with the terrain becoming ever tougher progress was slow and dangerous. Down below they had sometimes climbed unroped, but now they had no alternative but to belay each other carefully. When after four hours they finally reached the top of the Pyramid, Charlie was so tired and numb with cold that he had let his younger partners, Bob Craig and George Bell, press on to find the next campsite without him.

With the weather deteriorating, several men began wearing their new-style 'Bunny Boots'. Unlike traditional leather footwear, they were made of rubber and featured a sealed internal layer that acted as a thermal barrier, keeping the cold out and the heat in. They did make a difference but it was impossible to feel really warm.

The worst part of the expedition was the storm days which kept them confined to their tents and still showed no signs of letting up. On 28 July, as Dee Molenaar spent another day of 'pit time' at Camp 6, he mused in his diary about the dangers of frostbite and wondered how far he would be prepared to go to reach the top. The French climber Maurice Herzog, who summited Annapurna in 1950, had famously given all his toes and most of his fingers for the privilege of becoming the first man to climb a 26,000 ft peak. But as Dee asked himself, could it ever really be worth it?

> Will I – at that altitude and in that final stage of excitement at approaching the goal of months of planning – forget all future consequences of frozen feet and keep moving upward? Or will I, on the other hand, be able to clearly evaluate the worth of reaching that high goal against the probable fact of going toeless (or worse) the rest of my life.[2]

Dee was still feeling fit, but he had now spent enough time at high altitude to realise just how it dulled the senses and could make a climber behave irrationally. And it wasn't just a question of each man protecting his own extremities. Whatever happened to one man affected everyone else on the team, and, as Dee knew, it would be virtually impossible to carry a badly injured man off K2.

Frostbite was not the only danger. From a distance K2 looked like a huge solid lump of rock, but up close it became obvious that much of that rock was very loose and prone to avalanche if disturbed. The second time they headed for the Black Pyramid, aiming to set up Camp 7, Tony Streather was hit by falling rock. He emerged unscathed, but it was a close call and could have been serious.

Then, just when it looked as if conditions would never change, they woke up on the morning of 30 July to a cloudless sky and hot sun. Charlie hoped that a period of stable weather had arrived – after all, in 1938 they had enjoyed good weather for most of July and had only left the mountain in anticipation of bad weather, rather than in the midst of it. They had found a route through the Black Pyramid; all they needed now was a few good days in a row to set up the next three camps and they could start thinking properly about a summit bid.

Both Charlie's reverie and the good-weather window, however, were short-lived: within a few hours the clouds and the cold weather had returned. There was no alternative but to carry on going but they simply could not find the site for the next camp. In 1938 and 1939 both teams had placed their Camp 7 at around 24,700 ft, but they encountered no remains of any tents in the vicinity and no other clues as to where their predecessors had pitched their tent.

Only when Bob Craig accidentally broke through a slope and discovered a small ice cave were they able to hack out a tiny ledge, just wide enough to hold their smallest shelter. While Charlie and the others retreated to the cold comfort of Camp 6, Pete Schoening and Art Gilkey wriggled inside and tried to keep warm. On 30 July it was chemical engineer Pete Schoening's twenty-sixth birthday but it was difficult to celebrate inside a cramped tent, perched below a steep slope that looked as if it might avalanche at any minute.

Next morning they probed higher, hoping to discover a safer spot, but they had no luck. Evidently, avalanches had changed the whole topography since 1939. The hapless Dudley Wolfe had probably spent his last days up here alone but it was impossible to tell exactly where. The only good thing to come out of their efforts was the identification of a potential site for Camp 8, on a wide flattish area at about 25,500 ft, big enough to cope with four tents.

Climbing at this altitude was very tiring; Pete Schoening didn't feel too bad but he noticed that his current climbing partner, Art Gilkey, was getting increasingly irritable and finding the going very hard. Art had never been afraid of the cold. He'd spent two summers in Alaska, in the middle of the Juneau icefield, but this was by far the highest mountain that he had climbed, and like a lot of first-timers he was struggling. On 1 August they planned to make two carries up to Camp 8 but Art's feet were so frozen that they didn't leave their tent till after midday, by which time Charlie and the others had joined them.

It was all becoming very hard: cold, windy and incredibly exposed. The excitement and enthusiasm of the first weeks had been replaced by a sense of grim determination. No matter how good they were as climbers and how committed to the cause, the weather had become a relentless, unpredictable antagonist. It was a war of attrition and they were in the firing line.

The first night at Camp 8 was their worst so far. The wind battered their tents, making sleep impossible. Pete Schoening and Art Gilkey tried out an experimental army tent manufactured from impermeable cloth. It had several air vents but there was so much snow coming in that they blocked them to stay warm. Eventually, they did manage to fall asleep but, if it hadn't been for Pete's sixth sense, they might never have woken up. Some time after dawn he pushed his head through the tent flaps and found himself spluttering and gasping for air. The impermeable tent had done its job so well that they had only narrowly avoided carbon dioxide poisoning. They were both left with nasty headaches and nausea and Schoening saw double for several hours.

On the following day the weather played its usual games, starting with a beautiful sunrise before rapidly deteriorating. Bob Bates and Tony Streather came up from Camp 6 with the last loads of food and fuel. After ten hours' climbing in atrocious conditions, they finally stumbled into camp at around 6.00 p.m. to be greeted with amazement followed by very welcome hot drinks. It was day forty and all eight members of the climbing team were now high on K2. Compared to 1938 or 1939, this was an achievement in itself, but if they were to match or outperform Fritz Wiessner, they still had over 2000 ft to go to his highest point and a further 700 ft to reach the summit. Charlie tried hard to be optimistic: all they needed was three days of good weather and K2 would be theirs. Dawn, however, brought no improvement. If anything, the conditions were even worse.

For almost a week, they were pinned down by the most vicious storm so far. In his autobiography, *The Love of Mountains Is Best*, Bob Bates wrote that it was almost as if the mountain itself wanted to kill them. Even when sporting two sets of underwear, padded trousers and jackets, wind pants and double parkas, they still felt absolutely frozen. Worse still, it was so gusty that they just couldn't keep their stoves alight. That meant no hot food and no water. When as a last resort they tried to melt snow in their mouths, it only made them even colder. At one point, Bob Bates vainly tried to beat some snow into liquid in a metal mug, before he gave up in frustration.

On the night of 4 August, day number three of the storm, the impermeable tent finally gave way. For several hours Charlie Houston and George Bell lay inside, watching as more and more rips appeared in the canvas above their heads, knowing that if it collapsed they would somehow have to get into their boots and parkas in the dark. Then just after dawn the poles finally snapped and the canvas fell apart. All they could do was grab their sleeping bags and crawl into the nearest tent.

When he wrote about it years later, Charlie remembered these storm days as a character-building experience, but in the audio tape they recorded immediately after they returned to base camp, there was no mention of anything other than the sheer tedium and the relentless battle with the hostile elements:

> And you lie there in your sleeping bag, warm, with snow
> blowing in on you, the tent buffeting over your head, unable
> to cook, can't light the stove, can't melt snow for water – it
> seems impossible to endure it, and it goes on and on and on.[3]

Amazingly, they still weren't ready to give up. On 5 August,[4] in a brief lull, they held a secret ballot to choose the first two summit teams. The plan was simple: as soon as the wind died down, they would climb up to about 27,000 ft, the foot of the summit pyramid, and establish Camp 9, their final shelter before the summit. It would consist of a single two-man tent. The first summit pair would be left with enough supplies to hold for several days and would make their attempt at the first possible moment. If they succeeded, everyone would retreat down the mountain as fast as possible; if they failed, they would return to Camp 8 and be replaced by a second and if necessary a third summit pair. All they needed were those elusive three clear days: one to get to Camp 9, one to the summit, and one to get back down.

The Los Alamos nuclear physicist George Bell and the team's philosophy graduate Bob Craig were voted in as the first pair, with Pete Schoening and Art Gilkey as the second. In an era characterised by national competition, many teams arrived in the East festooned with flags to wave on the summit of their particular mountain, but

Charlie Houston had come out without any. The ever-resourceful Dee Molenaar painted a 'four-in-one' flag, combining the emblems of America, Britain, Pakistan and the United Nations.

Meanwhile, 7000 miles away in America, no one had any idea of what Houston's team was experiencing, but the success of the British on Everest and the Austro-German team on Nanga Parbat had led to an upsurge in press interest around K2. On 6 August the *Boston Herald* carried a story reporting that the American team were close to their objective and, according to messengers recently arrived in Skardu, were in the best of health and spirits. That day's real news was very different.

Charlie had woken up desperate for their luck to turn. Exactly nineteen years earlier, against the odds, he had battled his way to the summit of Mount Foraker in Alaska, on the expedition that first established his reputation as a force in American mountaineering. If only they could get a break in the weather, he maintained, there was so much skill and sheer willpower in this team that they were bound to succeed. But when he put his head out of the tent and was battered by the wind, he realised instantly how vain that hope was.

When Charlie did his daily rounds, his spirits sunk even lower. Two days earlier George Bell had been voted onto the first summit team, but now he had signs of frostbite on both heels. He stood no chance of climbing higher in that state. After a quick conference they decided that Dee Molenaar would take George down to Camp 6 to recuperate, leaving Pete Schoening to take his place on the summit team. Bob Bates and Tony Streather agreed to go with Bell and Molenaar down to Camp 6, and then climb back up with food and fuel.

When that evening Charlie radioed base camp to explain their change of plan, Ata-Ullah was quietly pleased to hear that the Americans were finally thinking about splitting the party. Down at 16,500 ft on the Godwin-Austen glacier, they had been enjoying comparatively good weather at base camp, but whenever Ata-Ullah looked above he could see clouds covering the upper half of the mountain and knew from Pakistani weather reports that nothing was going to change soon. Ata-Ullah thought he sensed some relief in Charlie's voice when he admitted that soon they might have to quit K2 altogether.

There was no let-up in the wind on the following morning but at least everyone felt that, for better or worse, something was about to happen. George and Dee were preparing to go down, Pete and Bob Craig were getting ready to go up to establish Camp 9. Bob had just taken out his camera when he noticed Art Gilkey emerging from his tent. Then, just as he pressed the shutter, Art fell over and collapsed in the snow.

He got up complaining that he'd been suffering from a cramp for the last few days, but when Charlie examined him he discovered that it was something far worse. Art had developed thrombophlebitis in his left leg. An inflammation of the veins caused by a blood clot, this condition more commonly affected elderly women. As far as Charlie could remember, it had never previously been reported on a mountaineering expedition but he had no doubt of his diagnosis.

If treated quickly, thrombophlebitis was not life-threatening, but high up on K2, where a climber's blood might be twice as thick as at sea level, it was just about the worst possible place for anyone with a blood clot. There was no alternative: they had to get Art down and get him down quickly. For the moment, at least, the summit would have to wait.

Chapter 8

MAN DOWN

For the second time in a row an American expedition had a man down on K2.

As a mountaineer, Art Gilkey could not be compared to the social-ite Dudley Wolfe. Art had worked as a professional guide in the Teton mountains, made a high-speed ascent of the famously difficult Devil's Tower in Wyoming, and spent a lot of time in the wilds of Alaska. A geologist by training and desire, he was used to long trips into the wilderness. On this expedition he had done much of the lead climbing and had impressed everyone with his skill and enthusiasm. He was going to be on the second summit team, and even cherished the hope that maybe everyone would reach the summit. But now?

Art put on a brave face and tried to play it down. It was just a 'Charlie Horse', a cramp that he'd had for a few days. He was really sorry and didn't want to be a burden on everyone else. Charlie Houston, however, realised the seriousness of the situation straight away. Thrombophlebitis might be as unlikely as smallpox on a moun-taineering expedition, but cursing your luck was not going to help anyone. He wrapped both of Art's legs in pressure bandages and went to consult the others.

Art's condition, he said, was not life-threatening at this point but if the blood clot enlarged or began to break up, it might go to his lungs and that meant almost certain death. The only answer was to get him off the mountain as quickly as possible – but could they do it?

The upside was that the whole team was together; unlike 1939, no one would have to make a long ascent from base camp to bring Art down. The downside was that whereas Dudley Wolfe was mobile but weak, their casualty couldn't really walk and he was 1000 ft higher up. Pete Schoening and Bob Craig both had experience of mountain rescue work. They thought it could be done but, as Charlie later wrote, their assurances 'lacked conviction'. Deep down everyone suspected that Art was unlikely to survive for more than a few days and that any rescue attempt would endanger them all, but what were the alternatives? Abandon him? Stay and watch him die?

At 10.00 a.m. they broke camp. They tucked Art into his sleeping bag and wrapped him in the remains of the collapsed impermeable tent. Then they packed their rucksacks: a small tent, sleeping bags, cameras, a little food and their precious diaries. Just before leaving, in a fit of good housekeeping, Charlie attempted to tidy everything up, collapsing the remaining tents and throwing any rations that remained over a nearby ledge. Before he could finish the job he was hustled out of camp.

As they struggled down the slope below, the soft powdery snow got deeper and deeper until it reached the tops of their hips. After a few hundred yards it was obvious that if they went any further, the whole slope would avalanche and take them with it. So they turned back. If getting Art down was tough, getting him back up was almost impossible. In an article written a few months later for the *Saturday Evening Post*, Bob Bates remembered the process vividly:

> It took an hour and a quarter to wallow back to camp with Art. We could not drag him, but he could stand up with the aid of his axe and then throw himself backwards while a man at each shoulder pulled. George is especially powerful and he, Art and Dee finally developed a winning system to defeat gravity and the deep snow.[1]

When they reached Camp 8, Charlie was glad that his earlier tidying fit had been interrupted. In the freezing wind they managed to repitch the tents that had been collapsed a few hours earlier but their mood was grim. They were trapped at 25,500 ft; it would take several days for the snow below them to consolidate and firm up, if it ever did. And the weather was getting even worse.

Doing nothing was not an option. Art was the immediate problem, but by now they had spent almost a week trapped in their tents and they were all suffering. As Dee Molenaar recorded in his diary, everyone looked gaunt, with his own weight probably down to just 140 lbs, 15 lbs below normal. One way or another they had to get down. Pete Schoening and Bob Craig volunteered to look for an alternative route. Two hours later they returned, with the good news that they had found one, following a rib of rock that terminated in a steep wall. From there it might be possible to lower Art to a point parallel to Camp 7, and then swing or drag him across the icy slope that lay in between. It wouldn't be easy, but at least they wouldn't set off any avalanches.

Charlie Houston found it hard to maintain his usual positive tone when he radioed down to Ata-Ullah at base camp that night. 'Morale remains high,' he said, but in almost the same breath added, 'This is a fight for our lives.' Earlier on in the expedition, Charlie and Ata-Ullah had discussed techniques for a high-altitude rescue, before both coming to the inevitable conclusion that 'if you got high on K2, you either walked off the mountain on your own two feet, or you stayed there.' When Charlie described Art's symptoms, Ata-Ullah agreed that it must be thrombophlebitis. He offered to come up and meet them halfway at Camp 4, but Charlie wasn't even sure that they would be able to get that far and did not want Ata-Ullah to get into trouble himself. Ata-Ullah's own news was equally sombre: they weren't the only ones to be suffering at the hands of extreme weather. On that same day meteorologists in Karachi, Pakistan's most populous city, had recorded the highest rainfall ever, with almost 10 inches falling in twenty-four hours. In the floods that followed, hundreds were feared dead.

Next morning, Art said he felt a little better so they decided to wait for another day, hoping that if he continued to improve it would be easier to take him down. Food was running low so Charlie, Tony Streather and Dee Molenaar attempted to go down to Camp 7 where they had left a small cache of supplies. After just 100 ft they were forced to turn back, in the face of yet another storm.

In a gesture born more out of defiance than hope, when Charlie went down, Bob Craig and Pete Schoening, in theory the first summit pair, went up to see how high they could get. The answer was not far. Low cloud made it impossible to see more than a few feet in front of them. On precarious terrain like the slopes above Camp 8, it would have been suicidal to continue.

Charlie came up with a new plan: he would stay high with Art and possibly one other person, everyone else could descend to Camp 6. When they recovered they could climb back and help Charlie and Art down. It would be just like the beginning of his 1938 expedition to K2, when he remained at Askole to look after Paul Petzoldt while the rest of the party carried on. No one, however, liked the idea of splitting the team – it was one thing to be on your own at a warm, well-provisioned village 100 miles from base camp, but something entirely different to have to look after a sick man at 25,500 ft.

The weather improved a little in the late afternoon, but Ata-Ullah only had more bad news to convey during their evening radio conference: yet another big storm was coming. This was not what Charlie wanted to hear. He had noticed that Art's right leg was now as tender as his left. More ominously, his high-altitude patient spent the night coughing. If the blood clot was on its way to his lungs, he would not last more than a few days.

They reached a new low point on 9 August. As the blizzard raged, Charlie did his rounds. Almost half the team were showing signs of frost-bite and Art looked as if he could not last much longer. Dee Molenaar began writing a letter to his wife Lee. The situation, he said, was 'as desperate as anything I've ever experienced'. His only comfort was that they had bonded so well as a team and were absolutely determined to look after each other.

> *There's no thought of 'every man for himself' in this desperate plight. We all come down or else.*[3]

Next morning that bond was tested to the limit.

At 9.00 a.m. Charlie radioed Ata-Ullah and told him that they were about to make a second attempt to get Art down. After synchronising watches, Charlie promised to call again in six hours. Then they took Art out, still in his sleeping bag, and wrapped him in a tent with a rucksack covering his feet. Charlie injected him with morphine to kill the pain, and then they attached four ropes to him, one at the top and bottom, one on either side. With both legs now affected, there was no question that Art could play a role in his own deliverance. He was like a baby: passive, roughly swaddled, utterly dependent. His face had gone blue grey, but when anyone spoke to him he tried to raise a smile and promised that he was feeling okay.

First to leave camp were Pete Schoening and Dee Molenaar. Their aim was to climb down the rocks below, scout the route ahead and then traverse over to Camp 7 to collect some rope, which might be useful for the rest of the descent. Then came the rest of the team and Art. On the flatter sections, they had to haul him through snowdrifts, on the steeper sections they struggled to stop him sliding too fast. Everyone was wearing several layers of clothes, but it didn't take long to become very cold because they were moving so slowly. Icicles hung from their beards and their eyebrows. The wind pummelled them, churning and scattering the snow, until they found themselves climbing down through a virtual white-out.

'Avalanche!'

Tony Streather saw the rope cutting through the top of a snowdrift but before he could warn his teammate Bob Craig, then 10 ft below him, a huge mass of freezing snow came pouring down covering everything in its path.

Bob was one of the youngest climbers on the team, but he was also one of the strongest. He had taken part in mountain rescues in the US, but he had never experienced anything quite as challenging as this. Right then he was unroped and out front, trying to help direct Art down a steep gully. Tony was further up, using shouts and hand signals to liaise between him and Houston and Bates, who were also each holding ropes attached to Art. When the avalanche hit, Charlie and Bob had just enough time to brace themselves. The rope held and Bob was able to hang on, but he was so shocked and chilled that he had to leave Art and traverse to Camp 7 to recover.

While he tried to warm himself and shake the snow from his parka, the others carried on lowering Art, trying to get him to a point parallel to Camp 7 and then somehow swing him across the icy slope that lay in between. As they got ready for what was going to be a very difficult manoeuvre, Pete Schoening took up position 60 ft above, securing Art with a single rope.

Map 6   The Gilkey Rescue, 10 August 1953

The others had taken the precaution of pairing up, with Bates and Houston on one rope, and Bell and Streather on another. When Dee Molenaar realised that he was on his own, he tied onto Art. The storm continued relentlessly.

Then suddenly, inevitably, someone slipped.

It was the 6 ft 5 in George Bell, climbing down to organise Art's ropes. Bang. He fell on his back and slid down the slope, pulling off Tony Streather. Tony attempted to arrest his fall but it was too late. Bang. He flew into the rope connecting Charlie Houston to Bob Bates. Bang. Charlie began tumbling down the mountain. Bob tried to get the head of his ice-axe into the snow to arrest his fall, but before he knew it he too was on his back, his hood over his head, sliding down over the hard ice. Bang. Someone hit the rope connecting Dee Molenaar to Art Gilkey, and Dee fell. Within seconds five men were sliding, rolling, flying down an icy slope, heading toward a 9000 ft drop to the Godwin-Austen glacier below.

'No sensation at all,' George Bell remembered fifty years later. Bob Bates was equally precise in his memory, and his sense of resignation: 'This was it. I'd had a long mountaineering career but this was the end.'[4]

High above, out of the corner of his eye, Pete Schoening saw George slip and drag off Tony Streather. There was nothing he could do to help, but just in case they got tangled up with Art, he turned into the slope and braced himself. The rope connecting Pete to Art ran first around his back and then around the shaft of his axe, which was wedged behind a rock. Seconds turned into milliseconds as he waited for something to happen. Then it hit. Ba-a-a-a-n-g. His ice-axe quivered and the nylon rope stretched and stretched until it was impossibly thin.

A few months earlier Pete's friend Tom Miller had loaned him his favourite ice-axe when he heard that Pete was going to K2. Instead of the usual European ash, Tom's was made from American hickory, a much stronger wood. It needed to be, for Pete was now holding six men: Art Gilkey and all the others apart from Bob Craig. All their ropes had become entangled into one giant rat king and the only thing keeping them from falling off was Pete Schoening and his hickory ice-axe. One flaw in the wood, one imperfection in the rope, one movement

171

in the rock in front of the ice-axe, and they would all be dead and Pete dragged off too.

Over at Camp 7, the snow flurries cleared for a moment and Bob Craig was able to see the slope he had just fled from. Nothing made sense. He spotted a solitary axe jammed into the ice, but all his team-mates had disappeared. Then the wind came back and whipped up the snow and blocked his view altogether.

For Bob's friends flying down K2, it was all surprisingly painless. There had been no rocks to crash into or arrest their fall. For Dee Molenaar it felt a bit like flying, for Bob Bates it was just so fast that he barely had time to react. With his ice-axe somewhere above, his hood jammed over his head and a tangle of ropes wrapped round him, he was as helpless as Art Gilkey. There was nothing he could do but wait for the inevitable moment when he lost consciousness altogether.

Then, all of a sudden, Bob stopped. It was impossible to move, but once he got his breath back he realised that he was perched on the top of a clump of rocks. He called out for help and to his amazement heard a voice from below. It was Dee Molenaar, bleeding from his nose and badly winded after the fall but on his way up. When Dee unravelled the ropes, Bob struggled to his feet.

Gradually voices and shapes came out of the mist: Tony Streather was 50 ft above, trying to clear the ropes tangled around his waist. George Bell was 60 ft below, climbing up out of the void holding his hands in front of him like a zombie. The nuclear physicist from Los Alamos had lost his rucksack, his glasses and his mittens; he was so short-sighted that he could barely see in front of him but he could feel his hands getting colder and colder. Luckily, Bob had a spare pair in his pocket but it wasn't easy putting them onto George's stiff and frozen fingers.

Then Bob saw a dark shape, lying just below some steep rocks. It was Charlie Houston, all crumpled up and still attached to his rope like a limp puppet. When Bob shook him, Charlie regained consciousness but he couldn't focus properly and had the faraway look of someone suffering from concussion. 'Where are we?' he said, and then repeated it over and over again. Bob glanced toward the solitary tent of Camp 7, the only shelter from the wind. Unless they got there soon, they would all be so badly frostbitten that no one would stand any chance of getting down. He might just reach it himself, but there was no way he could get Charlie there as well. So Bob paused for a moment and concentrated hard to remember the names of Charlie's wife and daughter. 'If you ever want to see Dorcas and Penny, you've got to climb up right now!' he bellowed above the wind.

It was the perfect card to play. Charlie immediately started climbing as if on auto-pilot, but getting everyone to Camp 7 was only half the battle; next they had to repitch the tent. The wind roared mercilessly, making it almost impossible to fix down – as soon as they secured one corner another came free, and even when they pegged the tent down with several pitons, the groundsheet still overhung the ledge.

While they struggled to make it secure, 60 ft above Pete Schoening was still gripping a rope attached to the immobile Art Gilkey who was fixed precariously on the snow slope. Pete no longer had the weight of the rest of the team but with frozen hands he could not hold on much longer. So Bob Craig climbed across to Art and anchored his rope to the slope with his ice-axe. A few minutes later, Tony Streather plunged in a second ice-axe to make Art absolutely secure.

About 150 ft to the right, Houston, Bell and Molenaar had now crammed into the tiny tent to get out of the storm. The others were working on a second platform for an even smaller, one-man bivouac shelter that someone had stowed away in his rucksack. They were amazed to have survived the fall but they were still in a desperate position. Charlie Houston had concussion and what sounded like a broken rib, George Bell could barely see without his glasses and had badly frozen feet and hands, Dee Molenaar had a gash above his nose, a deep cut in his leg and very sore ribs. Pete Schoening was very worried about his hands and Bob Craig still hadn't recovered from the avalanche that had engulfed him earlier. They could not see Art Gilkey because he was hidden behind a rib of rock but occasionally, above the wind, Bob Bates thought he could hear him shouting encouragement.

Just four months earlier, Art had been dashing around New York, before setting off on the greatest adventure of his life. At the age of twenty-seven, he was just at the point in his life when everything was falling into place. Back home, he had a Scottish girlfriend, a small apartment in Manhattan and, with his PhD finished, a promising academic career ahead of him. All that meant nothing now. He was inert, immobile, his destiny far outside his own control. If his new friends could drag him over to their tents, he might survive another night, but after that it would only get harder. There was still another 8000 ft to base camp, and in between lay the icy rock pitches of the Black Pyramid and the sheer drop of House's Chimney. It didn't bear thinking about.

His teammates, though, hadn't given up on him. As soon as the tents were erected and the most badly injured men inside, Bob Bates led a small party over to Art. He was about 150 ft away to their left, but it took several minutes to get close. They knew they didn't have the strength to haul Art back to their tents at Camp 7 but they had a little food for him and were hoping to scrape out a small ledge to make him more comfortable.

Tony and Bob were in the lead but they were both slightly snow-blind and everything looked hazy. When they crossed the rock ridge they expected to see Art at the centre of the narrow gully where they had left him, but for some reason he wasn't there. As they got closer, there was still no sign. Instead, there was a bare, smooth slope descending into the gloom.

With the two Bobs holding him carefully on a rope, Tony traversed over into the centre of the gully. Nothing. Art was gone. The slope was bare, apart from a small groove toward the bottom, the only sign of the avalanche that must have taken him. As Bob Bates later said, 'It was as if the hand of God had swept Art clean away.'[5]

It was a shocking climax to a shocking day. First Pete Schoening had somehow managed to save them from certain death, then Art had simply disappeared. If this was God's handiwork, why was he playing with them? Or by taking Gilkey, had he in fact saved their lives?

Back at the tents, the news was greeted with shock and disbelief. And numbed acceptance. No one spoke it out loud, but they knew that if they had carried on with the rescue, the odds were that none of them would have come back alive. As George Bell remembered almost fifty years later:

> *In so far as we were capable of feeling anything, we felt a sense of relief. With everybody injured and in bad shape, the thought of trying to continue lowering him down the mountain would have been more hopeless than ever.*[6]

Mercifully, that night the wind subsided but their tents still felt incredibly precarious. One false move and the canvas would rip or the whole thing might tumble down the slope. Tony, Bob Craig and Pete Schoening were squeezed into the smallest tent. Amazingly, Tony found some tea and sugar in the pocket of his parka and began to brew cup after cup. With a single stove it was impossible to melt much water, but he kept on going for as long as he could.

The other tent contained George Bell, Charlie Houston, Dee Molenaar and Bob Bates. It was bigger but not big enough for Charlie, who spent the night alternating between disturbed sleep and even more troubled waking moments. In his delirium he repeatedly called out to the various members of his team to check they were okay and tried to persuade Bob Bates to get more air into the tent. 'If you will just let me cut a hole,' he would say, 'and put my head out, I won't die. Otherwise I will die from lack of oxygen within 3 minutes. I know – I have studied these things.'[7] Bob did the best that he could to calm him down but it was a long, long night.

When dawn broke the following morning, the wind returned with a vengeance. It was too risky to stay put – even if they managed to anchor down the tents, the slope above them looked ready to avalanche. Getting down, though, even without Art, would be a huge challenge. George Bell's feet were now so swollen that it took a massive effort just to get them into his boots. Charlie Houston seemed marginally more lucid but he was still finding it hard to breathe and, as well as his concussion, his right eye was badly haemhorraged.

Below them, the cliffs and steep pitches of the Black Pyramid looked more intimidating than ever. 'Imagine climbing down the roof of a house, 1500-feet long, the slates covered in ice and snow,' Bob Bates later wrote.[8] 'And imagine doing it when you can't see properly and your feet and hands are frozen,' George Bell could have added. He was in better shape than Gilkey had been the day before, but he needed to be. It would have simply been impossible to carry his huge frame down through the slippery obstacle course below them.

As a precaution, this time they split into two groups. Tony Streather was on one rope, followed by George Bell and then Bob Bates and Dee Molenaar. Charlie Houston was on the other, sandwiched between Bob Craig and Pete Schoening. Charlie descended in bursts, every so often stopping to sit down and stare into space. Then someone would tug on the rope and after the usual 'Where am I?' Charlie would continue. Bob Bates was very worried by his best friend's behaviour. At any moment he might slip or climb in the wrong direction and take the others behind him. There was nothing Bob could do, apart from hope and pray that fate would be kinder today than yesterday.

After a few hundred feet they came across Charlie's ice-axe lost a day earlier, and then a little further down the splintered remnants of one of the other axes that had been used to hold Art. Worse was to come. Just above Camp 6 at 23,300 ft, they passed a tangled, bloody knot of ropes and the tattered remains of the sleeping bag that had held their comrade. It looked as if he had slid down the mountain and momentarily come to rest on the rocks, before being shot out of his bag toward the glacier below. They all hoped that his death had been fast, but climbing down past blood splotches in the snow was an experience that seared them all, and one which they couldn't talk about for many years.

The two tents of Camp 6 were still standing, but only just. Both were full of snow, and one had a large gash in the canvas. Dee Molenaar got to work trying to repair the hole while the others cleared out the inside. Fortunately, they found a good stash of food and were only too pleased to use the three sleeping bags left by the Sherpas in 1939 to supplement what they had with them. Even better, Tony Streather brought out a small bag that he had picked up on the way down. He assumed it must have come from Art's rucksack but in fact it belonged to George Bell and to his joy and amazement contained his spare pair of glasses – and amazingly, they were undamaged.

Down at base camp, Ata-Ullah had become convinced the whole party had perished after thirty-six hours of radio silence. He was astonished when Charlie called down using the spare walkie-talkie left at Camp 6 and was deeply moved to hear about their struggle to save Art. Ata-Ullah still had nothing good to say about the weather, though. Yet another storm was on its way. When it hit the following day, the wind was so powerful they couldn't leave camp. In a brief lull, Tony Streather and Pete Schoening scrambled down to Camp 5 but no one was able to follow until the following morning.

The last big hurdle was House's Chimney. The ropes they had fixed on the way up were still in place, but the men who approached on the late afternoon of Thursday 13 August were bare shadows of the team who had climbed up a month earlier. Back in July, the 1000 ft from Camp 5 to the top of the Chimney used to take just five minutes. Now, with heavy packs and weary limbs, it took over an hour.

Charlie Houston seemed to have recovered and insisted on being the last man to climb down. He and Bob Bates belayed the others and then lowered their rucksacks. It was a struggle to finish before sunset gave way to total darkness. Charlie's own bag snagged on a projecting rock in the middle of the Chimney and then tumbled into the distance along with his precious diary and the anthology of English poetry which he had taken on all his expeditions since the 1930s. In order to move faster and avoid another loss, Bob Bates decided to climb down carrying his rucksack but as soon as he reached the bottom he regretted it. Charlie was not following him.

Alone at the top of the cliff, he was debating what to do. There was no one left to belay him. He would have to use the fixed rope that Dee Molenaar and Bob Craig had put up back in May. But which one was it? In the dying light it was impossible to tell which was the new rope and which were the old ones from 1938 and 1939.

Charlie had always prided himself on being a safe mountaineer. He'd been very critical of Fritz Wiessner and his leadership of the 1939 expedition, but now he was on his way home with one man dead and at least one other badly injured and he had got nowhere near as high as Fritz on the mountain. The last thing he wanted to do was choose an old rope that would not take his weight, and end up as another casualty, another burden on his weary team.

Down below, Bob Bates and the others were getting more and more frightened. They just couldn't understand what Charlie was doing. Was he sitting down again staring into space? Or maintaining his habit of obsessive tidiness and clearing up? Nothing made any sense but it was getting darker and he still wasn't coming.

It was Charlie's moment of truth:

> *I had begun to realise that I couldn't do it. It was dark and I was still hurting and I remember saying, 'I'm going to jump off because if I fall down there, I'll knock them off'. And I stood there while they were shouting at me to come down and I said the Lord's Prayer and then I started down and the next thing I knew there I was at the bottom.*[9]

A few minutes later they wriggled into the tents of Camp 4 but everyone was so tired that they didn't even attempt to make any hot food. They had made it, survived storms, accidents, the Black Pyramid and House's Chimney. There was nothing K2 could throw at them now to stop them getting down alive.

13 August was their last night alone. On the following evening, fifty-six days after they first set foot on the mountain, Bob Craig and Dee Molenaar were the first American climbers into Camp 2. They were received with huge warmth and emotion by their Hunza porters, who had come out to meet them, roped together with what looked like washing line.

The remainder of the climbing team followed soon after, and before long were being feasted with gallons of tea and plates piled high with chapattis and rice cooked in milk. The Hunzas prayed and wept and filled the air with all the emotion that the climbers had been suppressing for so many days. When Tony Streather told them how Art Gilkey had died, he couldn't stop his voice cracking.

Next morning they saw the full sun for the first time in so many weeks and luxuriated in the simple pleasure of sitting outside barefoot, working their way through an enormous pile of letters. Their main worry was still George Bell's feet. His toes were black with frostbite and, as they warmed up, were becoming increasingly painful. Even though everyone had made the climb from Camp 2 to base camp many times, it took a massive effort to get George down without any further accident.

Ata-Ullah greeted them like men coming back from the dead. Six months earlier he had been totally thrown by Charlie Houston's letter, inviting him to join the expedition. When on impulse he took a chance and said yes, he had no idea quite what he was letting himself in for and the tumult of emotions that he would experience.

In the days since they heard the news of Art Gilkey's death, the Hunzas had been busy erecting a tall cairn as a memorial to Art on a rocky hill to the west of base camp, where the Godwin-Austen and Savoia glaciers met. Next day at noon, everyone hobbled over to pay their last respects to Art in a simple but moving ceremony. George Bell and Bob Craig were so badly frostbitten that they could only watch from a distance.

On top of the cairn, the Hunzas placed an aluminium kit box, topped by Art's ice-axe. Inside were flowers and a poem and a letter signed by everyone. The text was simple and heartfelt:

> *He was a gallant member of this expedition and a leader in our attempt on the mountain. His illness at 25,000 ft was an unexpected tragedy and his death during our desperate attempt to rescue him is a loss which all of us feel more keenly because of the closeness of our bonds during these trying times.*

Bob Bates read the 23rd Psalm, 'The Lord is My Shepherd', and with bowed heads they said their goodbyes to the young climber who had been such a keen and amiable companion.

On the next day, they prepared to leave base camp. George Bell's feet were so tender that he was unable to walk so the porters rigged an improvised stretcher, or dandy, made by lashing long tent poles to the sides of a canvas cot. It took four porters to carry his weight, but was so uncomfortable that they had to change team every fifteen minutes. On the most awkward sections of the Baltoro glacier it had to be abandoned altogether, leaving the biggest of the porters, a giant of a man called Mohammed Hussein, to carry George on his back.

The others were able to move under their own steam but no one was too proud to get the occasional lift across a glacial stream. Like on most exit marches, food, and getting as much as possible of it, was high on everyone's agenda. When they reached Paiju, the end of the glacier, they celebrated with a campfire, a spoon of caviar and a tot of whiskey, which they had saved with remarkable self-discipline. Then the floodgates opened. On one day, en route to Askole, George Bell wolfed his way through ten hard boiled eggs, two chickens and a huge pile of chapattis – and that was just lunch. The closer they got to Skardu, the more they gorged on fresh fruit and vegetables: grapes, apples, pears, cucumbers and endless bowls of apricots. Even if it played havoc with their digestive systems, they just ate and ate.

By the time they reached Skardu at the end of August, the world's press had caught up with the events on K2 and their story was all over the newspapers. Several focused on Art Gilkey's parents who had by then been cabled with the terrible news of their son's death. The headlines were stark – 'Climber Killed on K2', 'Parents Hear of Son's Icy Death', 'Himalayan Peak Kills American'.

At Skardu there were more dignitaries to meet and condolences to receive. In the absence of any newly processed material, Charlie Houston once again introduced a showing of his film about the 1938 K2 reconnaissance. It must have been a strange and gruelling experience. Then, early on the morning of 30 August, three months after their flight in, they climbed on board an Orient Airways Curtiss C-46 and took off for Rawalpindi. A short while into the flight, the pilot called them into the cockpit and pointed out a black peak on the horizon dominating the surrounding mountains. It was K2.

Just over an hour later, they touched down. Charlie's wife, Dorcas, was there to greet them, resplendent in a recently purchased sari, surrounded by photographers and journalists. The press was eager to hear more details of their story but even after they had interviewed the team, many newspapers still couldn't cope with the complexities of the story and reported that the whole party had been swept away in a giant avalanche, which had killed Gilkey and traumatised the others. Several newspapers informed their readers that Art's body was now buried under a giant cairn at the foot of the mountain and his local paper in America began raising funds to have it repatriated.

The newswire Associated Press took a different angle, wondering if, like Captain Oates, Gilkey had deliberately freed himself from the ropes and ice-axes that held him to the slope. Charlie Houston, however, 'discounted any suggestions that Gilkey committed suicide to relieve the party of the burden of caring for him'.

After a few more days of interviews and public functions, the 1953 K2 expedition broke up. The injured George Bell was the first to reach the United States. He went straight into hospital at the Massachusetts General, where he was informed that he had the thickest blood of any patient ever admitted. In the end he lost two toes but there was no permanent damage to his hands.

Bob Bates headed west, stopping off in Europe, but the three climbers from Oregon and Washington State – Bob Craig, Dee Molenaar and Pete Schoening – took a flight in the opposite direction across the Pacific. Twelve days after his return, Pete married his fiancée, Mell. Dee Molenaar's homecoming was not quite so romantic. His wife Lee, whom he had spent so much time thinking about on K2, was there at the airport to meet him, but on the way back home she told him that she wanted a divorce. He never gave her the final letter that he wrote at Camp 8.

Charlie and Dorcas Houston returned to Idlewild Airport on 11 September. A few weeks later 'the country doctor', as the press loved to call him, was back at work at his medical practice in Exeter, New Hampshire. After settling the expedition accounts and writing the last official newsletter, he set to work on the expedition film, due for broadcast by NBC in February of the following year.

There were plenty of offers of a book contract and, as in 1938, they decided to spread the writing around the team. Before it was released, in December 1953 two long articles appeared in the *Saturday Evening*

Post, written by Bob Bates and Bob Craig. The narrative was a stirring account of their eight weeks on the mountain and the tremendous hardships they faced. A central theme was the way they had bonded and, as in 1938, there was a powerful sense that even though they had failed to reach the summit, the expedition had been a success. As Bates wrote in eulogistic fashion:

> *The mountain showed no mercy, but a Higher Power may have been watching over. To fall and still be spared convinced us that we would live to climb again. In these moments we forged a bond of brotherhood that never can be broken and proved that man's spirit is far stronger than his body. We did not fail ourselves on K2. We won.*[10]

It was not quite as simple as that for Charlie Houston, however. He too had left the mountain convinced of the bond of brotherhood forged on its slopes but he also craved the simple victory of reaching the summit. He had barely reached Rawalpindi in August 1953 before he announced that he was coming back in 1954 to finish the job.

But it wasn't quite as simple as that either.

Just before he left for the US, Charlie unexpectedly encountered someone whose eyes were also set on the highest unclimbed mountain in the world, someone who also felt that K2 was 'his' mountain and, crucially, someone who had already applied to the Pakistani government to make an attempt in 1954. It wasn't Fritz Wiessner but a totally unexpected rival: Ardito Desio, an Italian explorer and geologist from Milan.

And while Charlie was beginning his long journey back across the Atlantic to the United States, Desio was about to fly in the opposite direction, to Skardu, the starting point for a reconnaissance of K2.

Chapter 9

THE OLD ROAD

But that wasn't quite how it turned out.

When Ardito Desio left Charlie Houston at Rawalpindi, he had indeed boarded a plane to Skardu, the starting point for his planned reconnaissance of K2, but on arrival events took a different course.

At the airfield there was a jeep waiting for Desio and his companion, the Italian mountaineer Riccardo Cassin, but instead of taking them toward K2, they were driven into the city for a meeting with the local political agent and asked to help with a problem that was far more important to the population than any mountaineering challenge.

For the last three months a huge glacier had been advancing down the Stak valley, a famous landmark halfway between Skardu and Gilgit, the ancient city in north west Pakistan. The Kutiah glacier had been growing at the staggering rate of just over a mile every month, 15 ft every hour, and had devoured acres of pastureland. Now it threatened to overwhelm the villages. Anyone else who had spent years trying to get to K2 would have listened attentively, expressed shock and concern and then made their excuses and left. But then again, if it had been anyone else, they would not have been asked to help.

Ardito Desio was very different from all the previous contenders for K2's crown. Short and thin with slicked back hair, a beak-like nose, and an air of purpose and energy, he was a geology professor and a prominent Italian academic. Aged fifty-seven, Desio was sixteen years older than Charlie Houston, and first and foremost a scientist rather than a climber.

He was born in 1897 in north east Italy and had studied geology in Florence before becoming a professor at the prestigious University of Milan. He first encountered K2 in 1929, nine years before Charlie Houston, when he had been appointed the official geologist to the little-known 1929 Italian expedition to the Karakoram mountains.

It was led by the Duke of Spoleto, the nephew of the Duke of Abruzzi, the Italian explorer who had played such an important role in K2's early history. On the twentieth anniversary of Abruzzi's pioneering expedition, Spoleto had hoped to lead a second Italian attempt on K2, which would finish off what his uncle had started. He had recruited a large team of climbers and geographers, including Ardito Desio, only to have his proposal turned down at the last minute by the Italian government.

The Fascist dictator Benito Mussolini had been very embarrassed a few years earlier when an Italian airship had crashed while attempting to reach the North Pole, so he had refused to invest any more of his country's prestige in anything so unpredictable as an expedition to one of the world's most dangerous mountains. Instead, the Duke of Spoleto had been forced to make do with a small scientific expedition to the Karakoram and promise not to set boot on K2.

Nevertheless, for the thirty-two-year-old Ardito Desio, the 1929 Karakoram expedition had been a defining moment: on his first visit to Asia the sight of K2 towering over the surrounding mountains had made an indelible impression. In the decade that followed Desio's star had risen in the Italian academic world as he led geological expeditions to Libya and Ethiopia, but once he had seen K2, he couldn't get it out of his mind. In the late 1930s he tried to organise another Italian K2 expedition but the Second World War had put an end to his plans. Too old to fight, Desio continued to work at the university and plan journeys to come, but post-war Milan was not an easy place to turn dreams into reality.

Italy emerged from the war a broken and divided country. The Christian Democratic Party won the 1948 general election with the covert support of the CIA but for years afterwards there were fears of an imminent Communist takeover. Coalitions formed and dissolved, and governments rose and fell as the economy slowly stuttered back into life.

The early 1950s didn't seem like a good time to raise money for another trip to K2, but after all the international attention generated by the French ascent of Annapurna and the British and Swiss expeditions to Everest, Italy's politicians had begun to show more interest. Government officials had made it known to the Italian Alpine Club that they might be willing to fund a large-scale overseas expedition if a suitable target could be found, and in 1952 the Italian Olympic Committee paid for Ardito Desio to visit Karachi to apply to the Pakistani government for permission to lead the second Italian expedition to K2.

When he reached Pakistan in August 1952, Desio was very disappointed to hear that he had been pipped to the post by Charlie Houston, who had already obtained the sole permit for the following year. But he wasn't willing to give up. There was no guarantee that Houston's team would succeed, and if they failed, it would leave the way clear for an attempt in the following year. So Desio asked the Pakistani authorities for permission to make a preliminary reconnaissance in the summer of 1953, aiming to return in 1954 with a full-blown expedition, if Houston and the Americans failed.

The authorities did not grant his wish straight away, but Desio was well known and well connected and at the time the Italian government was trying to foster good relations with Pakistan. Several large Italian firms were working in the north of the country on dams and infrastructure projects and it was hoped that in the future there would be more. When the Italian prime minister, Alcide De Gasperi, met his counterpart, Muhammad Ali Bogra, in Rome in the spring of 1953 he brought the matter up and a few months later Desio's reconnaissance was approved. This time the government-funded National Research Council covered his expenses and the Italian Alpine Club paid for Riccardo Cassin to accompany him.

When they left Rome on 18 August 1953, Desio and Cassin were on tenterhooks. As far as they knew, the Houston expedition was still on K2. If they had climbed it, there would be no 1954 Italian expedition. But had they? Reports in the Pakistani newspapers indicated that the Americans had suffered a setback but were just about to make a second attempt. With a news lag of about two weeks, no one knew about the death of Gilkey or Houston's retreat from the mountain. Just before he left Karachi, Desio heard reports that the American expedition had failed, but it wasn't until a few days later when he met Charlie Houston at Ata-Ullah's house in Rawalpindi that he found out exactly what had happened.

The Americans were very generous with their photographs and memories but Charlie also told Desio some less welcome news: he was planning to come back in 1954 to take a second crack and was convinced that the Pakistani government would approve. To add to the sense of international competition, Desio saw reports in the Pakistani press that Dr Karl Herrligkoffer, the successful leader of the 1953 Austro-German Nanga Parbat expedition, had also thrown his hat into the ring and hoped to lead a German team to K2 in 1954. According to *The Times of India*, Herrligkoffer was so confident that he had left a large cache of climbing equipment in Gilgit in the Hunza valley.[1]

Desio immediately made a long-distance call to the Italian Alpine Club, warning officials that there was now a fight on to secure the permit for 1954 and that 'our position is gravely menaced'.[2] Even if the Pakistani prime minister had already said yes to his counterpart, De Gasperi, it was only a verbal agreement and Desio had nothing in writing. America was obviously a much more powerful country than Italy and, as if that wasn't enough, the Italian ambassador to Pakistan had just left the country and his post was vacant. Desio wrote a letter to his sister, asking her to mobilise their friends and contacts in the government, warning that 'national prestige is at stake'.

The invitation to the Kutiah glacier had come at the worst possible moment. If Desio flew back to Karachi, he could lobby the Pakistani government directly over his permit for 1954 but it would mean sacrificing his reconnaissance. If he stuck to his original plans, and ignored the rogue glacier, he could see the reconnaissance through but it would seem undiplomatic. In the end science trumped mountaineering: instead of heading for the Baltoro or the political corridors of

Karachi, Desio and Riccardo Cassin began the long tortuous journey to the Stak valley.

They were odd tent mates, the sophisticated academic and the rough-hewn mountain man from north east Italy. Twelve years younger than Desio, Cassin was wiry and tough-looking. He had grown up in poverty, his father a peasant who left the family home for America when Riccardo was two. While Desio was studying at the University of Florence, Cassin was working as a blacksmith's assistant.

As a boy Cassin had been a talented and keen amateur boxer but in his late teens he discovered climbing and quickly realised that he had a gift for it. There was no stopping him: he climbed all the nearby mountains in Lombardy and was soon regularly venturing into the Alps. By the end of the 1930s Cassin was known as Italy's best rock climber. He had recently opened a climbing shop in Lecco in Lombardy, but when Ardito Desio invited him to join his K2 reconnaissance he had no hesitation in saying yes. Riccardo had never climbed outside of Italy and was thrilled at the chance of visiting the Karakoram.

After a five-day journey by jeep, pony and foot, Cassin and Desio reached the Stak valley and were indeed astonished to see the huge glacier, which had devoured everything in its path. Local shepherds told them that they had been forced to abandon their pasture and were afraid that their villages might also be overrun by this vast river of ice and rock. The advance of the Kutiah glacier had slowed in recent weeks, but the nearest house was just 2 miles away so everyone was worried.

The reports had not been exaggerated but, as Desio noticed, the other nearby glaciers were in retreat, so it did not make sense for the Kutiah to be advancing. After a more detailed inspection he worked out what had happened: some months earlier there had been a huge avalanche on a nearby mountain, Haramoush. The debris had fallen onto the Kutiah and had caused it to surge down the valley, but it was a one-off event and the rogue glacier was very unlikely to encroach any further. The shepherds might never get all their pasture back but their homes were safe. Without more ado, Desio and Cassin and their small troupe of porters set off for the Baltoro and K2.

For Riccardo Cassin it was a journey into wonderland, past spectacular mountains that made his beloved Alps look tiny. For Desio, it
was a trek down memory lane. At Urdukas in the middle of the Baltoro
glacier, he saw the tent platform that his porters had built for him in
1929 on the Duke of Spoleto's expedition and memories came flooding
back. He could not spare a lot of time for nostalgic reveries, though:
their diversion to the Stak valley meant that they didn't reach K2 base
camp until 26 September and there were already signs that winter was
approaching.

According to Desio's original timetable, they should have gone
round to the east face and climbed a high pass called Windy Gap to
get a good view of the mountain but Cassin and Desio got no further than Camp 1 at the foot of the Abruzzi ridge. They inspected
K2 through binoculars and compared what they saw to photographs
given to them by Charlie Houston, but with the skies threatening
snow and their porters almost out of food, after just one day on the
mountain they were forced to turn round and begin the long march
back to Skardu.

It was frustrating not to have done more but Desio was quietly
pleased. He had made good local contacts and their trip to the Stak
valley had been both fascinating and positive from the diplomatic
point of view. He was still desperate for written permission to return to
K2 in 1954 but after talking to government officials he now felt much
more confident. When he returned to Italy a few weeks later, it did not
take long to get the confirmation he craved. In a letter drafted in July
1953 but not dispatched until October, the Pakistani prime minister
confirmed that Professor Desio and the Italian Alpine Club would get
their wish. Italy was on its way back to K2.

This was amazing news and a real personal coup for Ardito Desio.
The only problem was time. It was mid-October and to stand a reasonable chance of success he would have to start organising straight
away. Desio's plans were on a different scale from anything attempted
previously. His aim, as he would repeat many times over the following year, was to 'conquer K2 not to make an attempt on it'.[3] This would
mean taking the same approach as the British on Everest in 1953, with

a large team and enough logistical support for a prolonged siege. And there was more: Desio didn't just want to conquer K2. While they were in the Karakoram he also wanted to run a second, purely scientific expedition, to build on the work he had begun in 1929.

All this was fine in theory, but lack of time was not Desio's only problem. He needed a lot of money, a team of crack climbers and the army of backroom boys that would be needed to train and equip them. He estimated that his expedition would cost about 100 million lira, or roughly $160,000,[4] around eight times more than Houston had spent and three times more than the 1953 British Everest expedition. This was an enormous sum of money but fortunately by autumn 1953 the Italian government was firmly behind the project. The National Research Council offered to put up 50 million lira and the Olympic Committee another twenty. The remaining money would come from the Italian Alpine Club, private individuals and future royalties from press articles and the expedition book.

For the second element, finding and equipping the team, Desio also turned to the Italian Alpine Club, which he had been a member of for many years. The club quickly set up a K2 committee, appointing Riccardo Cassin as the leader of the climbing team and Desio as overall president. Unlike the United States or Britain, where membership was comparatively small, the Italian Alpine Club was a large organisation with over 75,000 members. It owned mountain huts, had club houses in many towns and two publications. The club contacted their officials all over Italy and soon had a shortlist of twenty-three prospective climbers, aged between twenty-four and forty-seven. On 9 December letters were sent out inviting them to come to Milan in a week and informing them that if they got through the initial selection process, they would have to make themselves available for most of January, when the final team would be chosen.

Desio's approach was entirely different to anything seen before on K2. There would be no dilettante climbers like Dudley Wolfe or youngsters like Chappell Cranmer and George Sheldon. Instead of Charlie Houston's fireside chats to choose his perfect team, Desio planned to put his candidates through a series of medical tests and training exercises before whittling them down to an eight-strong squad of Italy's finest alpinists.

The selection process began with a lecture in which Desio outlined his plans and gave a detailed analysis of the successes and failures of previous expeditions. He emphasised that rigid discipline would be essential. The expedition, he said, would be organised along military lines, of a kind familiar to anyone who had served with a mountain regiment. Desio himself had fought with the 8th Alpine Regiment during the First World War and there were a number of candidates who had been *Alpini* during the Second World War.

After their initial briefing, the candidates were sent to two different areas of Milan University: the Medical Clinic and the Department of Human Physiology. They were subjected to blood tests, urine tests, maximum work-rate tests, electro-cardiograms, examinations of their lungs, feet, hands, and general physical and medical inspections. Once the results came back, six men were weeded out.

The rejection letters, sent at the end of December, thanked the unlucky few for their participation but informed them that their physical state was 'judged incapable of the exceptional performance that will be required for the leading climbers who will have to operate at above 8000 m'.[5] Everyone knew that first list was going to be reduced at some point but there were two big surprises. The first was the elimination of Cesare Maestri, a promising though headstrong young climber from Trento. The second rejection was even more shocking: the team's climbing leader, the legendary Riccardo Cassin.

His initial reaction was disbelief. At forty-four, Cassin was one of the older candidates but he was also by far the most experienced. He had won fame making the first ascent of the sheer north east face of the Piz Badile on the border of Italy and Switzerland and ascended the infamous Walker Spur on the Grandes Jorasses, one of the toughest challenges in the French Alps. Cassin had climbing routes and mountaineering equipment named after him and was highly regarded all over Europe. Crucially, he was the only member of the team, apart from Desio, who had actually been to the Karakoram. To reject someone who had only a few months earlier climbed to Camp 1 on K2 because he was not deemed fit enough to go to high altitude was incomprehensible.

So Cassin went for a second set of tests at the Italian Air Force's medical centre in Rome. The doctors told him not to worry: he was in excellent health, they said, and would have no problems. Their written assessments, they said, would soon follow and within a few months he would be on his way to K2. But the positive reports never saw light. Instead, at the end of January, Cassin was called to a meeting of the K2 committee and told that the examinations in Rome confirmed what had been discovered in Milan: he was just not fit enough.

A few weeks later Cassin sent the committee a registered letter, offering to help with equipment but resigning from the expedition. But if Riccardo was prepared to go quietly, his friends in the press were more vocal. The first in a series of controversies that would dog the expedition began on 27 January 1954 when the *Gazzetta Dello Sport*, Italy's most widely read newspaper, published a long article in which it questioned Cassin's exclusion, and the medical tests that led up to it. Why, it asked, had he even needed to be examined? After all, he had proved his climbing credentials many times over and, with national prestige at stake, shouldn't the Italian team have a strong climbing leader?

Ardito Desio told the press that it had nothing to do with him. He was the leader of the expedition and chairman of the K2 committee, but as he explained to journalists, though he would hand-pick the members of the parallel scientific expedition, it was up to the Italian Alpine Club to choose the climbing team. Cassin wasn't so sure. He did not really get on with Desio. During their reconnaissance in 1953, he had never felt like an equal. There had even been several occasions when Desio had flown but Cassin had been forced to travel by train.

When they had met Houston and the Americans four months earlier in Rawalpindi, Desio hadn't invited Cassin to accompany him to Ata-Ullah's house to get the full story of the American attempt. Instead he had had to make do with a snatched conversation at the airport before they left for Skardu. As far as Cassin could see, Ardito Desio just didn't want to share the limelight.

The dispute began to turn nasty with anonymous members of the committee briefing against Cassin, alleging that because of his varicose veins and problems with his liver, no insurance company was willing to provide cover for him. In the end, it was a fight that Cassin was bound to lose because Desio was simply too powerful a figure. A few newspapers campaigned to bring him back, or at the very least appoint a new leader of the climbing team, but nothing happened and the articles petered out.

Ardito Desio was the sole leader of this expedition and, even if it would soon be his fifty-seventh birthday and he wasn't regarded as an alpinist per se, he did not want a second in command. That could come later, on the mountain, far away from the press conferences and the radio interviews. What this expedition needed, as he said time and again, was rigid discipline and a strong leader. And besides which, by the spring of 1954 they had a much bigger crisis to overcome than the exclusion of a mere climber. The expedition needed money – and it needed it fast.

In February 1954, just two months before they were due to sail, Italy's latest coalition government fell apart and suddenly there was a question mark over the grant from the major backer of the expedition, the National Research Council. This body was supposed to put up half the money, but it had not arrived. To make matters worse, letters were appearing in the press questioning why the government was willing to put so much into a climbing expedition when the country had more pressing social needs. Even within the mountaineering community, there were people who questioned the wisdom of an attempt on K2, when Italy's current crop of climbers had no high-altitude experience whatsoever – apart from Riccardo Cassin, the excluded climbing leader.

The Italian Alpine Club held their nerve and borrowed 25 million lira, secured by the personal guarantees of individual club members and club property. They were confident that the outstanding money would come eventually and knew that if they were serious about mounting an attempt on K2 in 1954 they had no other choice. Equipment had to be procured and two training expeditions to the Alps had to be paid for.

The first took place in the Alps in mid-January when the climbers who passed the medical tests came together for a week of team building, tent pitching and equipment testing under the watchful, undercover eye of an officer from the Italian Army's Alpine Training School, who was employed by Desio and the club to identify the strongest, and weakest, candidates. At the end of the course, they were put through a third set of medical tests, which saw off another two men. The remainder were sent on a second nine-day camp high up on the Monte Rosa plateau, which involved further equipment tests and exercises to demonstrate leadership and teamwork.

Desio's original plan had been to take eight Italian climbers and three Sherpas from Darjeeling in northern India, but after the success of Tenzing on Everest in 1953, it was inconceivable that the Pakistani government would allow any Indian citizens onto its highest mountain.[6] So Desio forgot about the Sherpas and expanded the climbing team, taking eleven climbers plus a doctor, Guido Pagani, and a dedicated cameraman, Mario Fantin.

Of the final selection six were professional guides and ski instructors. Ubaldo Rey, Achille Compagnoni, Mario Puchoz and Sergio Viotto were 'Westerners' who plied their trade in the Italian Alps, mainly around Mont Blanc and the Matterhorn. Two, Lino Lacedelli and Gino Soldà, were 'Easterners' who worked mainly in the Dolomites, in north east Italy. Walter Bonatti, at twenty-three the youngest member of the team, ran a mountain refuge at the foot of La Grigna, the famous mountain in the Prealpi Lombarde, to the north of Milan.

The three non-professionals were all *accademici*, members of an elite section of the Italian Alpine Club who had done difficult climbs without the support of any guides. Cirillo Floreanini was a draughtsman from Udine, Ugo Angelino was a salesman from Biella and Pino Gallotti was a chemical engineer from Milan. Erich Abram, from Bolzano, straddled both camps, working sometimes as a guide and sometimes as a refrigeration engineer.

As for equipment, Desio did his initial research overseas. He met John Hunt, the leader of the 1953 Everest team, at Genoa in October

1953 and later travelled to England to see an exhibition of their clothing and equipment. He also visited Zurich to meet the organisers of the Swiss Everest expedition of 1952, and Vienna where he met climbers from the successful Austro-German team that made the first ascent of Nanga Parbat in 1953.

Like the British Everest Committee, Desio and the organisers of the Italian K2 expedition hoped that it might become a showcase for home-grown engineering and manufacturing. Several famous Italian firms were involved, including Olivetti, Pirelli and Perugina, which respectively provided the typewriters, rubber goods and chocolates, but time pressures meant the organising committee had to be pragmatic. They bought British boots for lower-altitude climbing and Swiss-made reindeer-skin boots for the higher camps. The Italian firm Gottifredi-Maffioli manufactured their rope from locally made nylon, and the French firm Moncler provided their duvet jackets. Desio decided that for the first time on K2 supplementary oxygen would be used. The cylinders came courtesy of the northern Italian metal foundry Dalmine, which supplied the expedition with 200 specially made lightweight models free of charge, but they also brought several sets made by Dräger, the German firm.

Though he was planning to do everything on a much bigger scale than his predecessors, Desio was very keen to talk to both Charlie Houston and Fritz Wiessner. In spite of their obvious rivalry, Charlie was gracious enough to send him more photographs and information. Fritz Wiessner was even more helpful. In the autumn of 1953, when he had learned of the failure of Charlie Houston's expedition, Fritz had briefly considered mounting a second expedition to K2, but when he discovered that the Italians had the permit, he dropped his plans and offered Desio whatever assistance he could give.[7] In early 1954 Wiessner and Desio met at Davos in Switzerland and soon began corresponding.

As ever, Fritz was very positive, though he warned Desio that acclimatisation, one of the key factors in the success or failure of an expedition, was very unpredictable: different men acclimatised at different speeds and some never did. As for sleeping at high altitude, he made the surprising revelation that in 1939 he had never slept soundly during the whole period when he was on K2:

> *The psychological effect of this will be damaging if a climber worries about it and believes that sound sleep is necessary. I am firmly convinced that sound sleep is not necessary as long as the body is at rest and the mind is free of worries and great mental problems.*[8]

Based on his discussions with Wiessner and Houston, and his research on previous expeditions, Desio provided each of the Italian climbers with a booklet, detailing the history of previous attempts on K2. Like Wiessner and Houston, he planned to take the by now familiar route up the Abruzzi ridge and use more or less the same campsites that they had. Vittorio Sella's photographs from 1909 remained a key visual reference point and expedition stores included the official account of both the Abruzzi expedition of 1909 and the Duke of Spoleto's follow-up in 1929.

As with all big expeditions there were plenty of last-minute crises, but in spite of everything they were able to dispatch a staggering 12 tons of supplies and equipment to Pakistan, over three times what Charlie Houston's team had taken, on the SS *Asia* on 30 March 1954. Two weeks later Desio flew from Rome to Karachi, followed soon after by his climbers. By the end of April, the four members of Desio's scientific team had also arrived and convened at Rawalpindi, to wait for the planes that would take everyone to Skardu.

As in 1953, Desio decided to appoint Mohammed Ata-Ullah as his liaison officer, but this time round the Pakistani doctor was an old hand, not an anxious novice. He found the Italians very different from the Americans. Apart from their leader, very few of them spoke any English so it was not so easy to bond. Ata-Ullah came to like and respect Desio but there was never quite the same easy rapport that he had enjoyed with Houston. Ata-Ullah's character sketch in his autobiography, *Citizen of Two Worlds*, gives a fascinating insight into what he saw as the contradictions in the Italian leader's character:

*Alternately he has two personalities: now the cool calculating
scientist, methodical, patient, precise, careful of the smallest
detail; now the intensely human man of action, freely indulging his moods in colourful speech and vigorous gesture. Like
the friendship that developed between us, his many friend-
ships were loyal and deep. His few enmities were implacable
and bitter. He was unusually kind, but he could be ruthless
when he thought it necessary.[9]*

Initially, Desio was distracted by all the dignitaries he had to meet and
the events he had to attend, but as the days passed and the planes for
Skardu failed to materialise he grew increasingly frustrated. In 1929 it
had taken fourteen days on foot to get from Rawalpindi to Skardu; this
time round they made the same journey in one and a half hours but
only after waiting around for ten days because of flight delays.

In compensation, when the planes finally arrived and ferried everyone to Skardu, Desio was offered an unexpected bonus: the opportunity to see K2 from the air. By 1954 there had been several flights
around Everest, but no aviator had ever ventured into the heart of the
Karakoram. The local flight operator, Orient Air, was willing to try, if
Desio footed the bill. It would be a dangerous flight, though: the DC3
had a ceiling height of 23,000 ft – 5000 ft below the summit of K2.
Just to get close they would have to fly over passes that rose to almost
21,000 ft. With the pilot's official map scaled at 1:1,000,000, the success of the flight would depend on Desio being able to translate his
ground-level knowledge of the terrain gained on previous visits into
a bird's-eye view.

It was risky but Desio was both confident and excited; in the 1930s
he had experimented with aerial mapping in North Africa, and when
he first conceived of the K2 expedition he had tried to interest the helicopter company Sikorsky in staging a series of air-drops to get equipment and supplies to base camp. It had come to nothing but Desio
was sure that in the future aircraft would become an important tool
for cartographers and geographers, so this was an ideal opportunity to
take aerial photographs of the region and get close to K2.

Just after dawn on the morning of 30 April, Desio, the expedition cameraman Mario Fantin and the three-man air-crew climbed aboard and slowly taxied down the airstrip. Their plane was not equipped with its own supplies of oxygen so they took five masks and seven bottles of gas that had been destined for the climbing team. After circling the airstrip twice to gain altitude, the DC3 headed for K2. At 20,700 ft the pilot donned his mask and eased his way up to 22,000 ft.

The weather was perfect with blue skies and the occasional wispy cloud. Mario Fantin, a bearded native of Bologna in northern Italy, was an experienced photographer and a keen amateur mountaineer. He had spent the last few days suffering from a stomach bug but he was determined to take part. He asked the team doctor, Pagani, to give him his most powerful medicine and he put up with a night of throbbing headaches as the pills worked their way through his system.

Now, as he shot roll after roll of film, Fantin revelled in the fact that he was capturing something that had never been photographed before. From above, the Karakoram range looked simply magnificent: Gasherbrum, Mitre Peak, Chogolisa, Staircase Peak, Broad Peak and finally K2, the 'mountain of mountains'.

With the plane cruising at 207 miles per hour, they did not have the luxury of time, so as Fantin's cameras clicked and whirred, Desio made a rapid visual examination of the summit of K2. It looked very, very steep and there seemed to be few options other than the route up the south east ridge outlined by Fritz Wiessner a few months earlier. As they flew past the east face, K2 reminded Desio of a vast medieval castle that would have to be attacked with 'all the means of assault that modern science could devise.'[10]

For the pilot, the flight required utter concentration. As he took his 95 ft wide plane down the Godwin-Austen glacier, he was only too aware that many of the surrounding mountains rose 5000 ft above his ceiling height. There was no question of turning round in the valley between K2 and Broad Peak, so he flew over Windy Gap to the north side of K2. Technically speaking, this meant entering Chinese airspace but there was no alternative.

Guided by Desio, he circled round the north and the west face, flying over an immense labyrinth of frigid glaciers and past dizzying peaks. Desio was tempted to carry on over the territory that he had tried to explore in 1929, but remembering the old Italian proverb 'Chi lascia la via vecchia per la nuova, sa quell perde e non sa quel trova' – 'if you leave the old road, you know what you'll miss but there's no way of telling what you'll find' – he told the pilot to return to the now familiar landmark of the Baltoro glacier. An hour later they landed in Skardu, packaged up Fantin's film and sent it back to Italy.

The flight round K2 had been wonderful and would be very useful for the K2 documentary but there was no time for rest. That morning, Gino Soldà, the oldest climber on the Italian team, marched off at the head of a column of 270 porters, the vanguard of a veritable army hired to carry the Italian team's equipment to the foot of the mountain. On the following day, former soldier Achille Compagnoni took the second gang of 172 porters, and on 2 April Ugo Angelino, the salesman from Biella and the team's logistics officer, followed with the final 60 Baltis, Ardito Desio and the remaining members of the climbing team. The conquest of K2 was under way.

The first stages of the approach march were the easiest. Over the last year, the Pakistani army had constructed several new bridges between Skardu and Askole, making the first half of the journey twice as fast as it had been for Houston's team in 1953. It took a while, though, for the Italians to get used to the strange stop-start rhythm of the porters. Although they had come equipped with twenty Urdu dictionaries, Ata-Ullah and his small team of Pakistani liaison officers played a vital role. As in 1953, there was a lot of petty pilfering, of everything from climbing gear to the very clothes that the Italians were wearing.

The main challenge for an expedition on this scale was to provide enough food for the porters. Each man needed about 2 lbs of flour a day to make chapattis. Over the course of ten days, that meant 500 men would consume around 10 tons. In the early stages a lot of that food was purchased in villages en route to the mountain, but after the last village, Askole, there was simply no opportunity to buy anything, so Desio had to hire another 100 men just to carry the flour for the main body of porters.

In addition to providing food, there was also the thorny issue of special equipment. Everything had been costed and weighed, so Desio had tried to get away with little more than a few tarpaulins for the porters to sleep under. This worked most of the time and, provided they were well enough paid, the incredibly resilient Baltis put up with little more than a blanket and the clothes they were wearing. However, the minimalist approach depended on good weather, and when the warm sun of the first week gave way to heavy rain and then snow, the porters became much more assertive.

By the time they reached Urdukas, snow was falling continuously. Last time round, on his reconnaissance in September 1953, Desio had enjoyed the lush grass and carpets of flowers, but when he awoke on the morning of 11 May, everything was covered in a thick blanket of white and the Baltis were huddled in groups, looking distinctly unhappy. With no protective clothing and no firewood to cook with, they refused to budge.

Ata-Ullah tried to persuade them to get going on the following day, offering extra baksheesh for anyone who reached K2, but Desio was worried. Every delay en route to the mountain meant another ton of flour had to be found somewhere. He briefly considered turning Urdukas into his base camp, as the Duke of Spoleto had in 1929, but it was too far from K2 to make any sense. The snow continued to fall.

Next morning around 120 porters declared they had had enough and turned back. The others continued to prevaricate until the sun came out at around midday. Then, after a lot of shouting, they picked up their loads and moved slowly back up on the glacier only to stop after a few hours.

That evening there was no new snow, but a bitterly cold night prompted yet more desertions. Those who stayed refused to leave camp but, rather than waste yet more hours arguing, Ata-Ullah advised Desio to carry on with the porters. Sure enough, when he looked back a few hours later he saw a line of men following him.

By the time they reached Concordia, the sun was blazing down. The mountains looked magnificent but the return of blue skies brought new problems. None of the Baltis had their own snow goggles, and though the Italian team had brought hundreds of pairs for this very reason, half of them had been abandoned at an earlier stage in an attempt to economise on loads. It didn't take long for many porters to become snow-blind.

Hundreds of them did get all the way to Concordia but most dumped their loads, grabbed their pay and left. By the end of the evening, Desio found himself surrounded by a sea of wooden crates, with no apparent way to get them any further. Next morning, he carried on to K2 base camp, but only one porter was willing to accompany him on the three-hour trek. To add to his problems, it started to snow again and didn't stop for two days.

The whole expedition had become a logistical nightmare with men and supplies spread out over three separate sites at Urdukas, Concordia and base camp. Desio was rattled and took out his frustration on the Italian climbers. When they arrived at Concordia, instead of a warm welcome, Desio read them the riot act, reminding everyone of the 'pact of obedience' they had signed back in Milan and demanding total discipline from now on.

Desio blamed Ugo Angelino, the thirty-one-year-old climber from Piemonte who had been in charge of the final column of porters, for the missing snow goggles and even threatened to send him back to Italy. Angelino had an easy smile and a gentle demeanour, but he wasn't going to be pushed around by Desio, especially when his leader was in the wrong. He retorted that it was Desio himself who had given the order to leave a crate of goggles behind. Furthermore, as the team's logistics officer, he insisted that he should be allowed to take an inventory of all the loads delivered so far. The other climbers supported Angelino, so for the first – and not the last – time in the expedition Ata-Ullah found himself acting as an intermediary between the expedition leader and his rebellious team.

When news of the delays reached the outside world, their porter troubles had been exaggerated to headline proportions. An American press agency reported that the Italians were lost somewhere in the Baltoro and Desio had become separated from the others. According to the *New York Times*, Dr Benedetto D'Acunzo, the Italian ambassador in Karachi, had asked the Pakistani Air Force to send out planes to search for the missing team.[11]

In Italy, the press was a little more circumspect. Desio's colleagues threw doubt on the reports, reminding journalists of his experience in the region. The fact that nothing had been heard from him for twenty-three days, they said, did not necessarily mean he was lost – after all, this was one of the remotest parts of the world and he was an experienced traveller.

Eventually, in early June, the Italian Alpine Club broke the tension with a press release based on a letter that Desio had dispatched from Urdukas. It reported that all was well; there had been problems and delays, but things were under control and, as the statement concluded, 'Everyone is in perfect health, the weather is getting much better and the landscape is undescribable'.[12]

It took many days to get all the climbers and equipment to base camp, but by the beginning of June everything was in place. Desio calculated that he was two weeks behind schedule but he was so pleased to have everyone there that he even gave his men a rest day.

Like everything else on the expedition, the Italian base camp was on a much bigger scale than anything previously seen on K2. The 'new Italopolis' centred around four large interlinked tents: the first was the communications room, with a radio transmitter powerful enough, in theory, to reach the nearest city, Skardu; the second was a common room and refectory with two long tables and a set of chairs; the third contained the expedition's food and equipment; and the last combined Desio's office and the expedition doctor's dispensary. In an ice cave nearby, they placed a small statue of the Madonna, presented to them by Cardinal Schuster, the celebrated Archbishop of Milan.

Though initially Desio had planned to model their rations on those taken by the British to Everest, their food had a distinctly Italian flavour, with plenty of pasta, rice and dried vegetables and, for special occasions, 4 lbs of culatello, the finest Parma ham money could buy.

Their favourite tipple was camomile tea, with hibiscus tea a close second. Victory would be celebrated with a large bottle of brandy.

Desio's climbing strategy was very different from that of Wiessner or Houston. Those expeditions were, he later wrote, lightweight 'attempts' on the mountain, as opposed to his 'heavy', much more single-minded, approach. Whereas Houston and Wiessner had given themselves about two months to climb K2, Desio had brought enough provisions for a much longer siege that could last into the autumn if necessary.

After a suggestion from Riccardo Cassin, the expedition's ousted climbing leader, they had taken 4 miles of rope, enough, one climber joked to *Life* magazine, to wrap K2 up 'like a package'. The plan was to fix permanent ropes all the way up the Abruzzi ridge, in order to allow climbers to move quickly up and down the mountain. In 1953 Houston's team had moved upwards en masse and in the middle stages had only climbed down very occasionally to collect mail. By contrast, Desio hoped that all the fixed ropes would enable his men to ascend and descend at will even from the high camps, and periodically return to base camp to rest.

If everything went according to schedule, they would spend the first half of June putting up five camps on the Abruzzi ridge, aiming to get above House's Chimney – or, as they renamed it, 'Il Camino Bill' – by the middle of the month. The second half would be devoted to the last three camps before the Shoulder. Then, all being well, they would try for the summit in the first two weeks of July.

At first, they made good progress, reaching the site of Houston's Camp 4 just under House's Chimney within two weeks. Desio split the team into two parties: the main climbing party which pioneered the route, and a support party which followed behind and consolidated each camp.

The leader of the climbing party was Achille Compagnoni, a former soldier turned mountain guide. He was broad-chested and stocky, with an expressive face that mixed toughness and good humour. Aged forty, he was one of the team's older climbers, but during the physiological tests at Milan University, he had shown himself to be amongst the fittest. From the outset, and especially during the Alpine training camps in January 1954, he had liked to take charge and had quickly become his leader's favourite.

The support party was led by Gino Soldà, a mountain guide who ran a sporting goods shop in the Dolomites. Aged forty-seven, he was the oldest member in the climbing team, but he had a reputation for being a brave and daring mountaineer, and was fit and strong.

As the Italians moved up the Abruzzi ridge they found food and fuel abandoned by Houston's party on their retreat down the mountain. At Camp 2 there was marmalade, ham and a supply of petrol; at Camp 3 there was more petrol and several tins of meat. There was no trace of Art Gilkey or his personal effects, but poignantly they did find the red embroidered K2 umbrella that Charlie Houston had brought from America in 1953. Mario Puchoz carried it down the mountain and presented it to Desio, like the standard of a fallen enemy.

As ever, the challenge was not just to get high on the mountain, but to haul up hundreds of kilos of supplies and equipment and set up a ladder of camps to the summit. Taking inspiration from the A-frame that Pete Schoening built in 1953, the Italians had brought a portable winch to haul gear and reduce the amount that had to be carried by porters. It worked so well that they improvised a second version attaching a pair of skis to some wooden packing crates. Working in tandem, it was possible to winch material all the way from the glacier to Camp 1 and then, after a brief muscle-powered transfer, from Camp 1 to Camp 2 at 19,900 ft.

If the winch worked better than expected, their Hunza high-altitude porters were initially a disappointment. In total Desio had ten men, specially selected by Ata-Ullah and their tribal leader, the Mir of Hunza. One man, Vilyati, had been on the American 1953 K2 expedition; two others, Amir Mahdi and Isakhan, had been with the Austro-German team on Nanga Parbat in the same year. None, however, seemed to be that keen to be on K2 this year.

This was a real problem, because unlike Charlie Houston who had not expected his Hunzas to go beyond the first few camps, Desio had hoped they would go much higher. The Italian climbers, however, found their new colleagues very difficult to work with. The Hunzas frequently complained that their loads were too heavy, so much so that the Italians had to reduce their weight to below their own. The only common language was English, but neither the Italians nor the Hunzas were anywhere near fluent, so they communicated using sign-language, cigarettes and smiles – backed, as the young climber from the Dolomites Lino Lacedelli remembered fifty years later, by the occasional threat with an ice-axe.[13]

In spite of their porter problems, work continued. By 20 June there was enough material stockpiled at the foot of House's Chimney for Achille Compagnoni to be thinking of taking the next step and moving on to the second half of the Abruzzi ridge. The weather was not great, but so far there had been none of the major storms that afflicted Houston's attempt in the previous year.

Everything was moving steadily forward until news came down to base camp from Camp 2 that no one had expected: Mario Puchoz, one of the strongest climbers on the Italian team, was dead.

Chapter 10

THE FLOWERS
OF ITALY

When young Walter Bonatti returned to base camp on the morning of 21 June and told everyone that Mario Puchoz had deteriorated, no one could quite believe it. Puchoz was the strongest Italian on the expedition, a bull of a man, short but powerfully built with a broad face topped by a wedge of dark brown hair. During the Second World War, he'd fought the Russians on the bloody Eastern Front and, unlike most of his regiment, had come back to tell the tale. Afterwards Mario lived quietly with his brother and sister in Courmayeur at the foot of Mont Blanc but everyone had a story to tell about him – how he'd carried a 143 lb box of ammunition through the mountains for fifteen days, how he and another guide, Eugenio Bron, recovered the body of a woman who had tried to climb Mont Blanc bare-legged, how he and his friend Albino had carried down an unconscious client... no mere cough or sore throat could hurt a man like Mario Puchoz.

Then an hour after Bonatti, the others came down. Nine men, weeping quietly, their faces marked with pain. Mario was gone. 'He had died in silence as he had lived,' wrote expedition photographer Mario Fantin, 'almost tip-toeing out of life in order not to disturb the people in the tent next to him.'[1]

Dead? Only a few days earlier, Puchoz had been humping loads up to Camp 4 beneath House's Chimney. He had seemed happy, in his element; some were already saying that he was strong enough to stake a claim on a place in the summit team. When Puchoz had radioed down to say he had a cough and was feeling bad, Guido Pagani, the expedition doctor, climbed up to see what was wrong, but he had gone more as a precaution than with any great fear.

When he arrived, Mario looked pale and admitted that he felt very low. Then he collapsed and Pagani realised that it was something far more serious. He had wanted to bring Mario back to base camp but the wind was so ferocious that it would have been madness to descend with a sick man. So Dr Pagani sent down for more medicine, and began administering antibiotics. When Puchoz's breathing grew strained, Pagani flooded the tent with oxygen but neither the drugs nor the gas were enough to save him. On the evening of 20 June Mario fell unconscious and a few hours later, at 1.00 a.m., he died.

As the returning men told their news, base camp fell quiet. No one could quite believe it. In 1939 Dudley Wolfe had been an accident waiting to happen, in 1953 Art Gilkey a long-drawn-out agony, but Mario Puchoz? One day he was carrying huge loads up the Abruzzi ridge, the next day gone. Dr Pagani called it 'galloping bronchopneumonia', a long word for a death that had come so quickly.

In a letter back to Italy, Ardito Desio's deep sense of shock was understated but all too apparent:

> I won't say anything else – K2 has taken another victim. All I
> say is that no one expected to lose a companion like this, even
> if on an expedition like ours you have to be prepared for things
> going wrong, sometimes seriously.[2]

Desio wanted to tell Mario's family in Italy as soon as possible but they still hadn't managed to make their radio transmitter work properly so the grim news had to be sent out by runner.

For the next three days a storm raged, confining everyone to base camp. Then, on the 25th, Lino Lacedelli, the mountain guide from the Dolomites, led a party of two Italians and three Hunzas up the Abruzzi ridge to retrieve Puchoz's corpse. The storm had left K2 covered in a thick layer of snow, making climbing both dangerous and exhausting. Two days later they returned in silence with a body bag. Just before base camp, Desio solemnly placed an Italian flag on top. Then Mario Puchoz was laid in his tent for one last night.

Early next morning they carried him to a grave dug into the rocks, close to the monument put up for the young American climber Art Gilkey eleven months earlier. Ubaldo Rey, another mountain guide based in Puchoz's hometown of Courmayeur, read an emotional funeral oration and they all sang 'Montagnes Valdôtaines, Vous êtes mes Amours!', the anthem of the local guides. After covering his corpse in soil and small stones, Puchoz's teammates planted a small wooden cross, engraved with a simple inscription:

Here lies Mario Puchoz, Mountain Guide from Mont Blanc,
Courmayeur January 1918, K2 the Abruzzi Spur June 1954.

The Hunza porters surrounded the cross with moss and wild flowers, then everyone filed back down to the mess tent at base camp to eat in silence.

Shock and trauma hung in the air. 'We had no idea how easy it was to die up here,' wrote Mario Fantin.[3] Back in Italy, the doctors at Milan University had warned them of the hidden dangers of climbing at altitude, but Mario Puchoz hadn't even been that high. He was at Camp 2, just under 20,000 ft. If K2 could take someone as tough as Mario in just a few days, then what hope was there for the rest of them?

Ardito Desio was rattled. It was 27 June and they were now almost a month behind schedule. According to his original plan, by now they should have reached Camp 8 on the Shoulder, the high plateau at 25,000 ft, and should have been preparing to put up the final camps before staging the summit attempt. They were nowhere near: their highest position was Camp 4 at 21,150 ft, almost 4000 ft lower.

Desio had to be firm. This was a decisive moment in the expedition and many of his men were now very nervous. So he made an announcement: the time for mourning was over, they should all get back to work straight away in spite of the continuing bad weather. There would be no better way to honour Mario Puchoz than to conquer K2.

Desio's motives might have been sound, but he misjudged the mood of his men. No one, apart from his favourite, Achille Compagnoni, was willing to go. Erich Abram, a very strong climber from Bolzano in the Tyrol, spoke up and said what they were all thinking: wouldn't it be better to wait for a decisive break in the weather before going back to the Abruzzi ridge? Desio went silent. He didn't like having his orders questioned.

Desio left the tent and the climbers split into groups to play cards. To an outsider it might have seemed strange, but as the Bolognese photographer Mario Fantin later wrote, this act of 'impotent rebellion' was the only way to deal with their fears and worries, and the sense of outrage they all felt at the idea of returning to the slopes of K2 on the very morning they had buried their comrade Mario Puchoz.

The team dynamics in 1954 were very different from the last three American groups. Charlie Houston's expeditions were generally happy and congenial: he was the leader and Bob Bates was his deputy, but they shared out the work and tried to give everyone a say in important decisions. Fritz Wiessner's 1939 attempt was much more hierarchical and ultimately more fractious, but, initially at least, there was a strong feeling of camaraderie. With Desio there was always a sense of distance; he would lecture and give orders, but, as Ugo Angelino later complained in a letter to the Italian Alpine Club, there were very few moments of kindness.

In many ways Ardito Desio had modelled his approach on the British Everest expedition of 1953 but his style was very different from that of its leader, Colonel John Hunt. Though Hunt was a serving soldier and a decorated war hero, he took a much subtler approach to man management than his Italian counterpart. Rather than deliver orders from on high, he would cajole and charm his men in order to get the best out of them. Hunt always tried to lead from the front, climbing high on the mountain, but Desio by contrast spent most of his time at base camp. To many he was a distant figure, always on the radio or at his typewriter, hammering out orders, but only rarely venturing upwards.

'Il Ducetto', 'little Mussolini', as some of the climbers were now calling him, was by instinct a strict disciplinarian. Before the team left Italy they had all been required to sign a document in which they agreed to follow his orders 'unconditionally and absolutely', but as the weeks turned into months, some of the climbers became unhappy with his leadership and the tone of the official 'messages' that he periodically issued.

Desio's words did carry weight, however; morale was low but no one wanted to give up yet. So next morning, Achille Compagnoni led the first party back up the mountain. A day later he and his good friend and climbing partner Ubaldo Rey managed to climb House's Chimney, 'Il Camino Bill', the climax of the first half of the Abruzzi ridge.

It was the Italian team's first big breakthrough in weeks but no sooner had Compagnoni radioed Desio to tell him the good news than the storms came back for a second swipe, trapping Compagnoni and Rey in their tents for almost a week. Eventually, the weather eased up but their bad luck continued. One of the most experienced climbers, Cirillo Floreanini, the draughtsman from the Friuli region, took a 700 ft tumble just above Camp 3 when an old fixed rope gave way. He escaped with bruises and cuts but it was a terrifying moment for both him and his companions.

To make life even more difficult, the arguments with their Hunza porters continued until finally Desio decided to make an example of three of the laziest men by sacking them. This made the others so angry they all threatened to down tools and leave the expedition altogether. It took a lot of persuasion from Ata-Ullah before they came back on board.

The biggest hurdle remained the weather. For years scientists had maintained that the monsoon, the heavy rains that hit India every summer and brought huge snowfall to the Himalayas, did not reach K2 and the Karakoram mountains. On the ground, however, it felt very different. Of the five previous expeditions that had attempted K2, three had been severely affected by storms and heavy snows and increasingly it looked as if 1954 would become the fourth.

Desio had come prepared for a long siege and grew weary of all the questions about the monsoon. He went back through his books and meteorological data and wrote a memorandum, telling his men to stop worrying. If necessary they could spend another two months at base camp, he said, and contrary to received wisdom they might even get good weather in August. His message climaxed on a patriotic note, and a threat:

> *If we were to return home before we had exhausted all the possibilities that remain to us of reaching the summit of K2, or without at any rate making a serious attempt on the peak, we would be breaking faith with the nation.*[4]

Desio's letters back to Italy, used for official press releases, were less strident: if only, he wrote on 12 July, they could get 'just one week of good weather',[5] they could get to the Shoulder and be in a position to attack the summit. It was a familiar refrain from 1939 and 1953, but as both Fritz Wiessner and Charlie Houston had discovered, wishing for clear skies was not the same as getting them.

In order to keep the momentum going, on 14 July Desio formally announced that Achille Compagnoni would direct the attempt on the summit. Compagnoni had been in the vanguard since the beginning and had shown his loyalty to Desio during the tense period after Mario Puchoz's death. While the other men might complain about their leader's manner, Compagnoni refused to get into what he regarded as futile arguments. As far as he was concerned, the boss was the boss, and their job was to follow orders.

Desio's message number 12, issued on 14 July, was his most bombastic yet:

> *I can assure you that the interest aroused by our undertaking is not less than created by the Everest expedition. Remember that if you succeed in scaling the peak – as I am confident you will – the entire world will hail you as champions of your race and your fame will endure throughout your lives*

and long after you're dead. Thus even if you never achieve
anything else of note, you will be able to say that you have
not lived in vain.[6]

Quite what the team made of this at the time is difficult to know but when, fifty years later, I interviewed Lino Lacedelli, the guide from the Dolomites who had become a key member of the team, he was scathing, saying, 'We just ignored him and got on with it.'

Aided by Desio's morale-boosting messages or not, his team was again making steady progress. On 18 July Achille Compagnoni and Ubaldo Rey made another significant breakthrough, reaching the Shoulder at 25,000 ft after a long gruelling day.

On the way up, Compagnoni passed a tangled knot of ropes, a blood-stained relic of the Americans' desperate attempt to bring Art Gilkey down. A little further on, there was more· a larger red shape with what looked like two arms swaying in the wind. For a few heartbeats Compagnoni thought it was Gilkey's body but when he came closer he realised that it was his jacket and sleeping bag, wrapped up in another mass of ropes. Evidently, as he fell down the mountain, Gilkey had become wedged in a rock before he was projected into the air. It was a frightening moment, a grim reminder of the dangers they faced.

Over the following days, aided by sterling work from Walter Bonatti, the young climber from Bergamo, they fixed ropes up a dangerous section beneath the Shoulder and established their seventh camp, a little higher up than Houston's. A new, unexpected problem emerged: Compagnoni and the lead climbers were moving so fast that the support parties, with food and tents, could not keep pace. The first six camps had been built up and stocked slowly and methodically, but there was now a much greater sense of urgency – if they were going to get up before August, they would have to move quickly.

Back home, the Italian press was getting very twitchy. The news of Puchoz's death was first reported on 7 July, prompting worried headlines. Now there were reports in two of Italy's biggest newspapers, Milan's *Corriere della Sera* and Turin's *La Stampa*, that the weather was so bad in the Karakoram mountains that no one could possibly climb

K2. In the spring of 1954 another Italian expedition, led by the well-known mountaineer Piero Ghiglione, had gone out to climb Mount Api in nearby Nepal. When reports came in that Ghiglione had lost three men, the mood grew even more pessimistic. If three experienced climbers could die on an expedition to Mount Api, a mere 23,400 ft, then how could anyone safely climb K2, 5000 ft higher?

In Milan, Vittorio Lombardi, the K2 expedition's treasurer, was forced to issue a statement denying the negative stories in the press. Yes, he admitted, it was not easy but, according to Ardito Desio's most recent letter, the expedition was still making progress and there was no reason to despair, quite yet:

> *Within a month whatever will happen will happen, because I don't think it will be possible to keep up the climbing effort any longer.*[7]

Over in America, as reports came in that the Italians had faltered, Charlie Houston wrote to Ata-Ullah, inviting him to return to K2 in 1955 with the fourth American expedition that he planned to lead. Ata-Ullah wrote back to say yes; like everyone else he held little hope that the Italians would succeed. Then something unexpected happened: the United Nations radio station in Skardu forwarded a message saying that the Karakoram was about to enjoy five to six days of blue skies. Was the long-awaited weather 'window' about to open?

High on the mountain it didn't feel like it. The meteorologists in Karachi might be predicting clear days but at 24,000 ft the winds were so violent, the climbers couldn't get any sleep. Remembering Charlie Houston's ten-day ordeal by wind a year earlier, morale sank. On 27 July Sergio Viotto and Ugo Angelino, two climbers who had coped really well so far, stumbled down into base camp, utterly spent after almost two weeks battling against the elements. K2 was taking its toll. Positive weather forecasts were not enough: if everyone was close to exhaustion, it didn't matter whether the skies were blue or grey.

Desio dispatched another letter to Lombardi in Milan, warning him that they might have to retire and try again in September. Some of the climbers would undoubtedly have to go back home but there was now so much fixed rope on the mountain, Desio wrote, that an attempt could be staged with a much smaller team. All he would need was four or five fresh men from Italy, and that elusive 'week of good weather'.

Desio hadn't quite given up hope on his summit team. On 29 July, accompanied by Mario Fantin, he took a short walk over the glacier to visit Mario Puchoz's grave and make a silent prayer that they might succeed. The expedition was coming to a climax and all they needed now was a little bit of good fortune.

Unknown to him, the climbers were once again making progress, albeit of the unsteady kind. A day earlier, Achille Compagnoni had led a five-man party out of the tents of Camp 7 and climbed up the Shoulder toward the final summit cone. With so much fresh snow it was a long slow grind, which didn't take long to see off Ubaldo Rey, Compagnoni's great friend from Courmayeur.

Rey was thirty-one, an Alpine guide and the guardian of a mountain refuge on Mont Blanc. Tall and thin with a gold tooth and a twinkle in his eye, he was a strong and cheerful companion on the rope. Achille Compagnoni had hoped that Ubaldo would be his partner on the final attack on the summit but after a few hundred feet Rey had to go back to Camp 7, defeated by the altitude. The others carried on, until they came to a high ice-wall at around 25,400 ft. The tip of K2 was just visible, though it was impossible to see the entire route to the summit.

In order to economise on weight, they had only carried up one small tent, so two of the climbers, Erich Abram and Pino Gallotti, followed Ubaldo Rey back down to Camp 7, leaving Achille Compagnoni and Lino Lacedelli to spend the night alone. Though he had never thought it possible that he would ever play a prominent role, Lino Lacedelli, the twenty-eight-year-old guide from the Dolomites, had now become the second member of the summit team.

In fact, Lacedelli had a far better climbing record than Compagnoni. Tall and thin with two prominent gold teeth, he was one of the famous 'Squirrels' of the Dolomites, the small but illustrious Italian climbing club.[8] He had already made dozens of first ascents of difficult routes and was also a member of the French club, Le Groupe de Haute

Montagne, which included some of the best climbers in Europe. Back home in Cortina D'Ampezzo, the exclusive mountain resort in north east Italy close to the Austrian border, Lino worked as a ski instructor and mountain guide.

Though he was well liked by the other members of the team, Lino had not really been thought of as a particularly ambitious character. He was a modest man, a little rough around the edges but a team player and a safe climbing partner. So far on the expedition he had done well but he had never warmed to Desio, and as one of the 'Easterners' from the Dolomites, he never felt that he was taken quite as seriously as the guides from the Alps, the 'Westerners'. All that, though, was in the past; however surprised he was to be in this position, Lino was determined to make the best of it.

Achille Compagnoni explained to him that the plan was to put up one more camp on the next day, in order to get as close as possible to the gully underneath the summit cone. It had defeated Fritz Wiessner in 1939, but the Italians hoped that, better equipped, they could climb it and then strike out for the summit. But before that could happen, someone would have to bring up the oxygen sets.

Originally, the Italians were supposed to have used supplementary oxygen from roughly 24,000 ft upwards. Neither Wiessner nor Houston had thought it necessary, but after the British triumph on Everest, Desio was convinced that oxygen would make the difference between success and failure. The Italian team had brought out 230 bottles and piled them up behind base camp but so far they had not been used for anything other than the flight around K2 and for medical purposes. The big hurdle, as the British Everest team had realised a year earlier, was getting the precious but heavy cylinders up the mountain.

Whereas in 1953 John Hunt had a twenty-two-strong team of Nepalese and Tibetan Sherpas to act as high-altitude porters, Desio had just nine Hunza porters, of varying experience and aptitude. So though a few oxygen sets were carried up, most of the gas was left languishing behind the mess tent at base camp. When the Italian climbers realised that they could get on perfectly well without it, that's where it stayed.

For the final attempt on the summit, however, it would be different. The term 'death zone', or 'zone fatale', was first used by Edouard Wyss-Dunant, the leader of the 1952 Swiss Everest expedition, to describe the region above 26,000 ft where there is not enough oxygen to sustain human life. In 1954 everyone on the Italian team was convinced that any attempt on the summit without supplementary oxygen would be fatal. Even if physiologically the Italians could have survived without it, psychologically oxygen was essential.

Its importance didn't make it any easier to carry, though; a complete oxygen set weighed roughly 40 lbs, a heavy load and an awkward one. On 29 July, while Compagnoni and Lacedelli ascended the ice-wall above their tent to locate a site for their final camp, their four teammates down at Camp 7 attempted to carry up two oxygen sets, along with more supplies and camp equipment. They didn't get far. Once again Compagnoni's friend Ubaldo Rey was defeated by the altitude and the Bolzano climber Erich Abram turned back with him.

The other two men in the support party, Walter Bonatti and the 6 ft 'beanpole' Pino Gallotti, were faced with a dilemma: should they

28,251 ft
26,600 ft
25,400 ft
SHOULDER
24,600 ft

Map 7   The final Italian camps on K2

carry up the two heavy oxygen sets or take a second tent and provisions for the summit party? In the end they decided on the latter and left the oxygen in the snow, aiming to carry the bottles up on the following day.

When Bonatti and Gallotti finally reached Camp 8 at 25,400 ft, they found the summit pair exhausted after a hard day's climbing. Compagnoni told the new arrivals that he and Lacedelli had managed to reach the top of the ice-wall above their current tent and had cached two rucksacks' worth of equipment in the snow. Rather than forge ahead and establish Camp 9, their final shelter, they had decided to wait another day. Without the oxygen sets, they couldn't make an attempt on the summit anyway. So the question was: when would they get them and who precisely would carry up the oxygen?

Pino Gallotti was brave, tough and easily the tallest man on the team. Back in Milan he worked as a chemical engineer, but he spent as much of his time as possible in the mountains and was one of the expedition's four *accademici*, elite climbers who had proved their skill on other mountains.[9] Fresh-faced Walter Bonatti was the baby of the team but he was already a rising star in the mountaineering world. He had been ill several times on the expedition, but his climbing skill and ambition were obvious to everyone, and as the expedition reached its climax, he seemed to be full of energy.

After a snatched supper, the four men held a council of war. The plan that emerged was more demanding on the support team than the summit pair. In the morning, Compagnoni and Lacedelli would re-ascend the ice-wall and carry on going until they found a suitable site for their final camp. In the meantime, Bonatti and Gallotti would retrieve the oxygen sets abandoned above Camp 7, carry them back up to Camp 8, and then follow in Compagnoni and Lacedelli's bootsteps as far as their final tent, Camp 9.

It was a huge challenge for the support team: in total they would have to descend 600 ft and then re-ascend a further 1000 ft. Between them, they would have to carry roughly 80 lbs of oxygen equipment but they would not be able to use any gas themselves. With a bit of luck, they might just be joined by their teammates Erich Abram and

Ubaldo Rey, who had retreated to Camp 7, as well as any Hunza reinforcements who had come up from below. However, if no one else was willing or available, somehow Bonatti and Gallotti would have to carry the heavy oxygen sets by themselves. It was a daunting prospect for Bonatti and Gallotti, but with the weather still uncertain and the expedition's supply chain overstretched, everyone realised that they had to move as quickly as possible.

After a bitterly cold night, the summit pair and their support party were up at 6.30 a.m. It took a good hour and a half before they were ready to leave; at high altitude, even small tasks like putting on their boots and crampons seemed to take forever. Then Compagnoni and Lacedelli headed up, leaving Bonatti and Gallotti to head down toward the oxygen sets they had abandoned a day earlier.

At Camp 7, reinforcements had finally materialised. A partially recovered Cirillo Floreanini, the climber who had taken a fall a few weeks earlier, had arrived with two more oxygen sets and two Hunza porters, Isakhan and Amir Mahdi. They were the strongest Pakistanis on the team, both veterans of the successful Austro-German expedition to Nanga Parbat of 1953. Ubaldo Rey was still feeling very sick so he had decided to descend with Floreanini, leaving the two Hunzas and Erich Abram, the resident oxygen expert, to assist the men above.

In the middle of the morning, Abram and the two porters met Bonatti and Gallotti just above Camp 7 and learned of the latest plan. Though there were now four oxygen sets available, the combined party decided to carry up just two, along with food and fuel and some spare sleeping bags and air mattresses. Then, with Walter Bonatti in the lead and Gallotti struggling behind, the three Italians and two Hunzas began the gruelling ascent back to Camp 8.

A few hours later they reached the tents at 25,400 ft and slumped down to make some soup. As he looked at his companions, Bonatti realised that he wasn't going to get much help for the next stage of his mission. His friend Pino Gallotti and the Hunza Isakhan both looked totally exhausted, and Erich Abram didn't seem much better. The other porter, Mahdi, was in surprisingly good shape but Bonatti wasn't sure that he would be willing to go any further. None of the Hunzas had been equipped with high-altitude boots because no one had expected that they would get this far.

Bonatti knew that if they couldn't get the oxygen up to Compagnoni and Lacedelli, the summit attempt would not take place. So as the Italian climbers had done many times on this expedition, he offered Mahdi a cash bonus and even hinted that if it all went perfectly, he might even reach the top himself. Tenzing's ascent of Everest a year earlier had brought him worldwide fame and rich rewards, so maybe the same thing could happen to Mahdi.

Fame, wealth, or just a few more rupees of baksheesh... whatever the reason, it worked. Two hours later Mahdi and Bonatti left camp carrying the oxygen sets, a small bag of tools and nothing else but their ice-axes and a length of rope. They carried neither sleeping bags nor a tent of their own; that night, they would either have to descend or squeeze in with Compagnoni and Lacedelli at Camp 9 and keep warm as best as they could. It wouldn't be comfortable but they simply couldn't carry anything else. Erich Abram offered to join them for a few hours of carrying but he warned that he would probably not be able to go all the way.

While the support party was organising itself, several hundred feet higher up Compagnoni and Lacedelli were approaching the final summit cone. When they reached the icy channel, or couloir, today known as the 'Bottleneck', they found it very different to Fritz Wiessner's description. In 1939 its surface had been hard ice, impossible to ascend quickly without crampons, but now it was choked with deep, powdery snow.

Compagnoni didn't like the look of it, either as a potential climbing route or campsite, so instead of pitching their tent at the foot of the Bottleneck as originally envisaged, they moved over to their left, carefully crossing some icy slabs of rock. It took almost an hour to find a large enough spot, though large was hardly the right adjective. At 6 ft 6 in long and 30 in high, their specially designed 'Super K2' tent was so cramped that their feet projected out of the flap.

Unlike Hillary and Tenzing, who had spent the night before their ascent of Everest feasting on tinned peaches, crackers and sardines, the Italians had brought very little food apart from soup and camomile tea. And whereas the New Zealander Ed Hillary had spent a lot of time carefully going over his and Tenzing's oxygen sets to make sure that all the valves were clear and the gas flowing freely, all Compagnoni and Lacedelli had in their rucksacks were the masks and connecting tubes. The rest of their sets and the precious oxygen cylinders had not yet arrived.

If they were worried, it was even worse for their support party. At around 4.30 p.m. Walter Bonatti reached the top of the ice-wall above Camp 8. He shouted up to Compagnoni and Lacedelli and was relieved to hear a response. They told him to follow their tracks but as the hours slipped by and the temperature dropped he became increasingly worried. Where was their tent? Why hadn't they put it lower down to make it easier for the support party arriving with the heavy sets? When the sun began to set just after 6.00 p.m., it became even colder. Erich Abram complained that one of his feet had gone numb so Bonatti stopped to massage it. Abram got some feeling back, but he had reached his limit so he left Bonatti and Mahdi to carry on alone and headed down to Pino Gallotti at Camp 8.

Higher and higher Bonatti and Mahdi climbed into the twilight, stopping only occasionally to take off their heavy sets and check the terrain above, but they could see no sign of their teammates' bright orange tent. Compagnoni and Lacedelli's tracks had disappeared, filled in by the snow and wind, so they just had to hope for the best. At one point, Bonatti contemplated abandoning the oxygen sets and descending but it was too risky. There was so much loose snow around, the oxygen could easily get covered up and never be seen again. So on they went, with Mahdi becoming more and more agitated and still no sign of the summit team.

Finally, a few hours later, with the sky growing ever darker, Walter Bonatti realised that they would never reach their comrades and there was no alternative but to stop and bivouac in the open. They were in the middle of a steep icy gully, around 650 ft high; he might be able to get down, but there was no way that Mahdi could descend safely. So Bonatti used his ice-axe to hack out a narrow platform, all the time cursing Compagnoni and Lacedelli for abandoning them. It didn't make any sense – why had Compagnoni and Lacedelli put their tent so high? How could they make an attempt without the oxygen?

Suddenly out of the gloom, Bonatti saw a small beam of light to his left. It was impossible to work out quite how far above them its source was, but Bonatti finally heard a voice. It was Lino Lacedelli and he could just about make out what he was saying.

'Have you got the oxygen?'

'Yes.'

'Then leave it where you are and go down.'

As the two Italians shouted at each other, Mahdi made a dash toward the light crying out to the sahibs above.

'Don't come up, it's too dangerous,' Lino Lacedelli shouted back. The icy rock slabs below their tent had proved treacherous to cross earlier in the day; it would be suicidal to attempt them at night. Mahdi kept on going and only stopped when the light disappeared. He desperately called out to the two sahibs above but there was no reply. Lacedelli had retreated out of the wind into his tent, sure that no one could possibly follow and that Bonatti and Mahdi were by then on their way down.

He was wrong. A few minutes later, Mahdi returned to Bonatti, but he was in no state to descend – the icy slope below them was steep and he was far too agitated for some tricky climbing in the dark. As Bonatti knew, their only hope was to hunker down for the night and descend at first light. A year earlier on Nanga Parbat, the Austrian Hermann Buhl had survived a bivouac, or night out in the open, at 26,000 ft. Now it was their turn to suffer.

They were an odd couple, thrown together by circumstances that neither could ever have envisaged. Walter Bonatti was a twenty-three-year-old free spirit, who had give up a safe job in the city to follow his passion as a mountaineer. Amir Mahdi was a forty-one-year-old porter from the village of Hasanabad in the remote Hunza valley of northern Pakistan. Tall with a sensitive face, he had proved himself to be one of

K2 from the Godwin-Austen glacier. (Mick Conefrey)

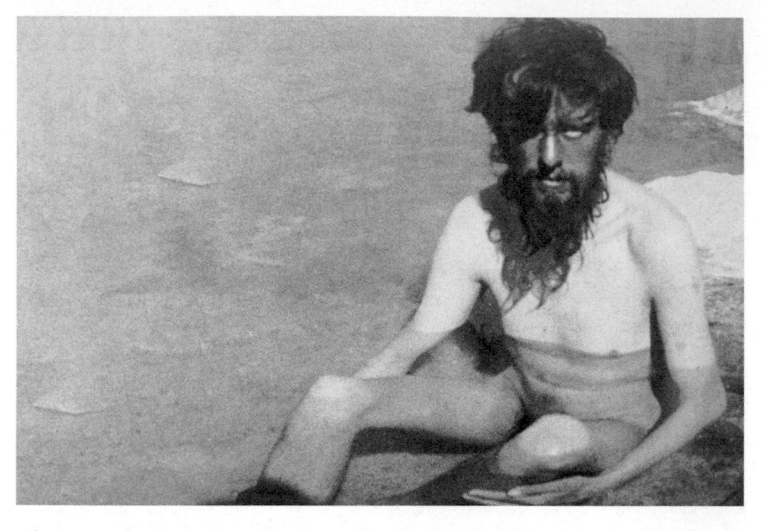

Aleister Crowley takes a bath on the way back from K2. He went for 85 days without washing. (Jules Jacot-Guillarmod)

The 1902 K2 Expedition. From left to right: Victor Wessely, Oscar Eckenstein, Jules Jacot-Guillarmod, Aleister Crowley, Heinrich Pfannl, Guy Knowles. (Jules Jacot-Guillarmod)

The returning 1938 K2 Reconnaissance expedition. From left to right: Bob Bates, Paul Petzoldt, Charlie Houston, Bill House, unnamed Baltis. (The Ed Webster collection)

Fritz Wiessner, a portrait from the 1940s. (The Wiessner Family)

Happy days: Jack Durrance, Fritz Wiessner, Dudley Wolfe, Genova 1939 before setting sail for K2. (The Wiessner Family)

The 1953 K2 Expedition pose with a flag painted by Dee Molenaar. From left to right: Bob Bates, Tony Streather, Charlie Houston, Dee Molenaar, George Bell, Bob Craig. (George Bell)

Charlie Houston, 2001, with his embroidered umbrella retrieved from K2 by the Italian 1954 team. (Mick Conefrey)

Art Gilkey, K2 base camp. (The Houston Family)

The 1954 K2 expedition. (Centro Documentazione Museo Nazionale della Montagna)

Walter Bonatti, left, at base camp August 1954 with a bandaged Lino Lacedelli. (Getty Images)

The contentious K2 summit photographs published in *The Mountain World* 1955 and then re-analysed by Robert Marshall in 1994 for *Alp*. Compagnoni, left and Lacedelli, right.

A frost bitten Achille Compagnoni, left, and Lino Lacedelli, right, at base camp August 1954. (Centro Documentazione Museo Nazionale della Montagna)

The Gilkey Memorial, 2000: since it was built in 1953 many more plaques have been attached to it. It is a moving memorial to those whose bodies are still lost on the mountain. (Mick Conefrey)

the strongest high-altitude porters in the previous year on the expedition to Nanga Parbat, but right now he was a desperate man.

Bonatti took off their crampons to help their blood circulate. For the next few hours, the two men clung to each other, massaging their limbs to keep warm and occasionally thumping themselves with their ice-axes to maintain their circulation. The Italian was desperately cold but he was grateful that the wind had died down. Then suddenly a storm sprang up and scoured their faces with a mass of icy, swirling snow. Bonatti tried to dig further into the slope for protection but the cold was excruciating.

As soon as the first glow of dawn hit the surrounding peaks, Mahdi decided to leave. Experience told Bonatti that it would be better to wait till the sun rose completely but, having restrained his companion several times during the night, he had no more energy to fight him. Instead he helped Mahdi put his crampons back on and watched as the Hunza porter tottered down the slope. They were anxious minutes for Bonatti; the storm had filled the gully with snow, which hadn't had time to consolidate. It would be very easy to set off an avalanche but fortunately Mahdi survived the descent, allowing Bonatti to breathe easier.

When the sun came up properly he too finally moved from his frozen perch but before going down he cleared the snow from the oxygen sets he and Mahdi had taken such pains to carry up. Then very carefully he began to descend without having seen or heard anything more of Lacedelli and Compagnoni.

When Bonatti reached the bottom of the gully and began threading his way through the maze of crevasses below, he heard a shout from above but he couldn't see where it had come from. He waved his ice-axe in the air in recognition and then carried on down. Just before he climbed down the ice-wall to Camp 8, Bonatti scanned the slopes above him for a last time, but apart from the brightly coloured oxygen sets, he could see nothing but snow, ice and the reddish rocks of the summit cone. Where were Lino and Achille?

For their part, Lacedelli and Compagnoni were utterly shocked when they spotted someone below. At first they weren't even sure whether the figure was ascending or descending but then it dawned on them that it must be either Bonatti or Mahdi, and that, incredible though it seemed, they must have spent the night bivouacking on the mountain. This didn't make any sense at all – no one would willingly risk a night out at 26,000 ft – but there was no other explanation.

After a difficult night of their own, spent shivering in and out of sleep, this was a disturbing start to the day, particularly for Lacedelli, who had been the last one to speak to Bonatti. Compagnoni was more bullish: whatever had happened there was no time to worry about their support party – if they didn't get going straight away, then they simply wouldn't make the summit. But what should they do about the oxygen sets? Climb down over the icy slabs of rock below to get them or set off for the summit under their own steam like Fritz Wiessner in 1939? For a moment Compagnoni thought it might be possible but just a few steps upwards convinced him he needed all the help he could get. So the two Italians headed toward the oxygen sets, taking a slightly longer and safer-looking route than they had used on the way up.

Lino Lacedelli was wearing all the clothes he could muster – three pairs of trousers, two pairs of gloves, two pairs of stockings, several shirts, an eiderdown jacket and a wind-suit – but he still felt very cold. Whenever he took off his heavy gauntlets to strap on his crampons or wipe the moisture from the inside of his snow goggles, he could feel his gloves getting damper and his fingers growing more and more numb.

When Compagnoni and Lacedelli reached the oxygen sets, they realised that they would have to abandon their rucksacks to keep weight down to the minimum. Both were carrying 35 mm stills cameras and spare rolls of film, but apart from a handful of sweets, neither took any food or water. Compagnoni carefully attached the small 16 mm movie camera that expedition cinematographer Mario Fantin had given him to the aluminium frame of his oxygen set. The official Everest film had climaxed with a still photograph of Tenzing on top, but Compagnoni was determined to go one better and bring back the first moving footage from one of the world's highest peaks.

If they had been asked six months earlier how the expedition would pan out, neither man would have dared suggest that they could be in this position now. Desio's team contained several climbers with much better track records; four were respected *accademici*, and amongst the professional guides there were others with more mountaineering experience. And yet here they were, Achille and Lino, aiming to make history and climb the hardest mountain in the world.

As they opened the valves and let the oxygen flow, they both got an instant boost. Each of their sets held three small bottles, designed to provide a total of around ten hours of gas. The main problem was the weight: 40 lbs of aluminium, steel and pressurised gas was a burden at any altitude and a real penance at 26,000 ft. The other question was whether the sets would work properly. Remarkably, this was the first time that oxygen had been used for climbing on the Italian expedition. Ardito Desio had taken several cylinders on his flight around K2 and Dr Pagani had treated the ill Mario Puchoz with oxygen, but most of these heavy cylinders were never used. Compagnoni and Lacedelli had no problems connecting up the tubes and masks but their oxygen bottles had spent the last two nights languishing in the snow – probably not what the engineers would have recommended just before a summit attempt.

When they reached the Bottleneck, their planned route to the top, they found it in no better state than on the previous day. In 1939, on his second attempt, Fritz Wiessner had been forced to retreat because it was so icy and he had no crampons. Fifteen years later, their problem was entirely different. They would have gladly cut steps or cramponed their way up but there was far too much loose snow to make such an approach possible.

Instead they moved leftwards and tried clambering up the nearest patch of rock. After two frustrating hours they had achieved nothing apart from depleting their oxygen reserves so they moved further across toward another wall of rock, closer to Wiessner's first route, and tried again. Compagnoni made the first attempt but fell back down after just a short distance. Then Lino, 'lo Sciattolo', the squirrel, took over.

It was too cold and overcast to climb bare-handed like Fritz Wiessner in 1939 but Lacedelli took off his outer gloves and his crampons before he started. Above him soared a very steep, awkward-looking rock pitch about 100 ft high. If he could reach the top, the angle eased off but it was a real challenge for anyone carrying a bulky oxygen set. It took several very tricky manoeuvres and a few prayers and curses but eventually he made it, brought Compagnoni up and let him take the lead.

The first bottle of oxygen ran out shortly afterwards, the second a few hours later. Their sets were designed so that empty cylinders could be thrown away thus reducing the burden. With each bottle weighing about 13 lbs, this was obviously a good idea though not an environmentally friendly one. Compagnoni and Lacedelli, however, were in too much of a hurry, or simply too unfamiliar with their equipment, to behave as the manufacturer recommended. They did abandon one of their empties but in spite of the weight carried on up with the other empty bottle.

The route was very mixed, with passages of hard ice interspersed with steep rock and even more dangerous stretches, where loose layers of snow made avalanches a real threat. Some sections were so difficult to ascend that they ended up hammering their ice-axes into the slope and standing on them. This unorthodox technique worked but it was always a little uncomfortable for the man below who invariably got showered with freezing shards of ice. Lino Lacedelli found his goggles kept misting up; every time he wiped them, his gloves grew damper and his hands colder and colder. Nevertheless, in spite of several slips and slides, they kept on going.

Then just when they thought they were winning came the moment that no one expected but everyone feared: their third oxygen cylinder ran out. Lacedelli felt as if his head was being crushed by a huge weight, and his legs went alternately hot and cold. For Compagnoni, it was as if a steel hand was crushing his temples. He unfastened his mask and sucked the air in.

For a few desperate minutes all they could do was stand still. Back in Italy, the physiologists had warned them of the dire consequences of running out of oxygen at high altitude, but after a few minutes to their surprise they realised that they weren't just about to die and that they could actually breathe. In order to check they were still capable of rational thought, they began naming the other mountains around them – Broad Peak, Masherbrum, Gasherbrum, Skyang Kangri.

Then unexpectedly, as if to urge them on, the band of cloud that had hung below all day suddenly parted revealing the tents of Camp 8 and five tiny specks craning upwards. The sight of their friends below was just the boost they needed.

Above stretched the final snow slope leading to the summit. It was impossible to tell how long it would take but there didn't seem to be any more rock climbing. So they put their heads down and kept on going, not even stopping to dump their now empty oxygen sets. In the rather sober account given in the official expedition book, *The Conquest of K2*, Compagnoni and Lacedelli recalled hearing a slight buzzing in their ears, but as they later admitted the experience was much stranger.

At one point Lino Lacedelli became convinced that his fiancée was behind him, and then later he saw a friend and fellow climber from the Dolomites, Guido Lorenzi. Compagnoni's hallucinations were equally vivid: first he saw their dead comrade, Mario Puchoz, following them, then he sensed a woman's presence – she was no relation to Lacedelli's fiancée, though definitely female. Compared to the 'flying teapots' that British climber Frank Smythe reported at 28,000 ft on the 1933 Everest expedition, their visions were rather mundane but they were disturbing nonetheless.

Down at base camp, Ardito Desio was burning with frustration. The last contact he had had with the advance party was three days earlier on 28 July. As the Italian radios worked only on line of sight and Camp 8 was not visible from below, it was not possible to talk to anyone without making a long risky trek up the Godwin-Austen glacier to Windy Gap. All he could do was wait and hope.

At Camp 8, it was very different. Bonatti and Mahdi had returned several hours before and were recuperating in their tents. The Hunza porter was in a bad way with frostbitten hands and feet but Bonatti had survived his ordeal remarkably unscathed. As he explained to his comrades, he had had no contact with Lacedelli and Compagnoni, bar a brief snatched conversation a night earlier. Where they were on the mountain, he really had no idea. All he and anyone else could do was stare upwards and hope to see them.

The first part of the route to the summit was hidden by the ice-wall but the rest was visible, though frequently obscured by clouds. At around 5.30 p.m., the Hunza porter Isakhan thrust his head into the tent where Bonatti, Abram and Gallotti were resting. 'A sahib is about to climb K2!' he shouted in English, echoing a famous line from the 1953 Everest expedition.[10]

As they ran out and craned their heads upwards, they saw two tiny figures slowly advancing up what looked from below like the last few feet, silhouetted against a clear blue sky. As Pino Gallotti wrote in his diary, it was an amazing moment:

> On the final slope, which was incredibly steep looking, first one tiny dot, and then a second, slowly made their way up. I may see many more things in this life, but nothing will ever move me in the same way. I cried silently, the teardrops falling on my chest.[11]

For Compagnoni and Lacedelli, their arrival on the summit of K2 was a moment of quiet realisation, rather than high drama. After a long slog, the final slope simply ran out, leaving them in the middle of a large open area, big enough, they estimated, to hold over 100 people. They linked arms, took a symbolic final step and embraced before falling back into the snow to finally get rid of their oxygen sets. The epic saga of K2 had come to a climax, with the mountain declared impossible by the Duke of Abruzzi in 1909 falling to an all-Italian team.

Unlike Hillary and Tenzing, who had famously buried a crucifix and some sweets on the summit of Everest as offerings to the gods, they had nothing to leave in the snow. They did, however, have their 16 mm movie camera and their two stills cameras to record their triumph. Lacedelli posed for a classic shot, standing next to the abandoned oxygen sets, his hands in his pockets, ice covering his beard. His photographs of Compagnoni were less formal, one showing his partner standing with a huge array of mountains behind him, another with his mask back on, trying to warm the incoming air.

Compagnoni unfurled three small silk flags: one Italian, one Pakistani and one a pennant from his local branch of the Italian Alpine Club in Valfurva. As they bristled in the wind, the two men took turns to film each other and even attempted a final roll with the camera set on automatic. They tried to smile and look positive, but looking at the photos now, you can see the discomfort etched on their faces. The sun was setting and the temperature had plummeted; every time they changed film, they had to expose their already frozen hands to the biting wind.

When Compagnoni realised that his fingers were severely frostbitten, he began to bang them against his ice-axe hoping to restore the circulation but he could feel nothing. He tried to put his large outer gloves back on, but the leather was so stiff and his fingers so swollen that he got nowhere. He took out a penknife and tried to enlarge the opening at the wrist but the wind rose up and the glove went tumbling down the mountain.

In an act of great self-sacrifice which virtually guaranteed that he would get frostbite, Lacedelli offered Compagnoni his own outer glove but it too had to be cut and enlarged before it would go over his partner's hand. Compagnoni was scared. Every climber in Europe knew the story of Maurice Herzog, the French climber who had come back from Annapurna with such bad frostbite that he lost all his toes and most of his fingers. Compagnoni had a wife, Enrica, and two young boys, but how could he support them if he too lost his fingers and could no longer work as a guide and ski instructor? When Lacedelli told him it was time to go down, Compagnoni refused to move, saying that he wanted to spend the night on the summit.

These were desperate moments for Lacedelli. Compagnoni seemed to have gone temporarily mad and now his own hands were starting to become numb. The longer they delayed, the worse it would become. 'We've got to go down,' he shouted, 'Now!' To make sure that Compagnoni got the point, he raised his ice-axe and threatened to hit him. Then, finally, Compagnoni came to his senses, gave one last look around and turned to go down.

If their ascent had been a·steady slog, the descent was an amphetamine-fuelled retreat. As experienced guides, they both knew that most accidents happened on the way down but they didn't have time to be careful. They swallowed a sympamine[12] tablet, a type of amphetamine used to ward off tiredness and boost performance, and hoped for the best.

It was impossible to repeat any of the tricky rock climbing they had done on the way up. Instead they always opted for the least demanding route. This time when they reached the Bottleneck, they avoided the rocks and ploughed straight down through the snow in the centre. Somehow they made it to the bottom without setting off any major avalanches and even managed to glissade down the lower section.

When they reached their abandoned rucksacks, Compagnoni fished inside his bag and plucked out a small bottle labelled 'Veleno', poison. Lacedelli didn't like the look of it but Compagnoni explained that it was his secret stash of brandy, which he didn't want anyone else to steal. The two climbers each took a swig and almost immediately felt drunk – an effect of the altitude not its potency. Then swaying slightly, they picked themselves up and continued down.

Lacedelli had a small torch but it soon ran out. There was one particularly big crevasse they remembered from the way up, but just when they were discussing how best to avoid it, they both slipped and found themselves tripping over it. Lacedelli lost his ice-axe but remarkably they both made it across unscathed.

The final hurdle was the ice-wall above Camp 8 and a second gaping crevasse in front of it. Compagnoni went first, working his way down the face while Lacedelli held him from above. It was all going well until he came to an overhanging section. Suddenly the slope seemed to disappear and Compagnoni found himself flailing around in mid-air. Lacedelli braced himself but his frozen fingers made it impossible to hold onto the rope between them. Compagnoni spiralled through the air and hit the snow with a thump. Once again he had been incredibly lucky, landing on the outer lip of the crevasse. When he checked, nothing seemed to be broken.

The danger was far from over. As Compagnoni lay in the snow he was convinced that within a few seconds Lacedelli would fly down on top of him, crampons first. Fortunately, his partner maintained his footing, but not for long. Though Lacedelli's descent was a little more controlled, it wasn't long before he had slipped and was flying through the air toward the crevasse below. Amazingly, he too managed to avoid it, landing on its outer lip. The soft snow that had made their ascent so tiring had come to their rescue on the way down, cushioning their landings whenever they fell.

On the slope just above Camp 8, the two men began to call out, hoping that their comrades would hear and help them back to their tents. No one responded. It was impossible to believe that they had all gone down, but in the dark there was a very real possibility that they might pass their tents without noticing. Then, at around 11.00 p.m., Compagnoni noticed a light below and within a few minutes they were surrounded by their ecstatic teammates, literally jumping for joy to hear that K2 had been climbed. At first their throats were so dry and sore they could barely speak, but after several cups of tea Lacedelli and Compagnoni were able to tell their story.

The warm tents of Camp 8 were a mixed blessing. As their frozen fingers began to thaw out, the agony began. Walter Bonatti massaged Lacedelli's hands and Abram worked on Compagnoni's but they couldn't get rid of the excruciating pain. The two Italians weren't the only ones to suffer the agonies of frostbite. Bonatti had survived his high-altitude bivouac on the night before the summit attempt remarkably well, but Mahdi came down with badly frostbitten toes. In a tent nearby, he spent the night crying out and moaning.

At base camp, the tension was growing. Would they soon be going home, or would they have to spend yet more months and endure many more storms at the foot of this huge mountain? Desio had plenty to do. His scientists and geographers were already in the field, and he was preparing to join them. But he too was desperate for news. Why no signal?

Then, just before midday on 1 August, several figures were spotted high up on the Abruzzi ridge. A few hours later, three rockets were fired into the sky from Camp 2. It probably signalled success, but 'probably' wasn't good enough. Why wouldn't someone just pick up the radio and put them out of their misery? A few of the men at base camp were so anxious to know that they set off up the glacier toward

Camp 1, hoping to intercept the returning climbers. They waited for three hours but saw no one.

Then, finally, the long wait was over. Just before 9.00 p.m. Ubaldo Rey and Cirillo Floreanini appeared out of the darkness and with faltering steps made their way toward base camp. As the others whooped and cried tears of joy, they told their news: Compagnoni and Lacedelli had made it, and reached the summit even after their oxygen ran out. Both had frostbitten hands and the Hunza Mahdi was badly injured too, but K2 had been climbed.

After ten weeks on the mountain, months of preparation, years of applications, decades of frustration... Ardito Desio finally had his wish. It was too late to contact the cable station at Skardu but he spent the night drafting telegrams and press releases. A letter written that evening to Vittorio Lombardi, the treasurer and press spokesman, beautifully captured the intensity of the moment:

> I still feel winded and have a lump in my throat that makes it hard to swallow. An hour ago the first two came down who announced the victory. At six o'clock yesterday afternoon, two of us finally reached the summit of K2!!! They got back into camp at 11 p.m. and left two oxygen sets with two bottles on the summit. For the last hour they had no oxygen. All the men are exhausted, I don't know how they have managed it. On the last day they climbed 900 m up and down. It still seems like a dream to me.[13]

Desio's frustrations weren't quite over yet. Transmission problems meant that he couldn't get a message out on the following morning and he had to wait until the end of the day before Compagnoni and Lacedelli finally arrived in camp. The conquerors of K2 were glad to be down but they were in a terrible state, their throats so badly blistered they could barely speak, their frostbitten hands getting more painful every hour. For now the detailed retelling of their story had to wait – all they wanted was to disappear into their tents and snatch whatever sleep they could get.

At 7.30 a.m. on 3 August, two and a half days after the ascent, Desio finally managed to get through to Skardu and send back a brief message:

Victory dated thirty-first of July. All well. Together at base camp. Professor Desio.

A few hours later, their victory was announced by the Pakistan Broadcasting Corporation. It was official: they had done it, 'lived their dream', as cameraman Mario Fantin called it. Now at last they could celebrate and stop thinking about the monsoon or coming back in September. Ardito Desio and his scientists still had two more months of work in the Karakoram but everyone else could go home.

By the late afternoon of 3 August the news had reached Italy. Mario Scelba, the new prime minister, made a formal announcement to parliament. 'The Italian flag is flying at 8611 m.' Luigi Einaudi, the president of the Republic, cabled his congratulations to Desio and, as Reuters reported, all over Italy flags were hoisted, bells tolled and public buildings illuminated.

Next day, the headlines roared across the front pages of Italian newspapers: 'K2 Conquered by Desio's Team', 'The Italian Flag on K2', 'Now K2 can be called Italian'. The news did not have quite the same international impact as the first ascent of Everest, a news event that had been supercharged by its coincidence with the coronation of Queen Elizabeth II, but there was no doubt of its importance to Italy.

The post-war years had seen continual industrial unrest, uncertain government and a faltering economy. The K2 story shared the front pages with articles about the high price of food and parliamentary debates about the risks of a Communist takeover, but in the summer of 1954 there was a feeling that just maybe the country was at a turning point. After ten years of Allied occupation, the city of Trieste was being handed back to Italy, the national broadcaster RAI had just started TV transmissions – its first programme an emphatic victory in a World Cup qualifying match – and now Italy had just climbed K2 – the world's hardest mountain, as journalists were keen to emphasise.

According to Turin's daily newspaper, *La Stampa*, the ascent of K2 was 'A flower in the button-hole of every Italian':

> *Because of this flag tied to the handle of an ice-axe, planted on the highest unclimbed mountain in the world, today we Italians can walk down the street as if we had a flower in our button-hole with more lively and happier hearts.*[14]

Dino Buzzatti, a friend of Ardito Desio and a well-known correspondent for *La Stampa*'s Milanese rival, *Corriere della Sera*, was even more effusive, proclaiming it the most important event for years:

> *Even if you're not interested in climbing, even if you've never seen a mountain, even for people who have forgotten what it means to love your country, all of us, at this happy news, we have felt something that we were no longer used to: a heartbeat, a palpitation, a pure disinterested feeling of happiness.*[15]

As news of the Italian victory on K2 spread around the world, messages came in from climbers everywhere. The British Everest Committee was one of the first organisations to send its congratulations, followed a few days later by Sherpa Tenzing, who was then in Switzerland at a guiding academy. The great Swiss climbers Raymond Lambert and René Dittert sent telegrams and there were goodwill messages from the Japanese, Austrian, French and American Alpine Clubs.

K2 had been ascended by an Italian team less than fifty years after the country's most illustrious mountaineer, the Duke of Abruzzi, had first made it famous around the globe. Everything that Ardito Desio and his backers in the Italian Alpine Club had hoped for had come true. The epic saga of K2 had reached a suitably Italian climax and now the whole world could rejoice in mankind's latest triumph.

Or could it? Within a few months the flower in the button-hole of every Italian would be showing its thorns.

Chapter 11

THE SPOILS OF
VICTORY

When Fritz Wiessner read about the Italian victory in the *New York Times*, he was thrilled and immediately sent an effusive message to Ardito Desio via his wife in Milan. Fritz was so happy for the Italian team that he even offered to write a chapter on the previous American attempts for any future expedition book. Charlie Houston's reaction, however, was much more complex.

When journalists caught up with him at his house in Exeter, New Hampshire, he too added his congratulations, but after several weeks of distinctly pessimistic press stories about the Italian expedition, he wasn't prepared for this moment and was already in the throes of organising another American expedition to K2. In a letter written to the *New York Times* on 4 August, Charlie was candid about his mixed feelings toward the Italian team:

> *I applaud their courage and their perseverance but I am too human not to be saddened for I held permission to take the fourth American expedition to K2 in 1955. Something is gone which has filled my thoughts for sixteen years since my first visit to K2, but I salute, with all my heart, the Italians and their success.*[1]

In a second letter, written the same day to Eric Shipton, the famous British climber who had been forced to resign from the Everest expedition of 1953, Charlie was more direct about his sense of loss:

There are other hills, other interests, but K2 has filled my heart
and head for sixteen years, as Everest filled yours. Nothing can
replace them, no second ascents, no other mountains.

I have neither means nor freedom to go to the Himalayas
again, so that phase of my life is over. Perhaps I shall grow up,
but right now I feel that I have grown down.[2]

If Charlie thought writing the letters would be cathartic, he was wrong.

On the following day, he set off on an errand to the nearby town of Nashua. When he arrived, his mind went completely, utterly blank. He forgot his name, his occupation, his address, his wife, his family. He forgot about K2 and his sixteen years of obsession, he forgot about Ardito Desio, he forgot about Fritz Wiessner. He forgot about everything.

After wandering about town distraught for several hours, Charlie ended up at the local hospital where they diagnosed a case of total global amnesia. Only when a policeman spotted the label on his tie and recognised it as coming from a shop in his hometown of Exeter, was he identified. His wife, Dorcas, and a friend came to collect him. After a long sleep his memory returned but the trauma was not over.

A few days later, Charlie set off on his summer vacation. A year earlier he had been high on K2, battling to bring down Art Gilkey; now as he drove along the country roads toward the family holiday home at Honnedaga Lake, he saw blood everywhere, seeping through the tarmac.

For almost three decades he had been obsessed with mountaineering but it was all over. After K2 he never went on another expedition again. 'His' mountain had been taken away from him and nothing would replace it. The glory was all Italian, and he would just have to live with it. But if Charlie could have stared into a crystal ball, he might have felt differently. Within a few months Desio's expedition would be mired in a series of controversies and the victors would be experiencing what Lino Lacedelli would later call the 'price of conquest'.

No one, however, had any inkling of the arguments to come at the beginning of August when the expedition broke up. There had been tense moments during their weeks at base camp and a lot of the men had not warmed to their expedition leader, but success was a great healer and now at last they were going home victorious.

Ardito Desio was the first to leave base camp, heading off with the geologist Bruno Zanettin on 7 August to begin a survey of the upper Baltoro. Four days later, the climbers said their goodbyes to K2 and began the long journey back to Italy. Before they left, they visited Mario Puchoz's grave and added the date of their ascent to a plaque placed nearby.

In spite of their joy at victory, they were leaving K2 a much weaker team than when they arrived at the end of May. Compagnoni, Lacedelli and Mahdi were still in severe pain from their frostbite and Gino Soldà, the oldest man on the climbing team, had developed thrombophlebitis, the same condition that had afflicted Art Gilkey in 1953. Soldà had to be carried on an improvised litter for the first few days.

Achille Compagnoni was very worried about his hands and wanted to get back to a hospital in Italy as quickly as possible. Lino Lacedelli, his summit partner, was also suffering, but he was not in quite such a hurry to go under the surgeon's knife. Guido Pagani, the expedition doctor, had convinced him that it would be better to wait than risk premature amputations.

Although everyone was very keen to get back home to their families in Italy, as cameraman Mario Fantin later admitted, there was also a tinge of regret that a great adventure was over. Though the climbers came from all over northern Italy, and few had been close friends before the expedition, over the last three months they had become a tight and effective team.

Desio's final message, number 13, issued before he left on his survey, warned them not to let future praise go to their heads and to 'remain calm and modest' during any celebrations to come. He finished by reminding them of the agreement they had made three months earlier, not to name the members of the summit team.

That decision had been made collectively at the beginning of the expedition, at the climber Cirillo Floreanini's suggestion. Everyone in the mountaineering world had been appalled by the squabbles that broke out after the 1953 Everest expedition over who had actually set foot on the summit first. As all climbers knew, a big mountain like K2 or Everest could only be climbed by teamwork, so it was wrong to give all the honour to one or two individuals.

Like so many good intentions, their pact of silence had unforeseen consequences. Almost as soon as the victory announcement was made on 3 August, the Italian press began asking who had actually reached the summit. If their names had been kept secret for a few days, it might have helped spread the glory. Instead, the Italian Alpine Club refused to release them until Desio got back to Rome, almost two months later, giving rise to endless speculation. The public wanted their heroes – 'the guys who got there first' as British writer James Morris wrote of Hillary and Tenzing – and refusing to say who they were helped create a niggling sense of uncertainty about the facts of the expedition.

Many journalists guessed immediately that Achille Compagnoni was one of the summiters. He was the leader of the climbing team and had been out in front from the beginning. The fact that he and Lino Lacedelli had frostbitten hands also seemed to indicate that they had done something special. On 6 August an American news agency named Compagnoni in print, though it did admit it had no official confirmation.

Many papers ran with the American story but some were not so sure. *La Stampa* put forward an opposing theory, arguing that the injuries suffered by Lacedelli and Compagnoni showed they had been members of the support team who had heroically carried up the oxygen. *La Stampa* concluded that Walter Bonatti and Pino Gallotti must have been the two men who reached the summit, because they had come back unscathed.

While the Italian press spent August speculating, a very different kind of controversy broke out in Pakistan when, after a long journey back, the Italian team reached Karachi, their final stop before Europe. It centred upon the Hunza porter Mahdi. As *The Times of India* reported:

> *The* Morning News *in Karachi charged that the Italians had prevented Amir Mahdi from reaching the summit.*

> *Mahdi, according to his own statement, was within 100 ft of the summit along with two Italians who finally scaled the peak, the newspaper said. 'He however was not permitted by the Italians to climb further because he was "not a full member" of the expedition team.'*
>
> *Apparently the honour of the final assault was jealously reserved for the foreign team, even though but for Mahdi and the Hunza porters, the team never would have got where it finally did.[3]*

The *Morning News* went on to compare the Italians unfavourably with the British Everest team which had allowed Tenzing to reach the summit of Everest in 1953, conveniently forgetting how the aftermath of that expedition was marked by months of bitter arguments. Fortunately for the Italians, the *Morning News* story received very little international coverage and was not widely reported in Italy. The Italian ambassador, Dr Benedetto D'Acunzo, did, however, feel compelled to bring Ata-Ullah and several members of the team together to draft a memorandum, which stated precisely what had happened during the build-up to the attempt.[4]

On 31 August, the same day *The Times of India* reported the spat in Karachi, *Corriere della Sera* published Ardito Desio's first account of the summit day. He still refused to give any names but inadvertently revealed the identities of the summit pair, when he specified that they both returned to base camp suffering from frostbite. When a few days later Compagnoni returned to Italy, he was given a hero's welcome at Rome Airport. According to one newspaper, in amongst the cheering crowd, a voice cried out:

> *'Have you suffered?'*
> *'I have suffered a lot,' he replied.[5]*

For the next two weeks there was almost daily coverage of Compagnoni's hospital treatment at a Milan clinic. He was given experimental plastic surgery, which involved painful skin grafts and required him to spend several days with his left hand sewn onto his abdomen in order to speed up recovery. The procedure was not as successful as the doctors initially hoped and he lost the tips of two fingers on his left hand. Compagnoni had come back in very poor shape and would eventually spend three months in hospital, suffering from pleurisy and then pneumonia.

While he languished in bed, his teammates were steaming back across the Indian Ocean on the SS *Asia*. Lino Lacedelli was still receiving treatment for his frostbitten fingers but it was a relaxed and enjoyable voyage, in comparison to Compagnoni's frenetic forty-eight-hour plane journey from Karachi to Rome.

When the ship arrived in Genoa on 22 September, the quayside was thronged by dozens of friends and family members but there wasn't quite the media scrum that had marked Compagnoni's return. There was still no official confirmation of the names of the summit team but the Italian Alpine Club had drip-fed the press a succession of photographs, including a pair showing Lacedelli and Compagnoni on the summit. As the journalist Fulvio Campiotti commented, the Italian public simply laughed at their inability to make a formal announcement. Everyone knew what the truth was.

Then, finally, on 8 October, Ardito Desio flew back into Rome to be greeted by a large crowd of supporters, along with official representatives of the Italian Olympic Committee and the government. At Milan Airport, his second stop, he was cheered by a large group of students from the university and carried on their shoulders in triumph. Echoing the excitement and hyperbole of early August, *Corriere della Sera* proclaimed him 'the man who all of a sudden, last July, changed every geography book in every language in every part of the world'.[6]

Four days later, the team came together for two days of celebrations in Genoa and to receive the Caravella D'Oro, a prestigious trophy awarded on Columbus Day for the most important sporting achievement of the year. Fritz Wiessner could not come, but the festivities were attended by Hermann Buhl, the Austrian conqueror of Nanga Parbat, and Edouard Wyss-Dunant, the leader of the Swiss Everest team of 1952. The guest of honour was none other than Charlie

Houston. In one of the more informal ceremonies, Lino Lacedelli presented him with the bright red embroidered umbrella that he had left on K2 in 1953.

At the climax of the celebrations on 12 October, in typically bombastic fashion, Desio finally made the announcement he thought everyone had been waiting for:

> *By agreement of the members of the Italian Alpine Club's expedition, I can finally end the secrecy over the names of the two Italians, who thanks to the collaboration and physical and moral strength of their companions, had the good luck and the merit to conquer K2, the second highest mountain in the world, on the 31st July 1954: Achille Compagnoni and Lino Lacedelli. The two friends reached the virgin summit in the same instant, holding each other affectionately, after a huge physical and spiritual effort.[7]*

His statement was picked up by *The Times* in London but the Italian press had by now grown so bored with the endless prevarication that it didn't generate the headlines that Desio undoubtedly expected.

A fortnight later, the celebrations at Genoa were followed by a day-long series of parades and official functions in Milan, but in spite of all the back-slapping and group photographs, something was not quite right. Charlie Houston had noticed it in Genoa. As he wrote afterwards in a letter to the other members of the American 1953 K2 team, he found Desio and the Italian climbers modest and unassuming and was hugely impressed by the enthusiasm for mountaineering in Italy, but 'make no mistakes about it, it was not a happy party'.[8]

It wasn't long before that unhappiness found its way into print. In November, the popular Italian magazine *Settimo Giorno* commissioned a series of articles entitled 'The True Story of K2' in which it was revealed that the climbers had argued with Desio over tactics on the mountain. The young climber Walter Bonatti got a lot of coverage in the press. In an interview with *Settimo Giorno* headlined 'The Night of 20 July when the Climbers Said No to Desio' he revealed that the decision to try for the summit had been made by the climbers, without the approval of their leader.[9]

In December, the journalist Fulvio Campiotto beat everyone to the presses, publishing his book *K2*, a long and detailed account of the 1954 expedition and the history of the mountain. Its overall tone was very positive but Campiotti wasn't afraid to criticise Desio's leadership. His book included a long interview with Riccardo Cassin, who made it very clear that he still felt bitter at his dubious exclusion on 'medical grounds' and believed that he had been dropped because Desio didn't want to share the glory with a mere 'climbing leader'.

Hard at work on his own book, as well as his duties at the university, Ardito Desio didn't take any of this too seriously, but in addition to the public controversies, behind the scenes the first of a series of legal cases was getting under way, which potentially had far more serious consequences.

It revolved around a dispute that had begun five months earlier in the Karakoram when Desio arrived at the village of Askole, hotfoot from K2 base camp. The climbing expedition was over and the mountaineering contingent was heading back to Italy but Desio and his scientists still had plenty of work to do. He expected to find a cache of 16 mm film to record their activities. As well as providing a valuable document of their endeavours, it would ensure that this aspect of the whole K2 adventure would make it into the official documentary. The only problem was that instead of finding a large stash of unexposed celluloid, there was nothing but an empty box.

Desio was furious and immediately decided that the blame must lie with Mario Fantin, the expedition cameraman. The two men had never liked each other and had argued continually during the expedition. Fantin bridled at Desio's imperious manner and was frequently frustrated by his refusal to let him climb up to the higher camps. Desio, for his part, had regarded Fantin as yet another drain on his precious resources and had not wanted him to interfere too much with the main climbing effort. It was a classic argument between an expedition leader and an expedition cameraman, but nothing was classic about what happened next.

As far as Desio was concerned, the missing film was the last straw, prompting a swift letter to the Italian Alpine Club on 27 August in which he demanded that henceforth Fantin should be treated as 'a non-participant' in the expedition and excluded from all official functions and receptions. They were strong words from a clearly very angry man but there were two problems. In the first instance, neither the Italian Alpine Club nor the members of the climbing team were willing to comply and made sure that Fantin attended all the celebrations. He was a popular character and, after spending so many weeks on K2 with him, no one was willing to deny him his share of the glory. The second, bigger problem for Desio was that he was wrong.[10]

In fact the missing film had been taken by one of Desio's own scientists, Bruno Zanettin. As soon as Zanettin realised his mistake he wrote to both men to apologise. Desio, however, for reasons best known to himself, refused to take back his accusations, so Fantin took him to court for defamation, declaring to his local newspaper in Bologna that 'honour is greater than any summit'.[11]

While Fantin's lawyer got the legal process under way, a far bigger dispute was brewing between Desio and the Italian Alpine Club over expedition finances. In the spring of 1954 when the previous government fell and the grant from the expedition's major supporter, the National Research Council, hung in the balance, the Italian Alpine Club had stepped in and taken out a huge bank loan, guaranteed by twenty-three individual club members. Naturally they were very pleased when, in November 1954, the latest Italian parliament passed a law confirming the retrospective grant of 50 million lira.

Before the club could get their hands on their money, they were required to provide detailed accounts, but Ardito Desio did not send in the paperwork straight away. Eventually, after a lot of ill-tempered to and fro, the receipts appeared but only for just over half the grant. As far as the Italian Alpine Club was concerned, the remaining money would be used to pay off other debts incurred for the sake of K2. Anything left over would go into a fund for future expeditions.

Desio, however, saw things differently and, with 23 million lira to fight over, he was prepared for a long-drawn-out battle. He argued that any fund should also be available for geographical and scientific expeditions. When he took a second, purely scientific expedition to the Karakoram in the summer of 1955, he assumed that his costs would be covered by the original grant. The Italian Alpine Club disagreed, and ultimately so did the National Research Council, forcing him to find financial support elsewhere.

Behind all the detailed financial arguments, a power struggle was being fought out for the legacy of the expedition. When officials at the Italian Alpine Club decided to dissolve the K2 committee, Desio responded by resigning from their central council. When they printed a long article in the club magazine about their problems with him, he shot back with a very detailed rebuttal and then, to add fuel to the fire, published a short book in which he argued that like King Lear he was much 'more sinned against than sinning' and that the club was treating him unfairly.[12]

From Desio's perspective, he had initiated, nurtured and brought the expedition to a successful climax. On top of which, he had agreed to donate all royalties from his official book and any articles about K2 to expedition funds. Weren't his critics simply being monstrously ungrateful? Officials at the club felt differently. They had become increasingly annoyed at what they regarded as his arrogance and his condescending manner toward the K2 climbing team. Now they had had enough. They published letters from disgruntled team members, complaining about Desio's patronising and unfriendly behaviour during the expedition, and refused to back down over the funding issues.

As if all this was not enough, in the summer of 1955 another and much more public controversy erupted in the press between Achille Compagnoni and the producers of the expedition film, *Italia K2* – the Italian Alpine Club and an independent film maker, Marcello Baldi.

After his long spell in hospital in the autumn of 1954, Compagnoni had gone back to his home in Breuil, worrying about what he would do next. His hands were far from recovered and he felt very weak. It was obviously going to be many months, if not years, before he could resume his career as a mountain guide so he needed to find a way to make a living. The Italian Alpine Club were not blind to his problems. They had awarded him a small stipend of 100,000 lira per month and backed a campaign to get state pensions for the two men who reached the summit and the family of Mario Puchoz.

Compagnoni had made money from product endorsements and, like everyone on the team, had been given a free Fiat 500 'Topolino', after the Italian Alpine Club struck a deal with Italy's talismanic car manufacturer. A few hundred thousand lira from advertising and a free car, however, were not enough compensation for his lost fingers. When, after a couple of weeks on national release, the K2 film started to make a lot of money, he asked to be given a share in the royalties. As he argued in numerous interviews, it was only fair – after all, he had lost two of his fingertips for the sake of filming on the summit.

There was a lot of sympathy for Compagnoni in the press. He was a popular and charismatic figure and, though his suggestion was surprising, it did not seem totally unreasonable. And, as every newspaper editor knows, controversy sells. Once their pages had been full of headlines proclaiming the glorious national victory; now they took great relish in detailing the arguments that had followed in its wake.

K2 was no longer the 'flower in the button-hole of every Italian'. In an article entitled 'The K2 Millions', *Epoca*, a popular weekly magazine, reported:

> *The time for flowers, flags and speeches is gone. Now what matters is how to apportion the spoils – how they should be divided, returned and assigned to the various organisations and individuals who claim them.*[13]

According to the article, in its first three months the expedition film had made somewhere between 200 million and 220 million lira. After the various cinema owners and distributors had taken their cut, the substantial profits were being split between Marcello Baldi, the film's producer, and the Italian Alpine Club. Would it not be fair for some of the money to go to Compagnoni and the other climbers?

The Italian Alpine Club said no. In the first instance, they had a contract with the producer, which they felt legally and duty bound to respect. Marcello Baldi might not have gone to K2, but he had put up his own money and taken on a lot of the financial risk. If the Italian team had failed in 1954, the film might have flopped and Baldi would have lost out. Besides which, a few months earlier Compagnoni had signed a declaration, as had everyone, which stated clearly that he would not seek any financial compensation from the expedition. None of the other climbers supported him and nor did his summit partner, Lino Lacedelli.

Lino had been keeping a low profile. After the expedition he had gone back to his home in Cortina D'Ampezzo, given very few interviews and made it known that he had little time for the press. In September 1954, just a few days after his return from Pakistan, an article had been published in a weekly magazine entitled 'How Compagnoni Dragged Lacedelli to the Summit'.[14] The source of the story had not been identified directly, but as most of the piece was based around an interview with Compagnoni, the implication was that it came from him, or at least one of his friends. On the same day that it appeared, Compagnoni issued a retraction, denying he had ever said such a thing, but it caused huge offence in Lacedelli's hometown and left Lino suspicious of journalists – and of his summit partner.

When in the autumn of 1955 Lino's local newspaper caught up with him to ask about Compagnoni's claim for a share in the film's profits, he was blunt but reserved:

> I do not share the thoughts and actions of Compagnoni... I do not want to say anything else. Do not ask me more, I've had enough of controversy.[15]

Desio had been absent from Italy during the first part of this latest debate, but when he returned to Italy he came out publicly on

Compagnoni's side, telling the press that his lead climber had 'fought like a lion and lost the use of two fingers on one hand, together with Lacedelli, for the sake of bringing back evidence of the victory'.[16] Desio insisted that he had no personal stake in Compagnoni's claim but argued that it was only fair that his climbing leader should profit from the film.

As the case headed inexorably toward the courtrooms, Lacedelli and the other ten climbers on the K2 team signed a public statement condemning the actions of their former teammate, but Compagnoni paid no heed, retorting defiantly:

> *They've left me on my own. It's not the first time but I will survive.*[17]

Over the next three years Compagnoni's claim worked its way through the court until eventually it was rejected in the summer of 1958, the judge declaring that though Compagnoni 'could claim the glory for reaching the summit, he had no right to claim compensation as one of the authors of *Italia K2*'.[18] Compagnoni appealed but lost for a second time.

Ardito Desio too lost all his battles over the financing of the expedition and was even forced to hand over his precious trophy from Genoa, the Caravella D'Oro, which he had guarded jealously since its award in October 1954. In 1957 it made a symbolic move from the Museum of Science and Technology in Milan to the Italian Alpine Club's mountaineering museum in Turin.

In 1964, after almost ten years of disputes, visits to court and sensational headlines, everyone got ready to celebrate the tenth anniversary of the historic climb. With all the mud that had been thrown, it was easy to forget what a tremendous achievement the first ascent of K2 had been and there were plans to bring over Ata-Ullah from Pakistan and hold a series of events in Milan.

Then, just when it looked as if they could get those flowers and flags out again and prepare more heroic speeches, another controversy erupted which would make what had gone before seem like a mere warm-up act. Whereas the previous arguments had essentially been about peripheral issues, financing and film making, the final controversy focused on the ascent itself and exactly how it had been achieved. Though no one would have guessed at the time, it would last for forty bitter years and would lead to a wholesale reassessment of the Italian expedition.

Chapter 12

THE BASE LIE?

As many Italian writers have commented, their country is full of con-tradictions. It has some of Europe's most beautiful landscapes and its highest rate of natural disasters. It has given us the artistic wonders of the Renaissance and pizza; it has the warmest and friendliest people you can imagine, and more organised crime than anywhere else in the Western world. Italy is a country where vendettas can run for centuries and legal battles for decades, where successive scandals have undermined faith in government and where, as Machiavelli put it, some prefer 'to look at things not as they really are, but how they wish them to be'. It is a perfect arena for a long-running and bitter controversy over the first ascent of K2, a mountain that combines the beautiful and the terrible in equal measure.

The figure at the centre of the longest running of all the post-1954 controversies is Walter Bonatti, a man acclaimed as one of, if not *the*, greatest mountaineers of the twentieth century. Bonatti achieved many things as an alpinist and a global adventurer and yet, during the last thirty years of his life, he devoted a lot of his energy to arguing about K2, a mountain that he didn't summit. He wrote three books and gave countless interviews to prove that Ardito Desio's 'official' account of the first ascent of K2 was fundamentally flawed. Today his version of events has become the new 'official' version, as far as the Italian Alpine Club and most historians are concerned, and he is revered within the mountaineering community. Whether Bonatti was right about every-thing, however, is open to question.

Walter Bonatti was born in Bergamo in northern Italy in 1930. His father, Angelo, was a small businessman, his mother, Tina, a housewife. Life was not easy. When his father refused to join the Fascist party, he lost his job and his house. His mother had to leave Bergamo to find whatever work she could. Aged four, Walter was sent to live with a series of relatives. He grew up a solitary child who in his teenage years escaped into a fantasy world of exploration and exotic travel, courtesy of the books of Jack London, Arthur Conan Doyle and Daniel Defoe.

After military service Bonatti worked briefly for the steel company Falck, but his passion was elsewhere; aged twenty-three, he gave up his job to devote himself to climbing, and running a mountain refuge. In 1954, though the youngest member of the K2 team, he already had a reputation for skill and daring. When he published his first autobiography, *My Mountains*, seven years later, that reputation had been cemented by a series of amazing feats – a solo ascent of the near-vertical south west pillar of the Aiguille du Dru in the Mont Blanc range, several first ascents in Patagonia in South America and then, on a return trip to the Karakoram in 1958, a first ascent of the 26,000 ft Gasherbrum IV, without supplementary oxygen. In 1961 he was ready to tell the story of those climbs and, for the first time, what *really* happened on K2.

Bonatti had always felt that his role had been misunderstood and neglected. He maintained that without the oxygen sets that he had carried up with the Hunza porter Mahdi, Compagnoni and Lacedelli would never have reached the summit, yet the expedition film *Italia K2* had initially made no mention of their efforts or the terrible night they had spent at 26,600 ft. Only when he protested had a few lines of commentary been added to recognise their high-altitude bivouac. Similarly, in Desio's 'official' book, *The Conquest of K2*, these events had received very little coverage. In the chapter on the summit attempt, based on interviews with Compagnoni and Lacedelli, Bonatti and Mahdi had hardly appeared.

The story he told in *My Mountains* was very different. It included a very detailed and precise set of timings and altitudes that were either missing from or, as he claimed, inaccurately reported in the official account. He was very critical of the summit pair and presented Achille Compagnoni in a particularly unflattering light. According to Bonatti, two nights before the final attempt, Compagnoni was so exhausted that he didn't look as if he could continue. Bonatti had almost suggested taking over his role on the summit team, but held back because he was worried that Compagnoni might not even be strong enough to retrieve the oxygen sets from the slopes above Camp 7, so no one would make it to the top.

Most of Bonatti's account focused on the dramatic events of 30 July, the day before the first ascent, when he and Mahdi had tried to carry the oxygen sets to Camp 9 and ended up spending a freezing night out in the cold bivouacking at 26,600 ft, with nothing to protect them apart from the clothes they were wearing. Vividly recalling the excruciating cold, Bonatti accused Compagnoni and Lacedelli of deliberately situating their tent in a position that was both impossible to reach and much higher than had been agreed. He had felt betrayed and abandoned yet neither in public nor in private had Compagnoni and Lacedelli apologised for their behaviour or thanked him for the risks he had taken.

My Mountains was well received but there wasn't any great outcry at his revelations or his criticisms of Compagnoni. Though he was a hero to the public and much of the press, Bonatti was never really part of the Italian mountaineering establishment, a brilliant climber but a lone wolf. In his book *Karakoram*, the story of the Italian expedition to Gasherbrum IV, the celebrated Italian writer Fosco Maraini tried to convey the complexity of Bonatti's character:

> *A closed book and a complicated one. In some deep recess of his personality, he concealed a terrifying superhuman force. It almost frightened him too, sometimes. You could be his mate for weeks. You had a companion whose manner was consistently kind and at times exquisitely thoughtful. And then a veil of steel might come down between him and the world.*[1]

Initially, Compagnoni did not comment publicly on Bonatti's book. He remained a hugely popular figure, regularly appearing in the Italian press accompanied by film stars and dignitaries who had come to visit him in Cervinia. The arguments over the royalties from the K2 documentary had been forgotten and life was good. He was getting plenty of business as a guide, ran a successful hotel and was forging his own movie career, playing cameo roles in two Italian feature films. In 1958 he had published his own book, *Men on K2*, based on his expedition diary. It was well received by critics and won a prize in Italy for mountaineering literature.

Then, in July 1964, just before the tenth-anniversary celebrations, an article appeared in the Turin newspaper *Gazzetta del Popolo*, based on interviews given by Compagnoni and Lacedelli to a well-known mountaineering journalist, Nino Giglio. It was billed as their response to Bonatti's critique in *My Mountains* and did not pull its punches.

Giglio wrote that far from risking his life for the expedition, Walter Bonatti had brought it close to disaster by his selfish actions. According to his sensational new version of the story, backed by quotations from Compagnoni, Bonatti had schemed to make an unauthorised bid for the summit with Mahdi. When it failed, he had abandoned his faithful assistant and raced down the mountain. Furthermore, Giglio suggested that during their bivouac Bonatti had used an hour's worth of Compagnoni and Lacedelli's oxygen – hence it had run out just before the summit.

The first article was followed a week later by a second, in which Giglio reported that Mohammed Ata-Ullah had recently arrived in Italy and confirmed that Bonatti had tried to persuade Mahdi to make an unauthorised dash for glory. In spite of its inflammatory content, the article finished with a quotation from Compagnoni in which he offered to 'bury the hatchet' – once Bonatti had given 'a frank and honest explanation' of what had happened.

If Giglio really thought that Bonatti would let such serious allegations go unquestioned, he was very wrong. Far from burying the hatchet, Bonatti was sharpening it. A few months later he initiated a writ for defamation against Giglio and his newspaper. While depositions were taken and evidence assembled, Bonatti carried on climbing, achieving in 1965 what many regarded as impossible: an ascent of the north face of the Matterhorn. In winter. Solo. Walter Bonatti was not someone who would give up easily and the fact that he had achieved such a prodigious feat on Compagnoni's favourite mountain, a mountain that overlooked Compagnoni's hotel in Cervinia, made it all the more piquant.

When the case finally came to court in the winter of 1966, Nino Giglio defended himself by arguing that he had only repeated what Bonatti had written in his book and what he had been told by Compagnoni. In *My Mountains*, Bonatti had written that at one stage he had suggested to Mahdi that he might become part of the summit team, in order to persuade him to help carry the oxygen sets up to Compagnoni and Lacedelli.

Even more ironically, Bonatti had also planted the seed in *My Mountains* for the claim he found most offensive: that he had used some of Compagnoni and Lacedelli's oxygen. In a passage describing their night in the open, Bonatti remembered fantasising about doing just that:

> All it needed was to turn a valve, and to hell with the [oxygen] masks and regulators, which in any event we did not have because they were in the rucksacks of Lacedelli and Compagnoni. Once the valve was turned, the thin air around us would be suddenly enriched by the precious gas, and for a few minutes (the time it would take for cylinders to empty) it would be like being at home. I was being ironic naturally. But I could not fail to recognise by what a fine thread the outcome of the expedition was suspended upon.[2]

The tone of the language showed that he was recalling a flight of fancy rather than something he had actually done but this was undoubtedly the source of Giglio's allegation. The most serious claim, that Walter Bonatti had abandoned Mahdi after their freezing bivouac, had come from Compagnoni's 1958 book, *Uomini sul K2*, but it was contradicted both by the team statement made to the Italian ambassador in Karachi in September 1954 and the diary of Pino Gallotti, who had been present at Camp 8 on the morning of 31 July and remembered Mahdi arriving there first.

After hearing all the evidence, the judge ruled in Bonatti's favour. He accepted that though Bonatti might have given Mahdi the impression that he could become part of the summit team if he helped carry the oxygen up, there was no real intention on his part to make an unauthorised summit attempt. He had simply been trying to cajole his Hunza porter into an onerous job. As for using up some of the precious gas, the judge acknowledged that without an oxygen mask it would have been futile to open the cylinders. There were anomalies – a very confusing deposition that had been made by Mahdi in Pakistan, which partially backed Giglio's claims, and some curious statements made by Ata-Ullah when he came to Italy for the tenth-anniversary celebrations – but it was undeniable that the three accusations against Bonatti were unfounded and defamatory. *Gazzetta del Popolo* was forced to print a retraction and pay damages, which Bonatti donated to a local orphanage.

In spite of winning this case, by the mid-1960s Bonatti had become very disenchanted with the mountaineering world. In 1965 he made a dramatic announcement: after almost fifteen years in which his professional and private life had been dominated by climbing, he was going to take up a new career as a roving reporter and photographer for the magazine *Epoca*. Over the next two decades, he sought out new, mainly horizontal, adventures in Antarctica, Africa, and many of the world's wildest places.

Bonatti never forgot about the events of 1954, however, and as the years went on he became increasingly exasperated with the way the K2 story continued to be told in Italy. Whether in maps, books or television programmes, it always seemed that the same old inaccuracies were repeated. Even though Bonatti had won the libel case, Compagnoni was still held up as the great hero of K2 and no one had corrected the errors and omissions in his or Desio's account.

So in 1985, shortly after the thirtieth-anniversary celebrations, he went on the offensive, publishing a short book, *Proceso al K2* (K2 on Trial). The first half recounted the libel case, with transcripts of the defamation writ and supporting materials. The second was a systematic refutation of the 'official' histories written by Desio and Compagnoni. Bonatti's verdict was damning and his language unequivocal:

the sites, altitudes, timetables and oxygen usage set out by the
summit pair (and transcribed by the official spokesman Desio
with neither criticism nor verification) do not correspond to
the truth.[3]

These were strong words, but there were more. Bonatti had made a detailed analysis of the summit day and had come up with a precise timetable of events. By comparing the capacity of the cylinders used by Compagnoni and Lacedelli and the duration of the ascent, Bonatti now argued that their story of the oxygen running out below the summit was blatantly untrue, 'mere words and humbug' as he put it. Their ascent had taken between nine and a half and ten hours; their oxygen cylinders had a combined duration of at least ten hours. Therefore the oxygen must have lasted all the way to the top.

This was a much more dramatic assertion than anything Bonatti had made before and had not been included in *My Mountains* or his testimony during the 1966 libel case. Previously Bonatti had been trying to set the record straight about his own experience but now he was going on the attack and aiming to undermine the credibility of both Desio and Compagnoni. From the very first letter sent back to Italy two days after the ascent, to the first press articles, to the expedition book, the moment when the oxygen ran out had been a key part of the narrative of K2. Compagnoni had written about it at length in his book *Men on K2* and claimed that it happened at 27,560 ft, almost 700 ft below the summit. Now Bonatti was calling both Compagnoni and Lacedelli liars and accusing Desio of falling for their false account.

Bonatti's book was like a hand grenade thrown into the heart of the Italian mountaineering establishment, but it did not go off. There was some coverage in the Italian press, but no one really seemed willing to take him seriously. Bonatti was bitterly disappointed, but not really surprised. In spite of his fame, he remained an outsider; the Italian Alpine Club regarded him as an irritation and refused to question the myth of the great patriotic victory over K2.

Then out of the blue came an unlikely champion: Robert Marshall, an Australian surgeon based in Melbourne. Marshall was no mountaineer but he was a keen trekker and an avid reader of climbing literature. Already a big fan of Bonatti, when he came across a copy of his book *K2 on Trial* Marshall became convinced that a great injustice had been done. He began corresponding with his Italian hero, and eventually wrote a long commentary on the whole affair.

Marshall was persuaded by the evidence set out by Bonatti but he felt that there was something missing: an explanation for Compagnoni's hostility and Desio's willingness to play along. What were Compagnoni's motivations and why had Desio fallen for his story so readily?

His starting-off point was simple: Compagnoni resented Bonatti's climbing skill and was jealous of his reputation. This was the root cause of both the libel case in 1964 and Compagnoni's selfish behaviour on the night of 30 July 1954. He had put Camp 9 in an inaccessible position, because he was afraid that if Bonatti reached their tent he would muscle in on the summit attempt on the following day and steal his rightful glory.

In the first respect the plan had succeeded: Bonatti had not reached Camp 9 and had not gone any higher than 26,600 ft. Ultimately, however, Compagnoni's ruse had backfired because, rather than descending immediately on 30 July, Bonatti and the Hunza porter Mahdi had spent a freezing cold night on the mountain with unforeseen consequences. Bonatti had emerged unscathed but Mahdi had developed severe frostbite.

According to Marshall's theory, when expedition leader Ardito Desio heard about the events and the injuries suffered by Mahdi, he became very worried that the Italian team would be accused of neglect and their victory on K2 sullied. To add to the pressure, Ata-Ullah, the Pakistani liaison officer, had been so shocked by Mahdi's frostbite that he had confronted Desio to demand an explanation for what had gone on: why had Mahdi been told that he might be part of the summit team, and why had he then been forced to spend a night in the open?

When Compagnoni arrived at base camp and learnt about Ata-Ullah's outrage and Desio's worries, he realised that he would be blamed because he had made the decision to move the final camp. So, according to Marshall, he had attempted to shift the responsibility for Mahdi's injuries onto Walter Bonatti. He played along with the idea that Bonatti really had intended to make an unauthorised summit attempt and concocted two mutually supporting lies that would demonstrate Bonatti's selfishness: firstly, he told Desio that Bonatti had survived his night out on the mountain unscathed by using some of the summit team's oxygen. Secondly, he made up the story about the oxygen running out early on the summit day, in order to reinforce the idea that Bonatti had used the gas the night before. Desio had swallowed Compagnoni's lies because it suited him to deflect criticism from his glorious summit pair and had even told the Italian ambassador in Karachi that Bonatti was to blame for Mahdi's frostbite.

It was a complicated theory but for Marshall it offered something new and important: a motive for Compagnoni's lies and an explanation for Desio's complicity. Both men wanted to save face and avoid criticism, so they had turned Bonatti, the youngest man in the team, into their scapegoat. As Marshall later commented, strange though it all sounded, the whole affair was in fact 'a piece of typical Italian Machiavellian bastardy'.[4]

Bonatti soon became friends with the unlikely Australian, and even offered to include Marshall's commentary in a new edition of his K2 book. It was never published, however, and as the years rolled by, it looked as if the whole K2 controversy was going to be forgotten. Then in 1993 Robert Marshall made what he thought was a sensational discovery.

Looking through a copy of *The Mountain World*, a Swiss mountaineering review from 1955, he found an article on K2 written by Desio which included a photograph that had not appeared in Desio's 'official account', *The Conquest of K2*. It showed Compagnoni on the summit – wearing his oxygen mask! If, as Bonatti had pointed out, it stretched credulity for Compagnoni and Lacedelli to have carried two empty 40 lb oxygen sets to the summit, then the idea that they had continued to wear those masks, even after the gas ran out, was simply unbelievable. Here was clear proof that Compagnoni had lied. Marshall conceded that there were no photographs of Lacedelli wearing a mask, but in the famous image of Lacedelli on the summit there was a ring of ice clearly visible on his beard, indicating that he had only recently taken his mask off.

Marshall wrote an article about the photographs, which was trans-lated and published in Italy in 1993. To the Italian press, the Australian surgeon was an intriguing outside voice from a professional back-ground; the fact that he had taken no previous part in the controversy added to his air of objectivity.

Coming a year before the fortieth anniversary, Marshall's article generated huge interest and led to repeated calls for the Italian Alpine Club to set up an official enquiry and settle the controversy once and for all. The club's president, Roberto De Martin, issued a statement offering 'to give Walter Bonatti a hearing'.

It never came, though, leaving Bonatti feeling even more frustrated. So in 1996 he succeeded in publishing a second book, *K2: Storia di un Caso* (The Story of a Court Case), which included Robert Marshall's article on the summit photograph and his original commentary on Desio's role in the controversy. Again there was a lot of press interest but no concrete action from the Italian Alpine Club.

Bonatti refused to give up and progressively became more and more exasperated about the injustice he felt had been done to him. When the Italian government awarded him a prestigious medal, the Grand Cross of the Knights of Italy, he sent it back because Compagnoni had been given the same honour. He told Robert Marshall that his disil-lusionment over K2 had stopped him from having children, for fear that their lives would be stained by the lies told about him after the expedition, and told other journalists that by putting their final camp out of reach, Compagnoni and Lacedelli hadn't just abandoned him, they had tried to kill him.

Even if no one in the Italian climbing establishment would take him seriously, abroad it was different. Robert Marshall spoke at vari-ous conferences and became the translator of a new English language edition of Bonatti's autobiography, *My Mountains*. Sympathetic articles began appearing in European and American climbing journals. In 2003 Bonatti upped the pressure by publishing a third book, *K2 – La Verità* (The Truth). It included dozens of supportive articles from all over the world, by journalists and pundits utterly convinced of Bonatti's cause.

Finally, at the beginning of 2004, after dragging its heels for so many decades, the Italian Alpine Club announced that it was going to appoint a commission to investigate the events, composed of three eminent Italian professors – *I Tre Saggi*, the Three Wise Men.[5] It was announced that they would examine all the available evidence, though they would conduct no new interviews.

For once things moved quickly. The *Tre Saggi* released their report a few months later, in April 2004. They endorsed almost all of Bonatti's claims and called for the Italian Alpine Club to produce a revised official account. Then, about a month later, by coincidence, Lino Lacedelli broke his fifty-year silence with his own book, *The Price of Conquest*, based on a series of interviews with the journalist and climber Giovanni Genacchi. Like Bonatti, Lacedelli's inside story of the expedition was very different from the official account, which he now said had principally been written by Desio and Compagnoni.

Lacedelli portrayed Desio as an autocratic leader, out of touch with all of his team, apart from his sidekick Compagnoni. When it came to the summit days, Lacedelli agreed with almost everything that Bonatti had said, revealing that he had not wanted to put the site of Camp 9 so high and had argued with Compagnoni about its position. Though he had not realised it at the time, Lacedelli accepted that Compagnoni might have changed its position deliberately, in order to stop Bonatti from taking part in the summit attempt. Lacedelli, however, stuck to the story of the oxygen running out but said that it had happened much closer to the summit than Compagnoni had.

As if all this wasn't enough, at the end of 2004 Bonatti received a letter from his former teammate Erich Abram, which seemed to offer unequivocal proof of what Bonatti had dubbed 'la menzogna di base', the base lie, about the oxygen. Abram, an engineer by trade, had looked after the oxygen at base camp and had, he wrote, chosen the sets used for the summit attempts. Because the Italian Dalmine oxygen bottles leaked, for the summit attempt he had opted for the tried and tested German sets made by Dräger. This wasn't all. He revealed for the first time that the Dräger bottles had been specially filled to high pressure, in order to provide twelve hours of continuous oxygen, a full two and a half hours more than Compagnoni and Lacedelli had taken to get to the summit. As Robert Marshall wrote triumphantly in his final book, *K2: Lies and Treachery*:

> It therefore seems that Compagnoni's story is at least partially correct. The oxygen did perhaps run out on K2 at 8,400 meters or so, 200 meters from the summit, just as he has always insisted – but if so, this must have happened on the way down, **not** the way up![6]

As for Lacedelli's continued claim that the oxygen really had run out before the summit, as Marshall saw it, he was simply attempting to 'preserve at least some scraps of his own integrity and heroic reputation.'[7] They were harsh words but, after so many years of arguing, Marshall was in no mood to compromise.

Unsurprisingly, Achille Compagnoni had become more and more angry about all the 'mud' that had been thrown on his reputation and the memory of the Italian victory. He was furious with Lacedelli for seeming to turn against him and, in perhaps the saddest moment of the whole saga, in August 2004 he gave an interview to *Corriere della Sera*, in which he insisted that he had been the first man to set foot on the summit of K2, and had not arrived arm in arm with Lacedelli as previously stated. As the newspaper noted, Compagnoni had become like a wounded bear, a pack leader abandoned by all the other wolves. And there were more desertions to come.

In 2007 the Italian Alpine Club published their definitive final account of the summit days, *K2 – Una Storia Finita*, incorporating both the *Tre Saggi* report and the more recent evidence of Erich Abram. The story, they announced, was over and the new 'historic record' would state that Compagnoni and Lacedelli used oxygen all the way to the summit and that Walter Bonatti and Mahdi's role was 'the decisive and absolutely essential factor for the success of the expedition'. Bonatti had been vindicated, Compagnoni and Lacedelli damned.

Today this has become the new 'official account', regularly repeated in most books and newspapers. Walter Bonatti died in 2011 but he remains one of the best-loved figures in Italian mountaineering and few people question his account of the events on K2.

But when it comes to the oxygen controversy, is the case against Compagnoni and Lacedelli quite so clear cut? When I began this book, initially I thought there was nothing new to discover, but having looked through a lot of original documents, films and photographs, I'm no longer quite so sure. Many commentators routinely dismiss Compagnoni and Lacedelli's account as false, but could they in fact have told the truth?

Before looking at the evidence which supports Compagnoni and Lacedelli's version, it's important to acknowledge that their story was an unlikely one. The idea that they had taken two empty oxygen sets to the summit seems to defy common sense. Why carry all that extra weight when at high altitude every pound hurts? Couldn't they have simply abandoned their sets on the way up?

It is also important to recognise that in many ways the summit pair were their own worst enemies. When it came to altitudes and times, Compagnoni tended either to be vague or to exaggerate. Sometimes he said that the oxygen ran out 330 ft below the summit, at other times 655 ft below, and he invariably qualified everything with 'around' or 'about'. Lacedelli said very little and would nod along with his partner even when he didn't agree. The fact that they were inconsistent and their story was unlikely does not, however, mean that they were liars. This was a mountaineering expedition, which climaxed at the summit of a 28,251 ft peak, not a laboratory experiment.

Over the years, the dispute between Bonatti and Compagnoni inevitably became increasingly personal, until it really became a question of character, rather than evidence. Who did you believe: Walter Bonatti, the greatest mountaineer of the twentieth century, or Achille Compagnoni and Lino Lacedelli, two decent climbers who did nothing of note after K2? For Robert Marshall, the answer was simple and unequivocal:

Should Bonatti's story be accepted in its entirety? Is he hiding
something? Is he a fraud and a liar? Impossible! His career
speaks for itself: his whole life has been dedicated to uncom-
promising struggle, striving to explore his own physical and
moral limits. No man of this stamp could lie and go on lying
more and more stridently if he were guilty. His outrage is too
obviously genuine, every word spells it out.[8]

But is this really a fair way to look at this story and judge the protagonists' actions? Even though Bonatti's outrage was genuine, at both
his enforced bivouac and the accusations in Nino Giglio's article in
Gazzetta del Popolo, and even though he was a sincere, honest man, it
does not automatically follow that his teammates were liars. After all, he
wasn't present on the summit. At root this should never have become
an argument about personalities, it is really about timetables and how
well the oxygen sets of the early 1950s functioned. Looked at from
this perspective, Compagnoni and Lacedelli are much more credible.

Bonatti's case against the summit pair was essentially mathematical:
he outlined a chronology for the final day, worked out how many hours
it took to reach the summit and then compared this to the duration of
the oxygen cylinders. Compagnoni and Lacedelli, said Bonatti, had
started using oxygen at about 8.30 a.m. and reached the summit at 6.00
p.m. Thus their ascent had taken nine and a half hours. Their sets held
ten hours' worth of oxygen; therefore, there must have been some left.
When Bonatti heard from Erich Abram that Compagnoni and Lacedelli
were equipped with high-pressure Dräger cylinders with a capacity of
twelve hours, the lie seemed even more flagrant.

But could Bonatti really be sure that they had started at 8.30 a.m.?
He insisted that he could. According to his timetable, the first person
to move on the morning of the summit day was his partner Mahdi, who
descended from their freezing bivouac site at around dawn, roughly
5.00 a.m. After clearing the snow away to reveal the two oxygen sets,
Bonatti left about an hour later when the sun came up fully. Mahdi had
arrived at Camp 8 just before 7.00 a.m. and Bonatti had arrived shortly
afterwards.[9]

On the way down, he had continually looked up at the oxygen sets for any sign of Compagnoni and Lacedelli, but he saw nothing. Therefore, he concluded, Compagnoni and Lacedelli could not have left Camp 9 until 7.00 a.m. Assuming it took an hour to get from their tent to the oxygen sets and half an hour to organise their equipment, they could not have started using their oxygen until 8.30 a.m. Both Robert Marshall and the Italian Alpine Club's *Tre Saggi* accepted this as fact.

Bonatti's timings, however, beg two questions: first, why would Compagnoni and Lacedelli have left their tent so late? Were they having a 'lie-in' on the morning of the summit attempt? Second, could Bonatti be absolutely certain that nothing moved above him? Is K2's topography really so simple and regular that he could have had a completely uninterrupted view of the slopes above during the entire time of his whole descent?

Bonatti's own testimony contradicts this. At no stage on 30 or 31 July did he see Compagnoni and Lacedelli's tent, and there were several moments on the night of 30 July when he heard their voices but had not managed to identify their location. On the following morning, on the way down to Camp 8, at one point he had heard a shout from above and responded by waving his ice-axe in the air, but again he could not identify the spot from which the shout came. So, if, by Bonatti's own account, there was one moment at least on the morning of 31 July, when Compagnoni and Lacedelli could see him but he could not see them, how could he be certain that they did not leave their tent until 7.00 a.m.?

According to Compagnoni and Lacedelli in *The Conquest of K2*, on the morning of 31 July they broke camp at dawn, 5.00 a.m., and spotted someone descending below them. They called out and the figure turned round, before continuing down. If their timings were right, this could have been Mahdi, who according to Bonatti had paused at one point in the middle of the slope below their bivouac site. Compagnoni and Lacedelli then descended and reached their oxygen cylinders at around 6.15 a.m.

This is clearly incompatible with Bonatti's testimony, and bearing in mind that he was very precise, whereas they were always vague, it is probable that they got their timings wrong. However, the two accounts are not entirely contradictory: it is perfectly possible that Compagnoni and Lacedelli left Camp 9 not at 5.00 a.m. but at 6.00 a.m. and saw Bonatti, not Mahdi, descending about half an hour later. Bonatti seemed to have assumed that Compagnoni and Lacedelli took the same route down to the oxygen cylinders that they had used on the night of 30 July, but in fact they took a different route, avoiding the slippery rock slabs that they had climbed on the way up. Their less direct route might very well have been invisible to Bonatti, and they could have arrived at the oxygen cylinders at around 7.00 a.m., the very moment when Bonatti was climbing down the ice-wall above Camp 8, rendering the slopes above invisible to him. If so, they could have set off for the summit at 7.30 a.m. and their ascent taken ten and a half hours.

This timetable does not match the 'official version' in *The Conquest of K2* but it does follow Lacedelli's account in *The Price of Conquest*. Bonatti did not mention the weather in *My Mountains*, but according to Compagnoni and Lacedelli and Pino Gallotti down at Camp 8, it was unsettled and misty, making visibility poor and Bonatti's claim that he could see everything above him during his hour-long descent even more questionable.

The second and much bigger problem with the case against the summit pair revolves around the Italian team's oxygen sets. Bonatti assumed that they were reliable and predictable but all the historical evidence runs against this. In the 1950s climbing oxygen was a crude, emerging technology. Before the Second World War, there had been several experiments with supplementary oxygen in the Himalayas, but the evidence was patchy as to its value and there was a lot of debate about the 'sporting ethics' of using it. Fritz Wiessner did not take any oxygen to K2 in 1939 and nor did Charlie Houston in 1938 or 1953, apart from a few cylinders for medical emergencies.

After the war, the consensus changed about the ethics of using supplementary oxygen, but though the equipment was better than anything available in the 1920s and 1930s, it was still unpredictable by modern standards. The French team that made the ascent of Annapurna in 1950, the first 26,000 ft peak to be climbed, took oxygen sets but did not use them because they were so difficult to operate. In 1952 both of the Swiss Everest expeditions had been equipped with supplementary oxygen, but neither had fared well. First time round, in the spring of 1952, Raymond Lambert and Tenzing got very high but came back complaining that their equipment had let them down and caused their summit attempt to fail. Their gear was so inefficient that users could only draw oxygen when they were stationary. Six months later, the Swiss tried again. This time they had superior German oxygen sets made by Dräger. They came back reporting that their equipment was much better, but they barely used their sets and did not get as high as Lambert and Tenzing. Most of their Dräger oxygen bottles were abandoned on Everest's South Col at 26,000 ft, the flat plateau 3000 ft below the summit.

In 1953 the Austro-German Nanga Parbat expedition was also equipped with Dräger oxygen sets, but once again they were barely used and played no role in the successful attempt. Hermann Buhl clambered to the summit of Nanga Parbat fuelled by amphetamines and sheer willpower, not supplementary oxygen.

In the same year Hillary and Tenzing did reach the summit of Everest on oxygen and even carried enough for the descent, but if you look in detail at the 1953 expedition, it was not a great advert. The British team had repeated problems with their equipment, even though they were by far the best-prepared and best-resourced Himalayan expedition so far. Cylinders leaked, valves and tubes iced up, adaptors were lost or forgotten, and climbers were forced to run their sets at low rates for fear of running out of gas.

The first summit attempt on Everest on 26 May 1953 by Tom Bourdillon and Charles Evans was doomed from the beginning because of a fault in Evans' oxygen set. The second attempt also might have failed when Tenzing's set became choked with ice at around 28,800 ft. Fortunately, because the British had experienced this problem so many times previously, Ed Hillary knew how to clear the blockage.

If you look in detail at the 1954 K2 expedition's use of oxygen, it becomes even more likely that their oxygen sets malfunctioned on the final day. Ardito Desio did not have the time or resources that the

British had in 1953. He wanted the K2 expedition to showcase Italian technology but no previous Italian expedition had used oxygen. He was very pleased to be offered the majority of his cylinders for free from Dalmine, a large northern Italian steel manufacturer, but the company had never been involved in mountaineering before.

To compound Dalmine's lack of experience, about a month before the expedition was due to set off for Pakistan, the company was paralysed by an industrial dispute that brought production to a halt. For a few tense weeks, it looked as if Desio would get no oxygen cylinders at all. Manufacturing eventually resumed and the consignment arrived on time, but Desio hedged his bets by taking a small number of German-made Dräger sets. Dräger was regarded as a leader in its field, but no one had successfully used one of its sets at really high altitude.

Early in the selection process, the Italian climbers were introduced to their oxygen equipment in a decompression chamber in Milan but there is no evidence that they did any field training before leaving for Pakistan.[10] When they reached K2, Desio had planned to employ supplementary oxygen from about 24,000 ft, but remarkably, the one and only time that it was used for climbing was on the final summit day.

Put all this together – the fact that Compagnoni and Lacedelli had so little experience and that neither their Italian nor their German equipment had been tested at high altitude – and it becomes much more believable that either their sets malfunctioned and didn't have the expected endurance, or that Lacedelli and Compagnoni did not use them properly.

Robert Marshall's article on the summit photographs was seen by many as a decisive intervention, but it too has to be re-assessed. In the first instance he claimed to have discovered photographic evidence that had been suppressed from the 'official version' and only published outside Italy, as if there was some kind of cover-up. Marshall was wrong on both counts: the two images that appeared in *The Mountain World* were in fact the very first two summit pictures released to the Italian press, published in *Corriere Della Sera* on 28 September 1954 under the headline 'The first photographic documentation of the events'. Far from being obscure, *The Mountain World* was a well-funded annual publication from the Swiss Foundation for Alpine Research and considered one of the world's leading mountaineering journals.

As to the image of Compagnoni on the summit, it is not surprising that Marshall questioned why he was wearing a mask, but he made an assumption that can't be substantiated simply by looking at the photograph: namely that the oxygen was connected and still flowing. The Italians were using open-circuit sets. The oxygen in their bottles was routed into a mixing box known as a lung where it was combined with ambient air, before travelling up a breathing tube into the mask. When the oxygen ran out it was still possible to breathe through the mask. You cannot tell from the still photograph whether or not the oxygen was still flowing and you cannot even see where the tube from Compagnoni's mask terminates.

When Compagnoni was challenged about the mask, he explained that he was using it to warm the incoming air. Robert Marshall dismissed this out of hand but it was supported both by Lacedelli and Erich Abram, the team's oxygen controller, who in 2004 confirmed that it was common practice amongst the Italian climbers to wear a mask and breathing tube, even when they were not carrying an oxygen set.[11] A year earlier, in 1953, two members of Charlie Houston's American team had worn 'Arctic breathers', a kind of sock on top of their mouths, in order to warm the incoming air. Then and now, in the Arctic and Antarctic, masks are worn for this very reason.

Marshall thought that the photographs offered definitive proof that Bonatti was right, but he didn't notice a small but crucial detail; namely, that Compagnoni and Lacedelli had in fact jettisoned one of their cylinders on the way up. Marshall maintained that Compagnoni and Lacedelli carried three cylinders, a full 40 lbs, to the summit, but this is not the case – they only carried around 26 lbs. The middle cylinder is missing from each set. This is hard to see in the black and white pictures but is clear in enlargements, and even clearer in the film footage and the colour photographs taken on the summit.

Like the British equipment taken to Everest in 1953, the Dräger and Dalmine sets were designed in such a way that it was easy to attach and remove cylinders. The theory was that every time a bottle ran out, it could be discarded; as each bottle weighed around 13 lbs even when empty, it clearly made sense. So why didn't Compagnoni and Lacedelli throw away their cylinders as soon as they exhausted them?

Compagnoni and Lacedelli were aware that taking their empty sets must have seemed odd, particularly to non-climbers. In *The Conquest of K2* they gave several explanations: it was late in the day and the sun was going down, the summit seemed very close and they didn't want to spend time on a complicated and dangerous manoeuvre. They also wrote that they wanted to leave some evidence of their achievement on the summit. This might sound strange, but a few days after Hillary and Tenzing climbed Everest, the Indian Air Force flew over the summit and brought back a series of aerial photographs, none of which showed any trace of their ascent, as some newspapers pointed out. Two oxygen sets would, however, be a big marker.

These explanations, whether or not you believe them, only refer to the final hour or so of their ascent, but they do not explain why Compagnoni and Lacedelli did not discard their empty bottles on the way up. Even if Bonatti was right, and one of their three cylinders still contained oxygen when they reached the summit, why did they each carry up at least one exhausted cylinder? There are only two credible answers: either they hadn't had the time or the experience to use their equipment in the way that it had been designed, or their oxygen sets had been assembled incorrectly, making it difficult to remove empty bottles. Either way it lends credence to Compagnoni and Lacedelli's claim that they knowingly carried their empties to the summit.

The most important photographic evidence, however, is found not in the still images but in the expedition film, *Italia K2*. Whereas most of the images taken on the summit were black and white, the expedition film was shot entirely in colour. One sequence filmed early on at base camp shows a long row of bright red Dalmine oxygen cylinders, topped by a smaller row of dark blue Dräger cylinders, the same cylinders that Compagnoni and Lacedelli were supposed to have used for the final attempt.

That colour combination, however, is repeated on the summit: the film shows that one of the Italian sets has dark blue bottles, the other bright red bottles. So, contrary to what the team's oxygen controller, Erich Abram, had intended, one of the oxygen sets that Compagnoni and Lacedelli took to the summit was loaded with Dalmine bottles. These had a lower capacity than the Dräger bottles, ten hours absolute maximum, and many of them leaked. Abram undoubtedly had intended to provide the summit team with good solid German sets, loaded with reliable, high-pressure cylinders, but, somewhere in the confusion of the last two days, that plan went awry and one Dalmine set was carried high, making it even more likely that at least one of the oxygen sets ran out before the summit.[12]

As for Robert Marshall's suggestion of a conspiracy involving Compagnoni, Desio and Ata-Ullah, this remains conjecture. It is attractively complicated and ingenious and has been repeated many times since in other histories of K2, but I found no documentary evidence to support it in any contemporary account, letter, diary or press article.

The idea of Ata-Ullah storming into Desio's tent to demand justice for his porter does not make historical sense: the Italian expedition had been personally approved by the prime minister, the Pakistani Army had built the bridges that enabled the Italians to reach K2 more quickly than any previous expedition, and Compagnoni and Lacedelli had planted the national flag on the summit of Pakistan's highest peak. Would Ata-Ullah really have had the temerity, or the desire, to create a scandal over Mahdi's injuries when he and everyone else were so thrilled at the ascent of K2?

In the 1950s frostbite was considered an occupational hazard for both climbers and high-altitude porters, and even though Desio would have sympathised with Mahdi, he would not have been worried about any scandal. After all, both Compagnoni and Lacedelli were also suffering from frostbite, and Mario Puchoz had given his life for the sake of climbing K2. In 1939 three Sherpas and one American had died on K2, and in 1952 one Sherpa had died on Everest and two others had been badly injured. Mountaineering was regarded as inherently risky, both for high-altitude porters and Western climbers.

The main problem with the conspiracy theory, though, is much simpler: the chronology does not make sense. The first mention of the oxygen running out an hour below the summit came in a letter written by Desio on 1 August, a day *before* Compagnoni returned to base camp, based on the report brought down the mountain by two other Italian climbers, Ubaldo Rey and Cirillo Floreanini. It was not a lie dreamt up by Compagnoni in response to Desio's worries about an international scandal, nor was it a response to criticisms by Ata-Ullah over Mahdi's injuries. Compagnoni and Lacedelli returned to base camp on 2 August but Mahdi and the other Hunzas did not return until 3 August, by which time the story was already in circulation.

As for the idea that Desio misled the Italian ambassador and was frightened by negative stories in the Pakistani press, this again does not match the chronology. Desio did not leave K2 with the climbing team; he stayed in the Karakoram for a secondary scientific expedition. When the critical reports were published in Karachi at the beginning of September, he was many miles away on the Biafo glacier and had no idea what was being written and could not have communicated with the Italian ambassador in Karachi. In addition, the press coverage did not focus on Mahdi's frostbite, but rather on the mistaken idea that the Italians had prevented the Hunza porter from reaching the summit, because they wanted to keep that privilege for themselves. In the affidavit made to the Italian ambassador, signed by Bonatti and Compagnoni, there is no mention whatsoever of Mahdi's frostbite.

Unlike Bonatti in 1966, Compagnoni did not take his critics to court. Instead he appealed to patriotic values and called for Bonatti to stop the mud-slinging. To some this might seem suspicious, but Compagnoni was seventy when Bonatti first made his accusations and almost eighty when Marshall's article on the summit photographs was published.

Compagnoni was a tough, sometimes abrasive character. There were mistakes and exaggerations in his account of events, and many of his detractors will never forgive him for his decision to move the final camp on the night before the summit attempt, and for failing to come to the aid of Bonatti and Mahdi during their awful bivouac. This does not mean though that he was a compulsive liar.

Both Walter Bonatti and Robert Marshall presented Lino Lacedelli as Compagnoni's toady, who slavishly backed up his partner's lies in order to save face. This doesn't stand up. The two men were neither friends before the expedition, nor afterwards. Compagnoni was a 'Westerner' from the Alps, Lacedelli an 'Easterner' from the Dolomites. After the expedition, they quickly went their separate ways. When in 1955 Compagnoni sued the Italian Alpine Club and the producers for a share in the profits of the film, Lacedelli did not support him and even signed a team letter condemning Compagnoni's actions. In his book, *K2: The Price of Conquest*, he was very critical of Compagnoni but yet he insisted that the story about the oxygen running out was true. When his co-author, the mountaineer and journalist Giovanni Cenacchi, pressed him on this point, he always had the same answer: whatever anyone said, whatever numbers anyone came up with to prove the point, their analysis was 'theoretical'. Lino knew that the oxygen ran out because he experienced it.

Walter Bonatti won the libel case against the *Gazzetta del Popolo* in 1966 because the judge rejected the accusations made in Nino Giglio's article. No one could seriously believe that Bonatti had used any of the summit team's oxygen because he hadn't had a mask. It doesn't follow from this though that Compagnoni and Lacedelli must have lied about their oxygen running out before the summit. The two events became linked in Giglio's defamatory article but no connection had been made previously by Compagnoni or anyone else. The simple version, that the oxygen ran out either because of equipment or operational failure, has holes and problems and contradictions, but which is more likely: that Compagnoni made up the story in order to slander a teammate ten years later, or that he and his partner were telling the truth?

As for the question of whether Compagnoni deliberately changed the agreed location of the the top camp to prevent Walter Bonatti from joining him, this is impossible to answer definitively. Compagnoni always insisted that it made logical sense to place it as high as possible, Bonatti was equally adamant that this was not what had been decided and that it made the final carry much harder and more dangerous for the support team. Neither ever backed down from their position, and it really is one man's word, and one man's memory, against the other's.

In retrospect, of course, it was not a wise move. It didn't gain Compagnoni and Lacedelli any extra time on the morning of their ascent and if the final camp had been lower, Mahdi would probably not have suffered such severe frostbite and Walter Bonatti would not have had to endure such a traumatic ordeal. It's hard to believe though that this was a deliberately cynical move on Compagnoni's part, in order to harm Bonatti or anyone else. Compagnoni didn't know precisely who was going to be in the support party, and with the death of Mario Puchoz just a few weeks earlier, it impossible to think that he would have behaved so callously. What you can say though is that Walter Bonatti behaved selflessly and heroically: if he hadn't kept his nerve, the porter Mahdi would probably not have survived the night, and without the oxygen sets they carried up, which Bonatti took such care over, the summit would undoubtedly not have been reached on the following day.

Where though did that oxygen in all likelihood run out? In the first extended interview given by Compagnoni in November 1954 to the magazine *Settimo Giorno*, he said, 'I think, though I can't be sure, that it was around 100m from the summit.' This matches another intriguing piece of documentary evidence from one of the eye witnesses. Both Lacedelli and Compagnoni remembered it happening at around the same time as the mist cleared, allowing them to see the tents of Camp 8 below and their teammates standing next to them. For Lino Lacedelli the sight of his comrades below was a tremendous pick-me-up – a sign that everything would work out and they should keep going. That same moment when the clouds parted was also recalled from the opposite perspective by Pino Gallotti at Camp 8. In his unpublished diary, he recalled being called out of his tent by the Hunza Isakhan, who was pointing at two tiny figures heading up toward the summit. It was roughly 5.30 p.m., about half an hour before Compagnoni and Lacedelli reached the summit.

The idea that they survived for 30–60 minutes without supplementary oxygen is feasible, and ties in with the first reports sent back to Italy by expedition leader Ardito Desio, as well as Lacedelli's later evidence. Maybe Compagnoni did exaggerate in some of his accounts but he always qualified his timings and altitudes by admitting that he could not remember anything precisely, and it is obvious from his testimony about the hallucinations on the way up and his breakdown on the summit that he was not in a very orderly frame of mind during the final stages of the ascent.

That such a momentous event in the history of mountaineering should end in acrimony is sad for everyone involved. All the climbers on the Italian team were operating at the limits of their ability and endurance; the final drama took place at extremely high altitude, where mistakes are common, memories uncertain and where the best-laid plans frequently unravel. Should Compagnoni and Lacedelli have thought more about their support party? Undoubtedly. Should they have given due credit to Bonatti and Mahdi? Certainly. Should they have kept a better record of their altitudes, taken more photographs, consulted their watches more frequently and behaved more rationally with regard to their oxygen sets? Maybe. Is it realistic to expect them to have done so? Of course not. All the great Himalayan ascents of the early 1950s were much more chaotic than anyone had envisaged. Exhaustion, ambition, hypoxia, altitude, cold, obsession, dehydration, danger – it is a potent cocktail, but not one that is ever going to lead to a simple, straightforward outcome.

What remains uncontested is that on 31 July 1954 at around 6.00 p.m. Achille Compagnoni and Lino Lacedelli became the first men to reach the summit of K2, fulfilling the ambition that Aleister Crowley, the Duke of Abruzzi, Charlie Houston and Fritz Wiessner had all failed to realise. They got to the top, were both very surprised to discover they could breathe freely without supplementary oxygen, enjoyed a few minutes of wonder, and then in a state of high anxiety recorded their triumph, before descending to their comrades, narrowly avoiding death on several occasions. K2 had been climbed, not conquered.

Epilogue

LIVING UP TO
YOUR NAME?

In September 1953, as the American climber George Bell was being stretchered off a plane with frostbitten feet, a reporter asked him for a comment on K2. His reply was succinct:

It's a savage mountain that tries to kill you.

Bell's spontaneous comment provided the title for the 1953 expedition book, *The Savage Mountain*, and went on to become the defining adjective for many later books about K2.

Many of the protagonists of this book experienced the savagery of K2, on and off the mountain. Pasang Kikuli, Kitar, Phinsoo, Dudley Wolfe, Art Gilkey and Mario Puchoz never came back. For Charlie Houston and Fritz Wiessner, K2 was their last major expedition. Neither Achille Compagnoni nor Lino Lacedelli climbed any more big mountains after 1954, and though Walter Bonatti went on to achieve a lot, his obsession with K2 stayed with him to the end of his life and gave him little peace.

In the sixty years since the first ascent hundreds of other climbers have pitted their wits against K2 and the ever-growing collection of plaques attached to the Gilkey memorial reflects how savage and lethal it remains. The big difference today is its accessibility. Whereas then an expedition to the Karakoram meant giving up at least half a year, today it is possible to do the same trip in just two months. K2 is by no means as busy as Everest, but every spring there are usually several expeditions camped out at base camp, eyeing the summit with a mixture of fear and excitement.

It hasn't always been thus. There was just one attempt on K2 in the twenty years after Desio's 1954 expedition. It was led by Bill Hackett, a charismatic major in the US Army, then stationed in Germany. His 1960 expedition was notable for being the first to include a woman, Lynn Pease, but like so many of his predecessors, Hackett was forced to endure appalling weather and did not manage to get above 24,000 ft.

For the next twelve years the Pakistani government refused to allow any further expeditions to K2 or any of the other Karakoram giants. The northern borders of India and Pakistan remained disputed and the two countries spent much of the 1960s at, or on the verge of, war. Pakistan did sign a treaty with China in which they formally agreed that K2 marked the frontier between their two countries but the Pakistani government was very sensitive about the whole region and preferred to restrict access rather than risk any incidents.

When in 1974 Islamabad had a change of heart, Bob Bates, Charlie Houston's great friend and expedition partner, was one of the first Westerners to get his application approved. He was now sixty-three and, though still climbing, was not intending to make a third attempt. Bob took his wife Gail and his Harvard friend Adams Carter, along with his wife Ann, on what they nicknamed 'the Memsahib expedition', planning to revisit and reminisce rather than settle old scores.

Bob hired Mohammed Hussein as the expedition's sirdar, or head porter. The last time they had seen each other was at the end of the traumatic 1953 expedition, when Mohammed had been one of the Baltis who helped carry George Bell out of base camp. After a shorter but no less thrilling approach march, they finally reached Concordia. Bob was disappointed to discover that a party of Japanese trekkers had beaten them to it but none of the interlopers ventured further. Leaving their wives behind for a couple of days, Bates and Carter hiked up to base camp and then went over to the west side of the mountain to look at potential new routes to the summit before heading back.

A year later, a large American party, led by the well-known climber Jim Whittaker, tried to climb K2 via the north west ridge but they were not successful and their expedition is remembered as much for Galen Rowell's book *In the Throne Room of the Mountain Gods* as for any mountaineering achievements. Traditionally, 'official expedition accounts' had avoided any reference to conflict, but Rowell's was a 'warts-and-all' memoir that seemed to positively revel in detailing all the arguments, schisms and personal infighting that occurred before the team gave up.

Three years later, Whittaker came back with a bigger, stronger party that included four members of the previous team. This time they were much more successful, with four climbers reaching the summit via the north east ridge that Eckenstein's party had pioneered back in 1902. The expedition book, with a preface by Senator Edward Kennedy, was much more celebratory. The title said it all: *The Last Step: The American Ascent of K2*.

Over the next few decades, K2 followed a familiar pattern established in the Alps and then repeated on Everest, with successive expeditions tackling its various ridges and occasionally having the temerity to venture out onto its even more dangerous faces. A new style of mountaineering emerged, known as 'Alpine style' climbing. Instead of laying siege to a peak with a large team and several camps before a summit attempt, a new generation preferred to move fast and light, climbing in small parties and rarely using supplementary oxygen. This approach became very popular in the 1980s when successful Alpine-style attempts were made on Everest and several other Himalayan peaks. When the same approach was tried on K2, in the infamous 1986 season, the world's second-highest mountain hit the headlines once again, for all the wrong reasons.

The season began with no fewer than nine separate teams assembled at K2 base camp. The old system of awarding one permit per year for one team had long been abandoned but this was an unprecedented number. There were more than forty climbers from all around the world: South Korea, Poland, Britain, Spain, Italy, Austria and Pakistan. A year earlier, eleven climbers had reached the summit so hopes were high that this would once more be a bumper season.

The Americans John Smolich and Alan Pennington were the first to perish, swallowed up by a huge avalanche. The French husband and wife team Liliane and Maurice Barrard were next. They took the now 'traditional' route up the Abruzzi ridge and reached the summit on the afternoon of 23 June along with their teammates, the famous Polish climber Wanda Rutkiewicz and the Frenchman Michel Parmentier. Wanda and Liliane thus became the first two women to reach the top of K2, but there was no time to celebrate. With darkness falling fast and the temperature dropping rapidly, the four climbers spent a miserable night at 27,200 ft. They had a tent but, like Fritz Wiessner in 1939, they had no sleeping bags. On the next day, Parmentier and Rutkiewicz made it back down but the Barrards disappeared on the descent. No one knows quite what happened, but toward the end of July Liliane Barrard's body was discovered 10,000 ft lower down. Maurice Barrard's body was not found until twelve years later.

These early casualties did not deter the other expeditions camped on the mountain that year and the deaths continued. The Polish climber Tadeusz Piotrowski made an amazing first ascent of K2's unclimbed south face but came off when descending on a steep ice-slope, close to the point where Art Gilkey had disappeared thirty-three years earlier. He was never seen again.

Six days later, the Italian Renato Casarotto died in extraordinarily tragic circumstances, after getting to within 900 ft of the summit via the so-called Magic Line up K2's south west pillar. It was his third attempt that year but with storms on the horizon he decided to play safe and descend. He was less than an hour from base camp when a snow bridge gave way sending him plummeting into a deep crevasse.

By chance, the Austrian mountaineer Kurt Diemberger saw him disappear and immediately alerted Casarotto's wife Goretta, part of his support team. She was able to speak to her husband via radio. He had survived the fall but knew that he was very badly injured. 'I can't last long,' he said. When a rescue team reached him, Casarotto was still alive but only just. Goretta tried to organise a helicopter to fly her husband to hospital in Skardu, but it was too late. When a second team arrived with a doctor, Renato Casarotto was dead. With the agreement of his wife, his body was lowered back into the crevasse, his killer become his tomb.

The long-drawn-out agony of Casarotto's death did not put an end to that year's attempts. Bad weather plagued the mountain during mid-July, but at the end of the month the climbing started again and so did the casualties. In early August, a small team of two Polish climbers and one Czech made the first-ever ascent of Casarotto's 'Magic Line', without supplementary oxygen. On the descent, one of them, Wojciech Wroz, began abseiling down a fixed line which unknown to him had come free from its anchor. When he reached the end of the rope, he was unable to stop himself from falling off into an abyss.

A day later, an ad hoc team composed of three Austrians – Hannes Weiser, Alfred Imitzer and Willi Bauer – the Polish climber Mrufka Wolf and the British mountaineer Al Rouse, and the famous climbing and filming partnership of Kurt Diemberger and his British friend Julie Tullis headed for the summit after climbing the Abruzzi ridge. Beforehand, they had all spent two nights on the Shoulder of K2, at around 26,250 ft, and no one was in great shape.

All but two of them reached the summit but as they descended the weather deteriorated. For five days they were virtually confined to their tents. It was just like the vicious storm that Charlie Houston endured in 1953, but whereas Charlie's team started out at least feeling healthy and positive, most of the seven climbers on the Shoulder of K2 in 1986 were already exhausted and close to the limits of their endurance.

Britain's Julie Tullis was the first to die, her final words a plea to the strongest of the Austrians, Willi Bauer, to get her partner Kurt back down safely. He was devastated but by then everyone was in a desperate state. There was no food left and when their supply of bottled gas ran out, no way to turn snow into water.

When the storm finally abated, three of the survivors were in no condition to descend: Al Rouse had not left his sleeping bag for over forty-eight hours and could not stand up. Alfred Imitzer and Hannes Weiser were so weak that fellow Austrian Willi Bauer struggled to persuade them to move. Less than 50 ft from their tent they collapsed, leaving him to carry on alone. Diemberger and Bauer made it back to base camp and raised the alarm, but Mrufka Wolf disappeared during the descent.

By the end of the season twenty-seven people had reached the summit and thirteen had died, seven of them on the way down after a successful summit attempt. As the details of the '1986 K2 Disaster' emerged, they prompted shocked headlines in Europe's press and a lot of soul searching in the climbing world. The British high-altitude expert Dr Michael Ward, himself a noted climber and a member of the 1953 Everest team, co-authored an open letter to *The Times* in which he blamed the events on the recent fashion for Alpine-style climbing without supplementary oxygen.[1] It might work for a few super athletes like the Italian Reinhold Messner, the greatest climber of his era, but it was too dangerous for most others.

Over in the USA, Charlie Houston echoed the sentiment in an article for the *American Alpine Journal* called 'Death in High Places', in which he asked whether any climber can 'violate physiological principles' and expect to survive. He did not mince his words, putting the deaths that year down to the combined effects of dehydration, oxygen starvation and hypothermia – brought about by a combination of 'bad judgment, bad manners and bad luck'.[2]

Houston noted that the events took place very close to the site and in the same week as his own 1953 tragedy, and there were others who made the comparison between his party's attempt to bring down the stricken Art Gilkey and the 'abandoning' of Al Rouse by his tent mates. This of course was unfair, considering the specific circumstances of 1986, but the questions were inevitable. As another veteran British climber, Trevor Braham, asked eloquently in the *American Alpine Journal*: had a new age of selfish competitiveness arrived, in which traditional mountaineering ethics were replaced by a new set of values, in which ambition trumped teamwork and brotherhood?[3]

In certain respects, the debate about 'Alpine climbing' echoed the arguments over Fritz Wiessner's 1939 expedition and the question of what constitutes a justifiable risk. This time, however, rather than being framed as an opposition between German and British values, the

LIVING UP TO YOUR NAME?

culture clash was between older and younger generations. The 1986 disaster could have taken place on any big mountain in the Himalayas or the Karakoram, but K2 with all its 'objective hazards' and unavoidable risks such as altitude and steepness, was the perfect stage for a modern-day mountaineering tragedy.[4]

That question of ambition and risk was given a strange new twist a year later when K2 reappeared in the press for altogether different, and even more unexpected, reasons. In March 1987 the *New York Times* ran an interview with George Wallerstein, an astronomy professor from the University of Washington in Seattle, who had made a dramatic discovery: based on measurements taken at the end of the 1986 season, he concluded that K2 was in fact 29,064 ft high – 814 ft higher than Lieutenant T.G. Montgomerie's original measurement and almost 30 ft higher than Everest.

Wallerstein's revelation made headlines all over the world and not unexpectedly received a lot of coverage in Italy. Did this mean that Compagnoni and Lacedelli had climbed the highest mountain on earth, not Hillary and Tenzing? The disastrous 1986 season had tarnished K2's reputation, but would it rise once more if it turned out to be Everest's superior? Appropriately enough, the man who offered to settle the dispute was none other than Ardito Desio.

He was by now almost ninety, but his appetite for work was undiminished. He went to Italy's National Research Council, the same body that put up most of the money in 1954, and persuaded them to fund an expedition that would begin at Everest and then move on to K2 and use identical equipment to measure the heights of both. Technology was evolving fast. George Wallerstein had relied on an early generation of US Navy satellites for his positional fixes, but Desio was able to get hold of the very latest GPS equipment which promised to be much more accurate. Twenty years later GPS would be commonplace in every mobile phone, but in 1987 it represented cutting edge technology and getting hold of it was a real coup.

Desio's team of nine included two survivors of K2's 1986 season: Kurt Diemberger, who came on board as the official cameraman, and the climber Agostino Da Polenza, who had summited in the previous year. In the end, for family reasons, Desio was unable to travel out with his expedition but he supervised everything in his usual thorough fashion and it all went smoothly. In early August they measured Everest and a few weeks later pitched up at K2. For once the weather gods were kind and they were able to carry out both sets of measurements in perfect conditions.

After comparing the data, Desio announced that K2 was indeed taller than its first surveyor, Lieutenant Montgomerie, had thought – but only by 16 ft. Everest too had grown, in his electronic estimation, by a full 79 ft, making the difference between the world's highest and second-highest mountains even greater. As for why the original measurements were no longer correct, though remarkably accurate for their day, Desio explained that both the Himalayas and the Karakoram were continuing to be pushed up from the earth's crust as the continental plates containing Eurasia and the Indian subcontinent rubbed against each other. Depending on whose estimate you chose, every year K2 was growing in height by anything from 1 cm to 3.8 cm.[5]

Though it is inevitable that they will always be compared, the recent histories of the world's two highest mountains have been very different. Since the mid-1990s, Everest has been dominated by commercial expeditions in which teams of Sherpas and mountain guides take ad hoc groups of paying clients to the summit, most using the so-called yak route up the south east ridge that the British and Swiss teams pioneered in the early 1950s. In return for tens of thousands of dollars, relatively inexperienced mountaineers reach the summit regularly. In 2012 over 548 men and women made it – almost as many in one season as in Everest's first forty years.[6]

There have been a handful of semi-commercial expeditions on K2 but its much greater technical difficulties make large-scale commercial guiding inconceivable. It is hard to imagine that the overcrowding which has been held responsible for several recent deaths on Everest will ever become the norm on K2. On the other hand, the practice of selling multiple permits did not stop after the deaths of 1986 and is equally unlikely to disappear. Though mountaineering and trekking do not play nearly so great a role in Pakistan's economy as they do in

Nepal's, there is just too much foreign money coming in to revert to the old system of one team per season.

Ironically, one facet of modern mountaineering which should make things safer is now adding to the dangers: the ability to predict the weather with a reasonable degree of accuracy. Today most expeditions arrive at K2 armed with satellite-phones and laptops. They report their progress on a daily basis and use the same technology to receive detailed weather forecasts. In the past, attempts might be spread out over weeks; today teams are much more likely to wait at base camp for a good 'weather window' and then all head for the summit at roughly the same time. This was the root cause of K2's second great tragedy in 2008.

It began with some 73 climbers, porters and Sherpas waiting at base camp for the break in the weather that would allow them to dash up the Abruzzi ridge to the summit. In 2007 there had been thirty-one ascents so the mood at base camp was confident, with climbers from Korea, Singapore, the Netherlands, Italy, the USA, Ireland and Serbia having converged on the mountain. Many of the participants were highly experienced, and for some this was their second attempt. June and July were both plagued by storms and heavy snowfalls but at the end of the month four separate forecasting companies reported that the weather was about to break, prompting several teams to collaborate on a mass attempt on the summit.

The practice of putting up long sections of fixed rope, initiated by the Italians in 1954, had now been extended higher and higher up the mountain. Instead of being roped up to each other for safety, climbers would clip on to long stretches of line attached semi-permanently to slopes with pitons and ice-screws. In theory it was safer, especially in bad weather when the fixed lines would provide both a route marker and a hand-rail to the top.

One of the crucial places where the rope had to be fixed was the Bottleneck, the narrow channel at 26,500 ft that leads up toward the summit. Unfortunately, careful planning at base camp did not translate into a successful operation higher up. In the early morning of 1 August, the various teams converged on the Bottleneck, only to discover that neither enough rope nor enough personnel had arrived the night before. With rope fixing still in progress, two dozen people were forced to wait in a high-altitude queue that no one anticipated or desired.

The first casualty was a Serbian climber, Dren Mandic. By about 11.00 a.m. he had reached the middle of the Bottleneck. At a certain moment, possibly needing to change oxygen cylinder, he unclipped from the fixed rope to allow other climbers to pass. Moments later he slipped and fell about 300 ft. By the time a rescue team reached him, it was obvious that he was dead. While trying to carry down his body, Jehan Baig, a Pakistani high-altitude porter, fell to his death.

Higher up the mountain the other climbers were slowly making their way toward the summit. The first arrived at 3.00 p.m. but it took another five hours before the remaining seventeen topped out. Getting there so late in the day committed almost everyone to making his or her descent in the dark.

At around 8.30 p.m. three members of a Norwegian team were making their way down toward the Bottleneck when a huge block of ice came tumbling down from above, taking one man, Rolf Bae, with it, and slicing through the fixed ropes. Ironically, Bae had not actually summitted that day but stopped around 300 ft short to await the return of his wife, Cecile Skog, who had continued without him.

With the fixed ropes cut and darkness falling, getting down the mountain was much more difficult. Most of the climbers were wearing head torches but no one had brought extra rope, and to add to the danger, sections of the route were now choked with broken ice. The fourteen climbers who remained were faced with a stark choice: descend in the dark without the safety of fixed ropes, or bivouac and make their way down at first light.

Of the seven climbers who chose the first option, six made it down, but one, the Frenchman Hugues D'Aubarede, fell to his death. The remaining eight shivered until dawn. In the confusion of the following day, as rescue parties were organised below, they attempted to descend. Though the precise sequence of events is still disputed only two of them succeeded, bringing the death toll to eleven climbers within forty-eight hours.[7]

To add to the panic and chaos, all this was happening in the era of high-speed communication. In the early 1950s, it took weeks for the families of Art Gilkey and Mario Puchoz to find out about their deaths, but the events of 2008 almost seemed to be happening in real time, with reports coming out of base camp via sat-phone and email within days and sometimes hours of events occurring. Unsurprisingly, mistakes were made about who had survived and who had not.

There were moments of great heroism and bravery, but the '2008 K2 disaster' almost had a whiff of excess about it: too many teams, too much technology, too many climbers trying to reach the same spot at the same time. For years lurid reports had been appearing in the press about queues of climbers high on Everest at the Hillary Step, but K2 had retained its reputation as the climber's mountain, where only the world's elite ventured.

Of course this was illusory: Guy Knowles and Dudley Wolfe had gone to K2 in 1902 and 1939 with little experience, and Wolfe had paid the price. When K2 was difficult and expensive to reach, numbers were limited, but the era of fast, cheap flights had arrived and you didn't need to have hundreds of thousands of dollars or months of spare time to take on K2 or any of the other Himalayan giants. One of the great joys of mountaineering has always been the fact that there are no 'official' rules, no external hurdles to climb over before you take on a particular peak – apart from those that you set up for yourself. On the other hand, the new era in which multiple expeditions attack the same route at the same time has thrown up ethical dilemmas that previous generations did not have to face.

For men like Charlie Houston and Bob Bates, the idea of the 'brotherhood of the rope', the sense of shared endeavour and the expectation of high levels of mutual support, was a central part of their mountaineering philosophy. But is there such a thing as the 'brotherhood of the fixed rope'? Do you have the same responsibility to climbers who you have never met before as you do to members of your own team? Today even big mountains have their lone wolves – individuals who turn up at base camp planning to solo the mountain with minimal equipment, and sometimes limited experience. If something goes wrong, is it everyone else's responsibility to look after them? These questions are not exclusive to K2, but because of its altitude and steepness the odds of things going awry are that much higher, so the dilemmas are more acute.

All this is a far cry from 1902 when Oscar Eckenstein and Aleister Crowley headed for K2 believing it offered 'no particular technical difficulties' and might easily be ascended in a few days. They were wrong, of course, but you wonder what Crowley would think about K2's current reputation as 'the world's hardest mountain'. In the 1900s the world was a much more mysterious place and the excitement about going there was not refracted through hyperbole in the same way as it is today.

History, or climbing history at least, has treated K2's pioneers relatively well. Back in 1902 Oscar Eckenstein and Aleister Crowley were considered mavericks, but both have now entered the pantheon of 'mountaineering visionaries', albeit of the eccentric kind, because of their espousal of climbing without the assistance of any professional guides.

Crowley outlived Eckenstein by twenty-six years and became much more famous, though 'infamous' is probably a more appropriate adjective. Denounced in 1923 as 'The Wickedest Man in the World' by one British newspaper, his experiments with sex, drugs and the occult endeared him far more to later generations than to his contemporaries. In 1967 he was immortalised on the cover of the Beatles' *Sgt Pepper's Lonely Hearts Club Band*, one of the 1960s most iconic albums. With other fans including Led Zeppelin's Jimmy Page and Ozzy Osbourne of Black Sabbath, for a while at least he was more famous in the world of rock and roll, than rock and ice.

Though arguably it was Crowley who first identified the south east ridge as the simplest way to the summit, he didn't manage to get his name on it or any other of K2's features. Its next suitor did, and today whenever any climbers start to ascend the Abruzzi ridge, they pay linguistic homage to the illustrious Italian Duke who did so much to make K2 famous.

As with Oscar Eckenstein, K2 turned out to be Abruzzi's last major climbing expedition. During the First World War he rose up the ranks of the Italian Navy to become a vice-admiral. When hostilities ended, he spent much of his time in the then Italian colony of Somalia, founding a model farming settlement. He died there in 1933 at the relatively young age of sixty, in a small house that it is said he shared with his secret Somali lover, Faduma Ali.

Charlie Houston, the next big character in the early history of K2, lived for much longer, passing away at the esteemed age of ninety-six in 2009. He didn't christen any of K2's features but his name will always be linked to the mountain. 1938 was in many ways a model reconnaissance, and though unsuccessful, his second attempt in 1953 is one of the most famous expeditions of the post-war era. As Reinhold Messner wrote, Houston's team may not have reached the top but they failed 'in the most beautiful way you could imagine'.

Several team members took part in further expeditions, but for Charlie Houston his second attempt on K2 was a turning point, an 'epiphany' as he later called it. Having come so close to death, and still feeling very guilty over Art Gilkey, he virtually stopped climbing and never went on another big expedition.

It wasn't easy, though, to give up something that he had been so passionate about. Mountaineering had been a central part of his life since his student days, and though he saw himself as being a very democratic leader, he clearly liked being in charge of teams. Over the next ten years while he struggled with periodic depression, Charlie's life took on an uncertain, rootless quality. He moved to Aspen to join a pioneering physical and mental health centre, spent a year trying to develop an artificial heart for America's National Heart Institute and then worked for the Kennedy government's Peace Corps before returning to the US to become a professor of medicine at the University of Vermont.

His new focus was supposed to be community medicine, but in the same year that he took up the post, Charlie was invited to take part in an ambitious project to set up a medical research lab high up on a plateau near Mount Logan in Canada's Yukon. Over the next decade he spent virtually every July on Logan, conducting numerous experiments on different aspects of high-altitude physiology and publishing dozens of academic papers.

In 1987 his life came full circle when he staged Operation Everest II, at a US Army research facility in Massachusetts. This time round it was on an even bigger scale, with eight subjects spending up to forty days in the decompression chamber while undergoing a simulated ascent to 29,000 ft. Whereas in 1946 the scope was limited, this time Charlie had a team of twenty-five scientists and much more sophisticated equipment and was able to study the complex way in which the human body reacts and adapts to altitude.

By the time Charlie died in 2009, he was acknowledged as a world expert in high-altitude physiology. He had not solved all its mysteries but had made a significant contribution to scientific understanding and inspired a future generation of researchers. For some of his friends, this was his greatest achievement, but for obituary writers around the world, the 1953 K2 expedition remained the touchstone of his life.

His credo, lived out on his expeditions, that the way in which you make an attempt is as important as whether you get to the top, is always going to be a hard sell in a world where competitiveness and individualism have become core values, but the undoubted courage and sheer humanity that run through the story of 1953 have given that expedition legendary status.

Ironically, considering their rivalry and intense mutual dislike, Charlie and Fritz Wiessner ended up living very close to each other. Charlie spent the last forty years of his life in Burlington, Vermont, the same town where Fritz had set up his ski wax business in 1946. Fritz lived nearby in Stowe. Both men came to be regarded as elder statesmen of the American mountaineering world, but they were never reconciled.

Like Charlie, Fritz did not go on another major mountaineering expedition after K2. His business, manufacturing and selling ski wax, took off during the Second World War and continued to thrive, with 'Wiessner's Wonder Wax' his bestselling and most famous product. In 1945 he married Muriel Schoonmaker and had two children.

When large-scale Himalayan expeditions began again in the early 1950s, he was too involved in his family and his business interests to want to disappear off to the far side of the world for months at a time but he couldn't quite shake off his fascination with K2. In the autumn of 1953, after the failure of Houston's expedition, he briefly considered organising another K2 expedition and even wrote to the American Alpine Club to find out if they would support him. Nothing came of it but Fritz did have a lot of contact with Ardito Desio, the leader of the Italian expedition.

His appetite for smaller-scale mountaineering never left him. Throughout his life he spent much of his holidays and recreation time on the crags and cliffs of North America, continuing to climb at a very high standard. He climbed all over the world from Mexico to Australia to the Alps to North Wales and even at eighty-six was leading on difficult routes. He never returned to K2 but in the early 1960s he visited India and spent time in Sikkim, in the far north of the country, with Pasang Lama, his partner in 1939. When years later Pasang fell on hard times, Fritz helped him financially.

Fritz Wiessner was not such an angst-ridden character as Charlie Houston and nor did he possess what Charlie's biographer Bernadette McDonald calls his 'messianic streak'. Whereas Charlie wrote articles and spoke out publicly about everything from climbing ethics to the impact of mass tourism on Nepal, Fritz kept a much lower profile, though he did do a lot of work for the American Alpine Club. Mountaineering was absolutely central to his life. As he once said, it had given him his 'greatest joys and most profound sorrows' and undoubtedly his most intense experiences had come on K2.[8]

As he regularly told journalists in his later years, if only Pasang Lama had agreed to follow him that windless night in July 1939, together they might have reached the summit, climbed back down, collected Dudley Wolfe and returned to America as heroes. So much of what followed hinged on that fateful moment when Fritz went against his own instinct and turned back for his Sherpa's sake.

When he died in 1988, tributes came in from all over the world, and even after the questions raised by Putnam and Kauffman's book on the 1939 expedition, Fritz's reputation has stayed very high. In spite of all the controversies, what remains unquestioned is that Fritz put in an extraordinary effort and got within a whisper of the summit.

The intriguing question is what could Houston and Wiessner have achieved, if they had climbed together in 1939 or even in 1953? Could they have reached the summit of K2? Both men were tremendously gifted and confident in their own skills. If Charlie had acted as Fritz's deputy in 1939, it is impossible to imagine that any camps would have been stripped before the lead party came down. Though in 1939 Fritz did not want to include Paul Petzoldt in his team, he later became convinced that they would have been perfect partners.

If Fritz had been invited on Houston's expedition in 1953, his knowledge of the mountain would have been invaluable. He would have been fifty-three, and considered past his prime, but in fact he would have been twelve years younger than Carlos Soria Fontán, the Spanish mountaineer who climbed K2 in 2004 at the age of sixty-five.

Hypothetical questions like this, of course, do not mean very much. Given a little more luck, Fritz might have succeeded in 1939 with Pasang Lama, and though Charlie would not have put himself forward for the summit team in 1953, it's perfectly possible that several other members of his team might have gone all the way if the weather had been better.

Equally, both expeditions might have fared even worse if they had been gifted the same atrocious storms that blighted Oscar Eckenstein's expedition of 1902. Luck plays an enormous part in any high-risk sport, and no matter how good a team is, the weather is almost always the decisive factor on any mountaineering expedition.

If Fritz Wiessner and Charlie Houston are now seen as key figures in K2's history even after failing to achieve their goal, it is ironic that the two men who actually succeeded, Achille Compagnoni and Lino Lacedelli, are regarded in a much more problematic light. Like so many of the other climbers in this story, neither went on another major expedition after K2. In 1954 Compagnoni was already forty, and by the time his law case against the producers of the K2 film reached its inevitable and unhappy climax, he was four years older and may have simply felt too old for a return to the Himalayas. He continued to work as a ski instructor and mountain guide and climbed the Matterhorn many more times before eventually retiring to run the hotel in Cervinia that still bears his name. His fame lasted for many years after K2 and he was honoured by organisations and governments all over the world.

Lino Lacedelli was ten years younger and well regarded as a climber, but though he continued to work as a mountain guide and run a climbing and skiing shop in the Dolomites called K2 Sports, he too never went on any other big expeditions. Immediately after his success in 1954, he talked about returning to the Karakoram to climb K2's unclimbed neighbour, Broad Peak, but after complications over permits the expedition failed to take off. Achille Compagnoni had a touch of the showman about him but Lacedelli did not enjoy all the publicity and attention that came with being a national hero, and preferred life out of the limelight. In 2004, at the age of seventy-nine, he was persuaded to make a commemorative trek to K2 base camp as part of the fiftieth-anniversary celebrations and impressed his much younger companions with his strength and resilience.

Walter Bonatti, of course, went on to become one of the most celebrated mountaineers of the post-war era and remains a towering figure in Italy. Today his role in getting the oxygen equipment up to the last camp and the unplanned bivouac at 26,600 ft is acclaimed as a key factor in the 1954 expedition's success. A few years later Bonatti tried unsuccessfully to raise money for a return to the Karakoram to make a second, oxygenless attempt on K2. It is only speculation, of course, but he probably could have made it. In *K2: The Price of Conquest*, Lino Lacedelli wrote that he thought he and Compagnoni could have reached the summit in 1954 without any supplementary oxygen at all, and the fact that Bonatti got very high on K2 in 1954 and reached the summit of nearby 26,000 ft Gasherbrum IV in 1958, entirely under his own steam, makes it likely.

It is difficult to know what history will make of Bonatti's long-running feud with Compagnoni. The available evidence points toward Bonatti being wrong about the oxygen question, his 'menzogna di base' or base lie, but there have been so many twists and turns to that particular controversy that it is too early to say that it is fully closed.

The 'caso di K2' is a very sad postscript to the K2 saga, but perhaps it is not so surprising, considering the tangled history of the mountain.

K2 has always attracted extraordinary people and frequently been an arena for extraordinary events. Looking at its early history and the later tragedies in 1986 and 2008, you might wonder why anyone would ever want to go.

There are many answers: K2 is incredibly beautiful, with the kind of pyramidal shape that makes it an iconic mountain. The very fact that it has a reputation for danger, for being the 'ultimate challenge', makes it attractive to a lot of mountaineers. With very few elite climbers interested in Everest's current incarnation as a commercial playground, K2 has become even more entrenched as the 'mountaineer's mountain'.

The epic saga of K2 is not a neat orderly story of methodical conquest. It is full of strange events and eccentric characters – from Aleister Crowley waving his revolver at Guy Knowles in 1902, to Dudley Wolfe dying in squalor at 23,400 ft in 1939, to Art Gilkey's mysterious disappearance in 1953, and Compagnoni and Lacedelli carrying their empty oxygen sets to the summit in the following year. K2 is a mountain where the extraordinary is almost the norm.

Every year the mountain gives up some of its victims: Art Gilkey's remains were found in 1993, Dudley Wolfe's in 2002. I vividly recall coming across a partially complete rib cage on the Godwin-Austen glacier when shooting a documentary for the BBC. There was no clothing or equipment nearby that might have identified who it was, so we said a silent prayer and moved on.

There's a line repeated in many articles and books about a mountain being a climber's best possible burial ground. This is comforting to grieving friends and relatives, but the people who I've met and interviewed for this book and the earlier documentary have all been drawn to mountains for life-affirming reasons rather than to dice with death for its own sake.

K2 is like its name: bare, simple, and slightly unworldly. If it has any ghosts, may they rest in peace.

ACKNOWLEDGEMENTS

Though most books have a sole author, they are invariably collaborative efforts to one degree or another. There are many people whom I would like to thank for the help they gave me over the years.

In the first instance, I want to thank the BBC team with whom I worked on the K2 documentary many moons ago which inspired this book. Clare Paterson, Tim Jordan, Alison Ramsey, Theresa Lydon, Richard Adam, Keith Partridge, Frank Bigg, Brian Hall and John McAvoy all played key roles.

Regarding the book itself, a big thank you goes to my agent, Anthony Sheil, and to Sally Riley and everyone else in the foreign rights department at Aitken Alexander, and to Mike Harpley, my editor, Tamsin Shelton, my copy-editor, and all the other staff at Oneworld.

The documentary we made in 2000 was principally based on interviews with survivors, their families and a range of historians and mountaineers. Sadly, some of them are now dead, but their testimony gave me a strong grounding in the story and I would like to thank all of them: David Roberts, Bill Putnam, Andy Wiessner, Ed Webster, Dudley Rochester, Charlie Houston, Bob Bates, Bob Craig, Dee Molenaar, Pete Schoening, George Bell, Tony Streather, Achille Compagnoni and Lino Lacedelli.

This book by contrast was largely based on archival documents and there's no doubt that it would not have been possible without the considerable help of librarians and archivists around the world, including Glyn Hughes of the Alpine Club in London, Katie Sauter and Dana Gerschel of the US Alpine Club in Colorado, and Alessandra Ravelli and Veronica Lisino of the Italian Alpine Club in Turin. I'd also like to thank archivists and librarians at the British Library in London, the Bodleian Library in Oxford and the Royal Geographical Society in London for their help and assistance.

For granting access to their private and family collections, I'd like to thank Andy Wiessner and Elda Compagnoni, and also Maria Lacedelli, Margaret Durrance, Paola Gallotti and Dee Molenaar for their help and assistance. I'd also like to record my gratitude to Nandini Purani of the *Himalayan Journal*, Ingo Welling from the Dräger Archive and Stefano Capelli from the Dalmine Archive in Italy. Norman Hardy, Stephen Venables, Jim Curran, Bernadette McDonald, Maurice Isserman, Stewart Weaver, Leonardo Bizzaro, Roberto Mantovani, Mirella Tenderini and Jennifer Jordan all helped with specific historical questions.

For reading the manuscripts and putting up with the copious typos, missing words and general grammatical errors that riddle my first drafts, I would like to say a special word of thanks to my friends John McAvoy and Jerry Lovatt, and particularly to Tim Jordan, who collaborated with me on the documentary and helped me a lot with this book.

As always my last word of thanks is to my lovely wife, Stella, and children, Frank and Phyllis, for putting up with my absences and the general tedium of living with anyone writing a book, for showing sincere interest in obscure oxygen equipment, and generally keeping me alive and well.

NOTES

PROLOGUE: THE MOUNTAIN WITH NO NAME

1 All 8000ers.com
2 *The Geographical Journal*, 1930
3 Younghusband, Francis, *The Heart of a Continent*
4 Conway, W.M., *Climbing and Exploration in the Karakoram Himalayas*, 1894, p. 326

1 THE BEAST AND THE PRINCE

1 Quoted in Thompson, S., *Unjustifiable Risk?*
2 Crowley, A., *The Confessions of Aleister Crowley*
3 Eckenstein, O., *The Karakorams and Kashmir*
4 Eckenstein, O., *The Karakorams and Kashmir*
5 Quite what this means is anyone's guess. Dapsang is another name for K2, but evidently the author thought it was a separate peak.
6 *The Daily Chronicle*, 13 May 1902
7 The term 'death zone' was not invented until the 1950s, by Edouard Wyss-Dunant.
8 Crowley, A., *The Confessions of Aleister Crowley*, p. 300
9 Chogori means 'big mountain' in Balti.
10 Jacot-Guillarmod, J., *Six Mois dans L'Himalaya*

11 Both Crowley and Jacot-Guillarmod give an altitude for base camp of 18,733 ft. This must be a mistake, as the description they give corresponds to roughly the same position adopted by subsequent expeditions, at around 16,500 ft.

12 Jacot-Guillarmod, J., *Six Mois dans L'Himalaya*, p. 231

13 Crowley later claimed that on his solo dash he reached around 22,000 ft but none of the others corroborated this.

14 Today the height of Aconcagua has been revised down to 22,841 ft. If Jacot-Guillarmod's aneroid barometer was malfunctioning, hence his overestimation of the height of base camp, it is possible that his maximum altitude of 22,000 ft is also incorrect.

15 Guy Knowles diary, 15 July 1902

16 According to an obituary in the *Alpine Journal*, it subsequently became one of his prize possessions, remaining on his mantelpiece for many years to come.

17 Quoted in Clark, Ronald W., *Great Moments in Mountaineering*, Roy Publishing, London, 1956

18 Guy Knowles diary, 1 August 1902

19 De Filippi, F., *Karakoram and Western Himalaya*

20 De Filippi, F., *Karakoram and Western Himalaya*, p. 218

21 De Filippi, F., *Karakoram and Western Himalaya*, p. 235

22 De Filippi, F., *Karakoram and Western Himalaya*, p. 324

23 *New York Times*, 26 September 1909

2 THE HARVARD BOYS

1 This does not include the abortive solo expedition by the American E.F. Farmer.

2 Undated letter, Charlie Houston to Henry Hall, 1936

3 12 April in Houston, C. and Bates, R., *Five Miles High*

4 Nabob is an Anglo-Indian word for a very rich person, their wealth usually made in the East.

5 Houston, C. and Bates, R., *Five Miles High*

6 Houston, C. and Bates, R., *Five Miles High*, p. 151

7 Houston, C., 'A Reconnaissance of K2', *The Himalayan Journal*, 1939

8   Today's climbers equipped with front-pointing crampons and spe-cialised axes for ice-climbing would not be daunted by 60° slopes, but in 1938 they would have been considered unclimbable.

9   Crowley had by then given up climbing.

10   Letter, Charles Houston to parents, as quoted in McDonald, B., *The Brotherhood of the Rope*

11   'One last mountain to climb', *Yankee* magazine, May 1997

12   Various notes, AAJ, 1938, vol. 3, p. 225

13   Letter, Fritz Wiessner to Henry Hall, 1938, Kauff Papers

14   Houston, C. and Bates, R., *Five Miles High*, p. 279

15   Houston, C., 'A Reconnaissance of K2', *The Himalayan Journal*, 1939

16   Houston, C., unpublished article, American Alpine Club Archives

17   See McDonald, B., *The Brotherhood of the Rope*

18   Houston, C., *The American Alpine Journal*, 1939

3 A CLIMBING PARTY

1   Letter, Henry Hall to Fritz Wiessner, 22 December 1938

2   http://www.nols.edu/alumni/leader/95fall/paultellshisstory. shtml

3   Cromwell, O.E., 'Spring Skiing in the Vale of Kashmir', *Appalachia* 23, 1940

4   Sixth expedition newsletter, 5 June 1939

5   Fritz Wiessner diary, 1 June 1939

6   Fritz Wiessner diary, 6 June 1939

7   Jack Durrance diary, 7 June 1939

8   Fritz Wiessner diary, 17 July 1939

9   Sheldon, G., 'Lost behind the Ranges', *Saturday Evening Post*, 16 March 1940, p. 126

10   Jack Durrance diary, 28 June 1939

11   Fritz Wiessner diary, 1 July 1939

12   Jack Durrance diary, 2 July 1939

13   Jack Durrance diary, medical notes

14   Jack Durrance diary, 9 July 1939

4 HIGH AMBITION

1   In the event thirty men turned up.

2   Fritz estimated it as between 27,450 and 27,600 ft.

3   Interview with Maix. Kauffman archive, original source unclear.

4   Fritz Wiessner diary, 22 July 1939

5   Jack Durrance diary, 24 July 1939

5 THE FALL OUT

1   Dornan, David, Profile of Fritz Wiessner, *Ascent*, 1969

2   Note that Fritz Wiessner says 17.

3   Letter, Fritz Wiessner to Alice Damrosch, 4 September 1939

4   When he first heard the news of the deaths on the mountain, George Sheldon wrote in his diary: 'The blame as has been said before lies mostly with Fritz. The great K2 expedition is over and they lost 4 men. Fine work.'

5   Testimony of Jack Durrance, quoted in Conefrey, M. and Jordan, T., *Mountain Men*

6   Letter, Henry Hall to Ellis Fisher, 2 January 1940

7   Unpublished MS, Fritz Wiessner

8   This note no longer exists. Like most of the papers from the original American Alpine Club investigation it has long since disappeared.

9   Letter, Bill House to Andy Kauffman, December 1986, Kauffman Collection, American Alpine Club

10   Rowell, G., *In the Throne Room of the Mountain Gods*, p. 215

11   Viesturs, E., *K2: Life and Death on the World's Most Dangerous Mountain*, p. 182

12   Letter, Andy Kauffman to Fritz Wiessner, 18 February 1982, Kauffman Collection, American Alpine Club, and unpublished MS, Wiessner Collection

13   Letter, Terris Moore to Andy Kauffman, February 1990

6 UNFINISHED BUSINESS

1   Ultimately, the expedition cost just under $31,000.
2   Letter, Charlie Houston to Fritz Wiessner, 8 April 1953, Wiessner Collection
3   As with many expeditions the precise number of porters that they used varies from account to account. In general when they have been available I have taken numbers and dates from the most contemporaneous documents (in this case the expedition newsletters).
4   Ata-Ullah, Mohammad, *Citizen of Two Worlds*
5   Interview, *Mountain Men*, BBC TV, 2001

7 TEAMWORK

1   20,700 ft, Bates, R. and Craig, B., 'We Met Death on K2', *Saturday Evening Post*, 5 December 1953
2   Dee Molenaar diary, 2 July 1953
3   Post K2 tape, recorded August 1953
4   There is a discrepancy in the various accounts over when exactly they held the vote on the summit teams. In some accounts written afterwards they say 3 August, in others 4 August. Dee Molenaar and Pete Schoening both agree in their diaries that it was in fact taken on 5 August.

8 MAN DOWN

1   Bates, R. and Craig, B., 'We Met Death on K2', *Saturday Evening Post*, 5 December 1953
2   Ata-Ullah, Mohammad, *Citizen of Two Worlds*, p. 257
3   Dee Molenaar diary, letter to Lee and Patti, 9 August 1953
4   Interview, *Mountain Men*, BBC TV, 2001
5   Interview, *Mountain Men*, BBC TV, 2001
6   Interview, *Mountain Men*, BBC TV, 2001
7   Bates, R. and Craig, B., 'We Met Death on K2', *Saturday Evening Post*, 5 December 1953

8   Bates, R. and Craig, B., 'We Met Death on K2', *Saturday Evening Post*, 5 December 1934
9   Interview, *Mountain Men*, BBC TV, 2001
10   Bates, R. and Craig, B., 'We Met Death on K2', *Saturday Evening Post*, 5 December 1953

9 THE OLD ROAD

1   *The Times of India*, 31 August 1953
2   Telegram, Ardito Desio to Club Alpino Italiano, 2 September 1953
3   *Corriere Della Sera*, 6 October 1954
4   http://famouswonders.com/italian-lira/
5   Club Alpino Italiano archives, letter 29 December 1953
6   Though Tenzing was Tibetan by birth and had grown up in Nepal, he was claimed by India as its national hero and took Indian citizenship in the late 1950s.
7   Letters, Fritz Wiessner to Ardito Desio, 1954, Wiessner Collection
8   Letter, Fritz Wiessner to Ardito Desio, 18 May 1954
9   Ata-Ullah, Mohammad, *Citizen of Two Worlds*, p. 269
10   Desio, A., *The Ascent of K2*, p. 101
11   *New York Times*, 9 June 1953
12   Press release no. 6, 8 June 1954, Club Alpino Italiano archives
13   See Lacedelli, L., *K2: The Price of Conquest*

10 THE FLOWERS OF ITALY

1   Fantin, M., *K2: Sogno Vissuto*, p. 53
2   Press release no. 8, from a letter 22 June 1954, Club Alpino Italiano archives
3   Fantin, M., *K2: Sogno Vissuto*, p. 53
4   Message no. XI, as quoted in Desio, A., *Il Libro Bianco*, p. 94
5   Press release no. 12, Club Alpino Italiano archives
6   Desio, A., *The Conquest of K2*, p. 156
7   Press release no. 10, 24 July 1954, Club Alpino Italiano archives. Desio's letters, which were turned into press releases, took several

weeks to get from Pakistan to Italy and sometimes arrived out of sequence.

8   *Gli Scoiattoli*, The Squirrels, was a small but highly regarded climbing club based in Cortina D'Ampezzo.

9   Three members of the climbing team – Floreanini, Angelino and Gallotti – plus Pagani, the expedition doctor

10 This in fact was a mistake made by a Sherpa who saw the first summit team, Tom Bourdillon and Charles Evans, reach the south summit, 300 ft below Everest's true summit.

11 Pino Gallotti diary, 31 July 1954

12 A common amphetamine. The Austrian climber Hermann Buhl is said to have taken three amphetamine tablets before beginning his descent of Nanga Parbat in 1953.

13 Press release no.16, 19 August 1954, Club Alpino Italiano archives

14 *La Stampa*, 4 August 1954

15 *Corriere della Sera*, 4 August 1954

11 THE SPOILS OF VICTORY

1   *New York Times*, 21 August 1954. It is impossible to say whether the newspaper delayed publication or Charlie Houston delayed sending the message.

2   Letter, Charlie Houston to Eric Shipton, 4 August 1954, American Alpine Club archives

3   *The Times of India*, 31 August 1954. In some of the early reports, Mahdi is spelt Mehdi but for consistency I have used Mahdi throughout.

4   For a transcript see Bonatti, W., *La Storia di Un Caso*, and Marshall, R., *K2: Lies and Treachery*

5   *Corriere della Sera*, 4 September 1954

6   *Corriere della Sera*, 9 October 1954

7   *Corriere della Sera*, 13 October 1954

8   Letter, Charles Houston, 20 October 1954

9   *Sette Giorni*, 18 November 1954

10 Letter, Ardito Desio to Amadeo Costa, 27 August 1954

11 *Visto*, Bologna, 25 December 1955
12 See Desio, A., *Il Libro Bianco*
13 *Epoca*, 31 July 1955
14 *Epoca*, 26 September 1954
15 *Alto Adige*, 8 September 1955
16 *Corriere della Sera*, 10 September 1955
17 28 September 1955
18 Press cutting, July 1958, Club Alpino Italiano archives

12 THE BASE LIE?

1   Maraini, F., *Karakoram*, pp. 249–50
2   Bonatti, W., *K2: Storia di un caso*, p. 31. The same material appears in *Proceso al K2*.
3   Bonatti, W., *K2: Storia di Un Caso*, p. 71
4   Marshall, R., *K2: Lies and Treachery*, p. 196
5   Fosco Maraini, Luigi Zanzi and Alberto Monticone
6   Marshall, R., *K2: Lies and Treachery*, p. 153
7   Marshall, R., *K2: Lies and Treachery*, p. 151
8   Marshall, R., *K2: Lies and Treachery*, p. 103
9   Their arrival time was corroborated by Pino Gallotti, who had kept a detailed diary and was then stationed at Camp 8.
10 There were two short films made of their Alpine training camps, but though the men were shown testing tents, stoves, winches and other pieces of equipment, there are no oxygen sets featured.
11 Bizzaro L., Gogna A., Pinelli C., *K2: Uomini, Esplorazioni, Imprese*, p. 111
12 The fact that Dräger bottles were blue was confirmed by the company archivist. When a report appeared in the Italian newspaper *La Repubblica* in July 2013 based on my research on the oxygen questions, Luigi Zanzi, one of the *Tre Saggi*, dismissed it, arguing that the colour of the bottles was irrelevant. He argued that the fact that Compagnoni and Lacedelli's oxygen sets ran out at the same time was an impossible coincidence which demonstrated that they were lying. However, Compagnoni and Lacedelli did not

say this – in Compagnoni's book *Men on K2*, he wrote that their sets ran out ten minutes apart. Elsewhere they said roughly the same time. It is possible, of course, that only the Dalmine set ran out before the summit, but bearing in mind the testimony of both men and the general chaos of both the last days of the expedition and the preparation of the oxygen sets in Italy, it is likely that both sets ran out before the summit.

EPILOGUE: LIVING UP TO YOUR NAME?

1 Michael Ward, Charles Warren and Peter Lloyd, *The Times*, 30 August 1986
2 Houston, C., 'Death in High Places', *The American Alpine Journal*, 61, 1987
3 *The American Alpine Journal*, 93, 1988–89
4 Objective hazards are issues such as climate and topography, constant dangers.
5 3.8 cm Ardito Desio
6 http://www.alanarnette.com/blog/2012/05/30/everest-2012-season-recap-a-study-in-risk-management/
7 For a detailed account of the 2008 disaster, see Bowley, G., *No Way Down: Life and Death on K2*, Harper Collins, New York, 2010, and Confortola, M., *Giorno di Ghiaccio*, Baldini e Castoldi, Milan, 2014.
8 'In Memoriam Fritz Wiessner', *The American Alpine Journal*, 63, 1989

BIBLIOGRAPHY

Ata-Ullah, Mohammad, *Citizen of Two Worlds*, Harper, New York, 1960

Bates, Robert, *The Love of Mountains Is Best*, Peter E. Randall, Portsmouth N.H., 1994

Bersezio, Lorenzo, *Il Mito di K2*, Capricorno, Torino, 2014

Bizzaro L., Gogna A., Pinelli C., Associazione Ardito Desio, *K2: Uomini, Esplorazioni, Imprese*, De Agostini, Novara, 2004

Bonatti, Walter, *The Mountains of My Life*, Penguin Classics, London, 2010

Bonatti, Walter, *Le Mie Montagne*, Zanichelli, Bologna, 1961

Bonatti Walter, *Proceso al K2*, Massimo Baldini Editore, Milano, 1985

Bonatti, Walter, *K2: La Verità*, Rizzoli, Milano, 2014

Bonatti, Walter, *Una Vita Libera*, Rizzoli, Milano, 2012

Bowley, Graham, *No Way Down*, Viking, London, 2010

Buffet, Charlie, *Jules Jacot-Guillarmod Pionnier Du K2*, Editions Slatkine, Geneva, 2012

Buhl, Hermann, *Nanga Parbat Pilgrimage*, Hodder & Stoughton, London, 1956

Cassin, Riccardo, *Fifty Years of Alpinism*, Diadem, London, 1981

Compagnoni, Achille, *Beyond K2*, Marsilio Editore, Venezia, 2014

Compagnoni, Achille, *Uomini sul K2*, Veronelli, Milano, 1958

Compagnoni, Achille, *K2 – Tra Storia e Memoria*, Bolis Edizioni, Azzano San Paolo, 2004

Conefrey, Mick and Jordan, Tim, *Mountain Men*, Boxtree, London, 2001

Conway, William Martin, *Climbing and Exploration in the Karakoram-Himalayas*, Fisher Unwin, London, 1894

Crowley, Aleister, *The Confessions of Aleister Crowley*, Mandrake Press, London, 1929

Crowley, Aleister, *The Spirit of Solitude*, Vol. 2, Mandrake Press, London, 1929

Curran, Jim, *K2: The Story of the Savage Mountain*, Hodder & Stoughton, London, 1995

Curran, Jim, *K2: Triumph and Tragedy*, The Mountaineers, Seattle, 1987

De Filippi, Filippo, *The Expedition to the Karakoram and the Western Himalaya*, Constable, London, 1912

Diemberger, Kurt, *The Endless Knot*, Grafton, London, 1991

Desio, Ardito, *La Conquista del K2*, Garzanti, Milano, 1954

Desio, Ardito, *The Ascent of K2*, Elek, London, 1955

Desio, Ardito, *Il Libro Bianco*, Garzanti, Milano, 1956

Desio, Ardito, *Sulle Vie della Sete dei Ghiacci e dell'Oro*, Garzanti, Milano, 2013

Eckenstein, Oscar, *The Karakorams and the Kashmir Himalaya*, Unwin, London, 1896

Fantin, Mario, *K2: Sogno Vissuto*, Tamari, Bologna, 1958

Golin, Augusto, *Erich Abram: Un Alpinista Bolzanino*, Citta di Bolzano, Bolzano, 2004

Herrligkoffer, Karl M., *Nanga Parbat*, Elek, London, 1954

Houston, Charles and Bates, Robert, *Five Miles High*, The Lyon Press, New York, 1939

Houston, Charles and Bates, Robert, *The Savage Mountain*, McGraw Hill, New York, 1954

Houston, Charlie, *Going Higher*, Swan Hill Press, Shrewsbury, 1998

Isserman, Maurice and Weaver, Stewart, *Fallen Giants*, Yale University Press, New Haven and London, 2008

Jacot-Guillarmod, Jules, *Six Mois dans l'Himalaya, le Karakorum et l'Hindu-Kush: voyages et explorations aux plus hautes montagnes du monde*, W. Sandoz, Neuchâtel, 1904

Jordan, Jennifer, *The Last Man on the Mountain*, W.W. Norton, New York, 2011

Kaczynski, Richard, *Perdubado*, North Atlantic Books, Berkeley, 2002

Kauffman, Andrew and Putnam, Bill, *K2: The 1939 Tragedy*, The Mountaineers, Seattle, 1992

Lacedelli, Lino and Cenacchi, Giovanni, *K2: Il prezzo della Conquista*, Mondadori, Milano, 2004

McDonald, Bernadette, *Brotherhood of the Rope: The Biography of Charles Houston*, The Mountaineers, Seattle, 1992

Mantovani, Roberto and Diemberger, Kurt, *K2: Una Sfida ai confini del cielo*, White Star, Vercelli, 2004

Maraini, Fosco, *Karakoram*, Hutchinson, London, 1961

Marshall, Robert, *K2: Lies and Treachery*, Carreg, Ross-on-Wye, 2009

Messner, Reinhold, *Walter Bonatti – Il fratello che non sapevo di avere*, Mondadori, Milan, 2013

Messner, Reinhold and Gogna, Alessandro, *K2*, De Agostini, Novara, 1980

Molenaar, Dee, *Memoirs of a Dinosaur Mountaineer*, CreateSpace, 2007

Moorehead, Catherine, *The K2 Man*, In Pinn, Glasgow, 2013

Neale, Jonathan, *Tigers of the Snow*, St Martin's, New York, 2002

Ortner, Sherry B., *Life and Death on Mt Everest*, Princeton University Press, New York, 2001

Petzoldt, Patricia, *On Top of the World*, Thomas Crowell, New York, 1964

Ridgeway, Rick, *The Last Step: The American Ascent of K2*, The Mountaineers, Seattle, 1980

Ringholz, Raye C., *On Belay*, The Mountaineers, Seattle, 1997

Rowell, Galen, *In the Throne Room of the Mountain Gods*, Sierra Club, San Francisco, 1977

Sale, Richard, *The Challenge of K2*, Pen and Sword, Barnsley, 2011

Sella, Lodovico, *Vittorio Sella with the Italian Expedition to the Karakoram*, Fondazione Sella, Biella, 1987

Symonds, John, *The Great Beast 666*, Pindar Press, London, 1977

Tenderini, Mirella, *Tutti Gli Uomini Del K2*, Garzanti, Milan, 2014

Tenderini, Mirella and Shandrick, Michael, *The Duke of the Abruzzi*, Baton Wicks, London, 1997

Thompson, Simon, *Unjustifiable Risk? The Story of British Climbing*, Cicerone, Milnthorpe, 2010

Tullis, Julie, *Clouds from Both Sides*, Grafton, London, 1986

Viesturs, Ed and Roberts, David, *K2: Life and Death on the World's Most Dangerous Mountain*, Random House, New York, 2010

Younghusband, Francis, *The Heart of a Continent*, Murray, London, 1896

Whymper, Edward, *A Right Royal Mountaineer*, William Clowes and Sons, London, 1909

BIBLIOGRAPHY

JOURNALS

Bates, Robert, 'The Fight for K2', *The American Alpine Journal*, Journal, 1954

Bates, Robert and Craig, Bob, 'We Met Death on K2', *Saturday Evening Post*, December 1953

Cromwell, Oliver Eaton, 'Spring Skiing in the Vale of Kashmir', *Appalachia*, 23, 1940

Cromwell, Oliver Eaton, 'Obituary Dudley Wolfe', *The American Alpine Journal*, 1940

Documenti e Notizie Sul K2, Il Club Alpino Italiano, 1956

Rivista Mensile, Il Club Alpino Italiano, Sept/Oct 1955

Rivista Mensile, Il Club Alpino Italiano, March/April 1956

Rivista Mensile, Il Club Alpino Italiano, May/June 1956

Rivista Mensile, Il Club Alpino Italiano, Sept/Oct 1956

Sheldon, George, 'Lost behind the Ranges', *Saturday Evening Post*, 16 March 1940

Streather, H.R.A., 'The Third American Karakoram Expedition', *The Alpine Journal*, London, 1954

The Swiss Foundation for Alpine Research, *The Mountain World 1955*, Allen and Unwin, London, 1955

Wiessner, Fritz, 'The K2 Expedition of 1939', *Appalachia*, 1956

DIARIES

1902 Guy Knowles (unpublished)

1939 Jack Durrance (unpublished)

Fritz Wiessner (unpublished)

George Sheldon (unpublished)

1953 Dee Molenaar (privately published)

Peter Schoening (privately published)

1954 Pino Gallotti (privately published)

Achille Compagnoni (privately published)

Index

References to maps are in *italics*.

Abram, Erich 193, 208, 213, 215, 226
  and Bonatti controversy 257–8, 260,
    265, 267
  and oxygen 216–17, 219
Abruzzi, Luigi Amadeo Savoia, Duke of xv,
  20–1, 284–5
  and expedition 22–3, 24–7, 28, 31, 48–9
Abruzzi ridge 50, 52–3, 54–8, 276, 277,
  281, 284
  and Desio expedition 188, 195, 202–4,
    206, 208–9, 229
  and Houston expedition 146–7, 150–2
  and Wiessner expedition 79–82, 87–8,
    99, 102, 104, 111, 113
acclimatisation 134, 135, 194–5
Aconcagua 15
Adams Carter, H. 32, 274
aerial reconnaissance 196–8
Ahdoo 41, 42
Alaska 32, 140
Alchori, Wazir of 10
Ali Bogra, Muhammad 185
Allain, Pierre 37
Alpine Club 1, 2, 8, 19; *see also* American
  Alpine Club; British Alpine

  Club; French Alpine Club; Italian
  Alpine Club
Alps, the 1, 3, 6, 29, 64
  and training 192–3
altitude 5–6, 61, 82
  and experiments 134–5, 286
  and pilots 133–4
  and Wiessner expedition 126–8, 129
  and world records 25, 27
altitude sickness 13, 89–90
American Alpine Club 31, 33, 34, 35,
  37, 58
  and Everest 138
  and funding 73
  and 1939 investigation 119, 120–3
  and Wiessner 67–70, 124, 287
American Alpine Journal (magazine) 62, 65,
  129, 278
Angelino, Ugo 193, 198, 200, 208, 212
Annapurna 138, 158, 262–3
Appalachia (magazine) 123
Ascent (magazine) 125
Askole 3, 9, 10, 22, 78
  and 1953 expedition 145
  and Houston expedition 39, 44–5

Ata-Ullah, Col Mohammad 142–3, 145, 162, 179
  and Bonatti controversy 250, 252, 254, 267, 268
  and Desio 195–6, 198, 199, 200, 209
  and Gilkey 167, 168–9, 177
  and Houston 212
  and radio 151, 152, 154, 156–7
avalanches 169–70, 174

Bae, Rolf 282
Baig, Jehan 282
Baines, A.C. 22, 23
Baldi, Marcello 242, 243, 244
Baltistan xiv, 8–10, 22, 39, 41–2
Baltoro glacier 10, 11, 18, 27
  and Houston expedition 39, 45–6
  and Wiessner expedition 95
Barrard, Liliane 276
Barrard, Maurice 276
base camp:
  and Crowley expedition 12
  and Desio expedition 201, 229–30
  and Houston expedition 47, 51, 53, 54
  and Wiessner expedition 79, 82, 102–3, 104–5
Bates, Bob 31–2, 37, 38, 44, 63, 181–2
  and 1974 expedition 274
  and Baltistan 41–2
  and descent 175–6, 177, 178
  and food 36
  and Gilkey 166, 169, 171, 172–3, 174, 179
  and K2 climb 45–6, 47, 48–9, 51, 53–4, 55–6, 59
  and second expedition 135–6, 141–3, 145, 146, 151–2, 160
  and Second World War 133
  and team building 34, 35, 139, 140
  and tooth extraction 154
Bauer, Willi 277, 278
Bell, George 139, 153, 154, 161, 273
  and descent 176
  and frostbite 162, 179–80, 181
  and Gilkey 171, 172, 173, 175
  and weather conditions 155
Black Pyramid 87, 157, 158, 175–6
  and Houston expedition 56, 57, 58, 59

Bonatti, Walter xv–xvii, 193, 205, 211, 226, 247–8, 271, 289
  and oxygen mission 216–18, 219–21, 225
  and summit controversy 236, 239–40, 248–62, 268–70
Bottleneck 218, 223, 228, 281–2
Bourdillon, Tom 263
Braham, Trevor 278
British Alpine Club 64, 138
British Everest Committee 232
British India xii, 7, 43, 68, 136
British Indian Army 6
Broad Peak 46, 289
Brocherel, Alexis 21, 25, 26
Brocherel, Henri 21, 25, 26
Brown, T. Graham 46
Bruce, Lt Charles Granville xv, 131
Buhl, Hermann 153, 220, 238, 263
Burdsall, Dick 34, 37, 46, 62
Burton, Sir Richard 2
Buzzatti, Dino 232

Campiotto, Fulvio 238, 240
Canada 32, 33, 67
Caravella D'Oro trophy 238, 245
Casarotto, Renato 276–7
Cassin, Riccardo 183, 185–6, 187–8, 189
  and rejection 190–2, 240
Cenacchi, Giovanni 269
Central Asia xiii, 136
Chapman, Freddie Spencer 34
China xiii, 52, 136
  and Pakistan 142, 274
Cho Oyu 97
Chogolisa (Bride Peak) 27, 46
Chrysler Building 93
Cima Grande 64
Climbing and Exploration in the Karakoram-Himalayas (Conway) xiv–xv
clothing 36, 140, 194; *see also* footwear; goggles
Colima 3
Compagnoni, Achille xv, 193, 198, 208, 209, 210, 288–9
  and Bonatti controversy xvi, xvii, 248–50, 251, 253, 254–6, 257, 258–9, 268–71

INDEX

and frostbite 235, 237–8
and House's Chimney 202–3, 204
and K2 film 242–4, 245
and oxygen controversy 260, 261–2, 264, 265, 266–7
and the Shoulder 211, 213, 214, 215
and summit 218–19, 221–3, 224–9, 230, 236
Concordia 11, 18
and 1953 expedition 146
and Desio expedition 200
and Houston expedition 46
and Wiessner expedition 79
Conquest of K2, The (Desio) 248, 255, 261, 262, 266
Conway, Martin xv, 3–4, 8, 27
Corriere della Sera (newspaper) 237, 238, 264
Cortanze, Marchese di xiv
Craig, Bob 139, 149, 150, 152, 153, 159, 181–2
and descent 176, 178
and Gilkey 166, 167, 169–70, 172, 173
and Rawalpindi 142
Cranmer, Chappell 67, 69–70, 71, 74
and Baltoro glacier 95
and illness 79–81, 82, 91
and investigation 120, 123
Crocé-Spinelli, Joseph 135
Cromwell, Tony 34, 69, 70, 74, 75, 109
and expedition 83, 84, 85, 86, 88, 89, 91, 95, 104
and investigation 122, 123
and Wiessner 115–16, 117, 119–20, 124
Crowley, Aleister xvii, 1, 2–3, 4–5, 6–7, 8–10, 284
and illness 13, 14, 16
and K2 11–12
and Kanchenjunga 19–20
and Wessely 10–11
Crystal Peak 11
Curran, Jim 129

D'Acunzo, Dr Benedetto 201, 237
Da Polenza, Agostino 279–80
Dalmine 194, 257, 264, 265, 266–7
Damrosch, Alice 69, 108, 117

Darjeeling 39, 144
Dartmouth College 31, 67, 72, 73
D'Aubarede, Hugues 282
Dawa 109, 110, 128
De Filippi, Filippo 21, 23–4, 25, 26, 28
De Gasperi, Alcide 185, 186
De Martin, Roberto 256
'death zone' 6, 126, 215
decompression chambers 134–5, 264, 286
Dengue fever 45
Desio, Ardito 182, 183–4, 185–9
and 1987 expedition 279–80
and Bonatti controversy 253, 254, 255–6, 257, 267, 268
and Compagnoni 244–5
and equipment 193–4
and expedition 201–2, 212–13, 225
and Fantin 240–1
and flying 196–8
and funding 241–2
and leadership 208–11, 240
and oxygen 263–4
and porters 198–201
and Puchoz 206, 207
and teambuilding 189–92, 193
and victory 229–31, 235, 237, 238, 239
and Wiessner 194–5
Devil's Tower 68, 165–6
Diemberger, Kurt 276, 277, 278, 279
Dittert, René 232
Dornan, David 108
Dräger 194, 257, 264, 265, 266–7
Durrance, Jack 69, 72–5, 76
and expedition 78, 82–6, 88–90, 91, 95, 96, 98–9, 102–3, 105
and healthcare 77, 79–80
and investigation 120, 121–2, 123, 127–9, 130–1
and Wiessner 116
and Wolfe rescue 109–10, 112, 113–14

Eckenstein, Oscar xv, 1–5, 6–7, 8–9, 10, 284
and illness 12–13, 16, 17
and Jacot-Guillarmod 18, 19
and leftovers 26–7
Eddie Bauer 140
Eiger Mountain 64–5

Einaudi, Luigi 231
Elkins, Katherine 20
Empire State Building 93
Epoca (magazine) 243–4, 252
equipment xii, 71–2, 140
    and Abruzzi expedition 21–2
    and Crowley expedition 6, 8, 9
    and Desio expedition 193–4
    and porters 199
    and Second World War 133
Estcourt, Nick xi
Evans, Charlie 263
Everest, *see* Mount Everest

Fantin, Mario 193, 197, 213, 231
    and Desio 240–1
    and Puchoz 205, 207, 208
    and victory 235
finances 35–6, 68–9, 140, 241–2
    and Desio expedition 189, 192
Fisher, Ellis 68, 72, 73, 116
    and investigation 119, 120
flags 161–2, 227
Floreanini, Cirillo 193, 209, 217,
    230, 235
Folio 44
Fontán, Carlos Soria 288
food 8, 9, 140–1
    and Desio expedition 201–2
    and Houston expedition 36, 50
    and porters 11, 198–9
footwear 83, 85, 194
    and 'Bunny Boots' 140, 157
    and *pabus* 11
Fraser, Lt Col Denholm de Montalte
    Stuart 116
French Alpine Club 37–8
Freshfield, Douglas 17
frostbite 85, 86, 91, 157–8, 179–80
    and Compagnoni 235, 237–8
    and Desio expedition 227, 229
    and Mahdi 267

Gallotti, Pino 193, 213, 216–17, 226
    and summit theory 236, 270
Gandhi, Mahatma 43
Gasherbrum IV 248, 249, 289

Gasherbrums 46
Gazzetta del Popolo (newspaper) 250,
    252, 260
Gazzetta Dello Sport (newspaper) 191
Genacchi, Guido 257
Germany xiv, xvi
Ghaffar Sheikh 41
Ghiglione, Piero 212
Giglio, Nino 250, 251, 252, 260
Gilkey, Art 140, 141, 152, 159, 160
    and death 173–5, 176, 178, 179, 180,
        181, 211
    and monument xi
    and remains 290
    and rescue 163, 165–71
Godwin-Austen, Henry Haversham xiii,
    xv, 41
Godwin-Austen glacier xi, 11, 12, 47
Golden Throne 46
GPS technology 279
Great Britain xii–xiii, xiv, xvi
    and permits 32, 33–4
Great Game xiii
Great Trigonometrical Survey of
    India xii
Groth, Edward 117–18

Hackett, Bill 274
Hadow, Maj Kenneth 75, 116, 117
Hall, Henry 58, 70, 120, 122–3
hallucinations 225
Haramukh xii
Hargreaves, Alison xi
Harrer, Heinrich 64–5
Harvard 31, 32
Hendricks, Sterling 68
Herrligkoffer, Dr Karl 186
Herron, Rand 33
Herzog, Maurice 138, 158, 227
Hidden Peak 37–8, 53, 57
Hillary, Edmund 153, 219
Himalayan Club 111–12, 117
Himalayas xiv, 3–4, 5, 141; *see also* Mount
    Everest
House, Bill 35, 37, 44, 49, 50, 63
    and investigation 119, 120–1, 122
    and K2 climb 51, 52, 54, 55–7, 59

INDEX

House's Chimney 56, 57, 58, 153,
    155–6, 177
  and Desio expedition 202, 209
  and Wiessner expedition 84, 85, 88
Houston, Charlie xv, 31–3, 34–5, 36,
    38, 182
  and 1986 season 278
  and altitude 133–5, 285–6
  and Ata-Ullah 212
  and concussion 175, 176
  and descent 177–8
  and Desio 186, 188, 194, 195,
    233–4, 238–9
  and family 149–50
  and Gilkey 165, 166–9, 171,
    172–3, 181
  and healthcare 42, 44–5
  and K2 climb 46, 47–9, 51–2, 53–5, 56,
    57–8, 59–62
  and porters 43–4
  and risk 62–3, 65
  and route 39
  and second expedition 141–3, 145,
    146–7, 150–2, 153–7, 158–9, 161–2
  and Solu Khumbu 136–7
  and team building 138–9, 140
  and Wiessner 73, 119, 123, 131–2, 288
Houston, Dorcas 149–50, 157, 180–1
Houston, Oscar 36, 37, 136, 150
Hunt, John 143, 193–4, 208
Hunza porters 144–6, 151, 152, 178, 179
  and controversy 236–7
  and Desio expedition 203–4, 209
Hussain, Akhtar 142
Hussein, Mohammed 180, 274

Imitzer, Alfred 277
In the Throne Room of the Mountain Gods
    (Rowell) 275
India xiii, 6, 38, 274
  and independence 136
Indus River 43, 145
injuries 42, 77
Irvine, Sandy 131
Isakhan 203, 217, 226, 270
Italia K2 (film) 242, 243–4, 245,
    248, 266–7

Italian Alpine Club 21
  and Bonatti controversy 253, 256,
    257, 258
  and Compagnoni 242–3, 244, 269
  and Desio 185, 186, 189, 192, 201
  and funding 241–2
  and victory 236, 238
Italy xiv, xvi, 184–5, 186, 192, 201, 247
  and news reports 211–12
  and victory 231–2

Jacot-Guillarmod, Dr Jules 4, 7, 9, 13,
    14, 17
  and Crowley 20
  and Eckenstein 18, 19
  and K2 12
  and north-east ridge 15–16
Johnsons scandal 70–1

K2 4, 273–5
  and 1953 expedition 143–7, 150–63,
    175–82
  and 1986 season 275–9
  and 2008 disaster 281–3
  and Abruzzi expedition 21–8
  and Crowley expedition 5, 6–7, 8–19
  and Desio expedition 188–9, 198–204,
    205–32
  and funding 68–9, 73
  and Gilkey rescue 165–74
  and height 279–80
  and history xii–xvii
  and Houston expedition 34–7, 38–62
  and Italy 184, 185–6
  maps 7, 40, 48, 81, 137, 170, 215
  and Wiessner expedition 77–92, 94–115
K2 – La Verità ('The Truth') (Bonatti) 256–7
K2: Lies and Treachery (Marshall) 258
K2: Storia di un Caso (The Story of a Court
    Case) (Bonatti) 256
K2: The 1939 Tragedy (Kaufmann/Putnam)
    129–30
K2 – The End of the Story (Italian Alpine
    Club) 258–9
K2: The Price of Conquest (Lacedelli) 257,
    262, 269, 289
Kanchenjunga xii, 19, 20, 31, 32

Karakoram range xii, xiii, xiv, 3, 5, 184
  and aerial photography 197
  see also K2
Karakorams and Kashmir, The
  (Eckenstein) 4
Kashmir xii, xiii, 4, 6, 7–8, 144
Kauffman, Andy 124, 125–30, 131
Kipling, Rudyard 41
Knowles, Guy 4, 5, 6, 8, 9–10, 18–19, 19
  and illness 13, 16–17
Knowlton, Elizabeth 33
Kraus, Hans 129
Kutiah glacier 183, 186–7

Lacedelli, Lino xvi, xvii, 193, 204, 211, 289
  and Bonatti controversy 249, 250, 253,
    255–6, 257, 258–9, 269–71
  and Compagnoni 244, 245
  and frostbite 235, 238
  and oxygen controversy 260, 261–2, 264,
    265, 266–7
  and the Shoulder 213–14, 216
  and summit 218–19, 220, 221–9,
    230, 236
Ladakh xiv
Lake District 3
Lambert, Raymond 232, 263
Last Step: The American Ascent of K2, The
  (book) 275
Lerco, Roberto xiv
Lindley, Alfred 68
Lombardi, Vittorio 212, 230
Loomis, Farnie 32, 34–5

McCormick, A.D. xv
Maestri, Cesare 190
Mahdi, Amir 203, 217, 218, 219–21, 225
  and Bonatti controversy 250, 251, 252,
    254–5, 260, 267, 268, 271
  and frostbite 235
  and summit controversy 236–7
maharajahs 22
mail services 18, 56, 83, 98, 150
Maix, Kurt 97
Mallory, George 131
Manaslu 141
Mandic, Dren 282

maps 28
  1902 expedition 7
  1938 expedition *40, 48*
  1939 expedition *81*
  1953 expedition *137, 170*
  1954 expedition *215*
Maraini, Fosco 249
Marble Peak 11
Margherita, Queen of Italy 20
Marshall, Robert 253–6, 258, 259–60, 261,
    264–5, 267–8, 269
Masherbrum 46
Mason, Kenneth 123, 124
Matterhorn 64, 250–1, 288
Men on K2 (Compagnoni) 250, 253
Messner, Reinhold 278, 285
Mexico 3, 6
Miller, Tom 171
Minya Konka 34
Mitre Peak 11, 46
Molenaar, Dee 139, 141, 145, 150, 153,
    157–8, 181
  and descent 176, 178
  and family 149
  and Gilkey 168, 169, 171, 172, 173
  and Rawalpindi 142
  and weather conditions 155
Mont Blanc 248
Montgomerie, Lt Thomas George xii,
    279, 280
Moore, Terris 119, 131
Morning News (newspaper) 237
Morris, James 236
Mount Api 212
Mount Crillon 32
Mount Everest xii, xv, 6, 31, 34, 97–8, 138
  and 1953 expedition 141, 143, 153, 162,
    188–9, 214, 236, 237
  and altitude 134
  and funding 35–6
  and height 279, 280
  and Nepal 136, 137, 138
  and oxygen 263
Mount Foraker 32, 162
Mount Lucania 32
Mount Rainier 139
Mount Waddington 33, 35, 68

mountain sickness 6
Mountain World, The (journal)
    255, 264–5
mountaineering 283–4
    and Alpine style 275, 278–9
    and risks 64–5
Mussolini, Benito 184
My Mountains (Bonatti) 248–9, 250, 251,
    256, 262

Nanda Devi 32–3, 34, 35, 60
Nanga Parbat xv, 31, 33–4, 141
    and 1934 expedition 57
    and Buhl 153, 162
    and oxygen 263
Nansen, Fridtjof 29, 31
National Research Council (Italy) 185, 189,
    192, 241, 242, 279
Naval Air Force 134–5
Negrotto, Federico 21, 23, 27
Nepal 6, 21, 39, 136–7
New York Times (newspaper) 201, 233
newsletters 150
North Twin 67
Norton, Edward 97, 98, 131

Odell, Noel 32–3, 60
Olympic Committee 185, 189, 238
'Operation Everest' 134–5, 286
Orient Air 196
oxygen 87, 134, 150–1
    and 1954 controversy 250–3, 255–6,
    257–8, 259–67, 270
    and Desio expedition 194, 214–18,
    219–20, 221, 222–4
    and flying 197

Pache, Alexis 19
Pagani, Guido 193, 206, 235
Pakistan 136, 138, 142, 267
    and permits 185, 186, 188, 274, 280–1
Parmentier, Michel 276
Pasang Kikuli 39, 43, 46, 57, 59, 62
    and Wiessner 71, 76, 95–6, 103
    and Wiessner expedition 82, 85, 89–90, 91
    and Wolfe rescue 110–14
Pasang Kitar 95–6, 109, 110, 111, 112, 114

Pasang Lama 90, 92, 103, 104, 117, 287
    and summit attempt 94–5, 96–8, 100–1
Patagonia 248
Pathan mercenaries 8
Pease, Lynn 274
Pennington, Alan 276
Petigax, Joseph 21, 25, 26
Petigax, Laurent 21, 25, 26
Petzoldt, Paul 34–5, 37, 43–5, 46, 49, 51, 63
    and food 50
    and Johnsons 70–1
    and K2 climb 54–5, 56, 57–8, 59–62
Pfannl, Heinrich 4, 10, 13–15, 16, 18, 20
Phinsoo 109, 110, 112, 114
photography 21, 27, 28, 40, 197, 222,
    226–7, 238–9
    and summit controversy 255–6, 264–6
Pico de Orizaba 3
Piotrowski, Tadeusz xi, 276
pitons 38, 87
ponies 8, 40, 43
Popocatépetl 3
porters 8, 9, 13, 17
    and Abruzzi expedition 22, 23, 24, 25–6
    and Desio expedition 198–201
    and Houston expedition 39–40, 43–4,
    45, 47
    and Wiessner expedition 78, 79, 95, 113
    see also Hunza porters
Processo al K2 (K2 on Trial) (Bonatti)
    252–3, 254
Puchoz, Mario 193, 203, 204, 205–7
Punjab 8
Putnam, Bill 124, 125, 126, 127, 128–9

radio 147, 152, 153, 156, 201
rajahs 8–9, 22
Rawalpindi 6–7, 21
    and 1953 expedition 142
    and Houston expedition 38–9
Rey, Ubaldo 193, 207, 209, 211, 230
    and altitude 213, 215, 217
Roberts, David 124, 125, 127, 130
Robinson, Bestor 68, 71, 72, 119
Rocky Mountains 67
rope bridges 77
rope 38, 56, 194, 202, 281–2

Rouse, Al 277, 278
Rowell, Galen 124–5, 275
Royal Geographical Society xiv
Russia xii–xiii, xiv
Rutkiewicz, Wanda 276
Ruwenzori range 20

Savage Mountain, The (book) xvi, 273
Scelba, Mario 231
Schacht, Hjalmar 74–5
Schlagintweit brothers xiv
Schmid brothers 64
Schoening, Pete 139, 141, 145, 155, 159,
　160, 170, 181
　and descent 176, 177
　and Gilkey 166, 167, 169, 170,
　　171–2, 173
Second World War 116–17, 118, 131,
　133–4, 184
Sella, Quintino 21
Sella, Vittorio 21, 23, 25, 27, 28, 31, 48
　and Desio 195
　and Wiessner 73–4
Sette Giorni (magazine) 239–40
Shawangunk mountains 68
Sheldon, George 69–70, 74, 114–15
　and Baltoro glacier 95
　and expedition 78, 82, 84–5, 86–7,
　　88, 91
　and investigation 120, 123
Sherpas 38, 39, 41, 43, 62, 144, 193
　and reputation 111–12
　and Wiessner expedition 76, 99, 110–11
　see also porters
Shigar River 44
Shipton, Eric 97–8, 233–4
Shoulder, the 57, 59, 81, 211, 213
Sivel, Théodore 135
Skardu 9, 22, 78, 212
　and 1953 expedition 144–5, 180,
　　183, 201
　and Desio expedition 196, 198, 230
　and Houston expedition 42–3, 44
Skog, Cecile 282
Skyang Kangri ('Staircase Peak') 27
Smith, Clifford 119–20
Smolich, John 276

Smythe, Frank 97–8, 225
snow-blindness 12, 79, 200
Soldà, Gino 193, 198, 203, 235
Solu Khumbu 136–7
Somervell, Howard 97
Spoleto, Duke of 184, 188, 195
Srinagar 4, 6, 7–8, 22
　and Houston expedition 39
　and Sikh sect 70–1
　and Wiessner expedition 75–6
Stak valley 183, 187, 188
Stampa, La (newspaper) 211–12, 232, 236
Streatfeild, Norman 38–9, 42, 49, 53, 54, 62
　and porters 44, 45, 47
Streather, Capt Tony 142–3, 145–6,
　158, 160
　and descent 176–7
　and Gilkey 171, 172, 173, 174
　and weather conditions 154, 155
Strutt, Col Edward 64
Swiss Foundation for Alpine Research 265
Switzerland xvi

Tendrup, Tse 91, 95–6, 99–100, 103–4, 105
　and departure 109
　and investigation 121, 122, 128
Tenzing Norgay 153, 193, 218, 219, 232, 237
　and oxygen 263
Teton mountains 68
Tibet 6, 21, 136
Tichy, Herbert 97
Tilman, Bill 32–3, 34, 60, 136–7
Times, The (newspaper) 36, 42, 62
Times of India (newspaper) 115,
　186, 236–7
Tirich Mir 143
Tissandier, Gaston 135
Trango towers 46
Tre Saggi 257, 258, 259, 261
Trench, George 76, 88, 89, 90, 95, 109
　and Wiessner 115, 116
Tsering 110, 111, 112–13
Tullis, Julie 277

United States of America xvi, 31–2, 33,
　35–6, 67–8, 93; *see also* American
　Alpine Club

Urdukas 23, 78
and Desio 188, 199
and Houston expedition 46
US Army 133, 139, 140, 286

Viesturs, Ed 125
Vilyati 203
Viotto, Sergio 193, 212

walkie-talkies 147, 156, 177
Wallerstein, George 279
Ward, Dr Michael 278
Warren, Ava 138
Washburn, Brad 32
weather conditions xii, 146–7, 281
and 1953 expedition 154–5, 157–61, 162–3
and Crowley expedition 12, 13, 14
and Desio expedition 209–10, 212–13
and Houston expedition 57
and Wiessner expedition 78–9, 84–5
Webster, Ed 124, 130
Weiser, Hannes 277
Wessely, Victor 4, 6, 10–11, 13–14, 20
and expulsion 18
and north-east ridge 15–16
Whitney, Roger 68
Whittaker, Jim 275
Whymper, Edward 20
Wiessner, Fritz xv, xvi, 67–70, 71–2, 76, 286–8
and Cranmer 80–1
and Desio 194–5, 233
and expedition 78, 79, 81–2, 83–4, 85–6, 87–8, 90–2

and Houston 35, 37, 58, 59, 139, 141
and investigation 118–22, 123
and Kaufmann 126–7
and Nanga Parbat 33–4
and reputation 124–6, 129–32
and Second World War 133
and summit attempt 94–5, 96–8, 100–2, 103, 104–5
and voyage 74–5
and Wolfe 89–90, 108, 112, 113–14, 115–18
Wiessner, Polly 125
Wolf, Mrufka 277, 278
Wolfe, Dudley 69, 70, 71–2, 74, 75, 107–8
and conditions 78
and death 116, 117, 119, 121
and expedition 82–3, 84, 87, 88–90, 91–2, 101–2, 103
and remains 290
and rescue 111, 112, 114
and technique 108–9
Wood, Walter 119, 122
Wroz, Wojciech 277
Wyss-Dunant, Edouard 215, 238

Yale 31, 35
Yosemite National Park 68
Younghusband, Francis xiii–xiv, xv, 22, 23
Yuno 43–4

Zanettin, Bruno 235, 241
Zoji La pass 41, 77
Zugspitze 67, 68